A Human Values Pathway for Teachers

Suma Parahakaran • Stephen Scherer

Editors

A Human Values Pathway for Teachers

Developing Silent Sitting and Mindful
Practices in Education

 Springer

Editors
Suma Parahakaran
American University of Sovereign
Nations
Sacaton, AZ, USA

Stephen Scherer
Virginia State University
Petersburg, VA, USA

ISBN 978-981-16-0199-6   ISBN 978-981-16-0200-9   (eBook)
https://doi.org/10.1007/978-981-16-0200-9

This Springer imprint is published by the registered company Springer Nature Singapore Pte Ltd.
The registered company address is: 152 Beach Road, #21-01/04 Gateway East, Singapore 189721, Singapore

Foreword

With great delight, I take this opportunity to write the foreword for this book entitled *Developing the Child of the Future: Human Values Pathway for Teachers.* This book has been written by educators, teachers, and community builders who believe that human values are fundamental to education. The authors are currently working in their respective fields to equip teachers and other practitioners with tools to draw out the human values that are inherent in us all. The tools of silent sitting, visualization, and mindfulness exercises are the focus of this book. The use of these tools can empower each child from within to enjoy the true essence of their nature, which is joy, happiness, courage, and a sense of self. Children who have assimilated these values and their practice in daily life can play their part in bringing peace, harmony, and happiness to their families, friends, and communities.

Some chapters address problems and challenges that can be experienced by teachers and by the young people whom they teach, arising from the pressures of today's society. Engaging in silent sitting and mindful practices can help them to secure peace of mind and happiness. The tools described in this book highlight the fact that the benefits of silence are everyone's birthright and that it is not restricted to any particular culture or creed. As well as providing some theoretical background and research findings about positive impacts of these tools on children and teachers, the book also offers practical examples for teachers and other educators to explore.

The ideas presented in this book are not restricted to just teachers in schools. They are also suitable for nongovernment organizations (NGOs) and trainers in all fields to empower their people. It is fitting for everyone, young and old, to develop the concept of morality; to be ethical in their innovations; to contribute to society and not place materialism as the most important thing in the world. Human values go beyond the body and mind. They touch the soul of the learner.

It is my hope that all teachers, trainers, and other educators will take hold of a copy of this book and use the ideas in their own ways. They will enjoy the experience of guiding the young people of today and tomorrow to live peacefully in nonviolence with one another, to love and respect one another, and to walk the path of righteousness that will serve as an invisible armor to protect themselves, their peers, and their fellow citizens.

Sathya Sai Academy for Human Values,   Ir. G. Reddy
Petaling Jaya, Malaysia

Acknowledgements

The editor would like to acknowledge with gratitude the support of the members of the Sathya Sai Academy, volunteer teachers from the Sathya Sai International Organisation, Malaysia, and teachers from the Sathya Sai School who facilitated education in Human Values program in Malaysia.

The editor wishes to thank the following for their contributions to the preparation of this manuscript: Dr. Stephen Scherer for proof-reading of chapter drafts and Dr. Margaret Taplin for proof-reading and her vital contribution by substantial revision to chapters.

Contents

1   **Introduction: Why Do We Need Education in Human Values?** 1
Margaret Taplin and Suma Parahakaran

2   **An Overview of Sathya Sai Education in Human Values and Silent Sitting/Visualization** 7
Margaret Taplin and Suma Parahakaran

3   **Guided Visualizations for Integrating Education in Human Values into Curriculum Subjects** 17
Margaret Taplin

4   **Light Meditation and Other Silent Sitting Techniques** 33
Lalini Reddy

5   **A Conceptual Framework for a Mindfulness Intervention** 41
Cheryl Talley, Stephen Scherer, and Oliver Hill

6   **Mindfulness and Silent Sitting in the Classroom** 55
Stephen Scherer, Cheryl Talley, and Oliver Hill

7   **Silent Sitting in School Counselling: An Educational Practice to Improve Academic Performance and Personal Well-being** 79
Kevin Francis

8   **Humanizing Education through Moral Education** 89
Vishalache Balakrishnan

9   **Silent Sitting and Visualization Techniques and the Environment: A Mindful Tool for Developing Awareness** 99
Suma Parahakaran

10   **A Reflective Practice Model for Introducing Teachers to Silent Sitting and Visualization Strategies** 113
Margaret Taplin

11 **Teachers' Perceptions of Silent Sitting as a Buffer
    to Their Problems** 125
    Margaret Taplin and Li Lingli

12 **Silent Sitting and Meditation: Building Teachers' Acceptance,
    Implementation, and Self-awareness in a Malaysian School** 151
    Suma Parahakaran

13 **Students' Acceptance of Silent Sitting/Visualization and Its Effect
    on Their Affective Dimensions** 165
    Suma Parahakaran

About the Editors

Suma Parahakaran is a trainer and researcher in Education in Human Values. She is a Visiting Professor for the American University of Sovereign Nations and is specializing in Bioethics and Education. She is a research consultant with the Southeast Asian Ministers of Education Organization Regional Centre for Education in Science and Mathematics (SEAMEO RECSAM) and selected schools in Southeast Asia since 2004. She was also an education training consultant for HUMANA Child Aid Society (Sabah) and has worked with schools in Thailand and Malaysia. The focus of her work is in the integration of education in human values for the curriculum (education and environment) and teaching related pedagogies. Silent sitting is one of the main teaching pedagogies which She is interested in implementing in educational systems. She is a member of Sathya Sai Academy, Malaysia and currently works as a tutor and a module writer for Wawasan Open University, Malaysia. Her major contribution includes training Southeast Asian teachers for Human Values-based water, sanitation, and hygiene education, a project by the United Nations Human Settlements Program (UNHABITAT).

Stephen Scherer is a research and supervising clinical health psychologist whose research interests lie primarily in the field of emotion and emotion regulation, with a focus on mindfulness as a mediator of emotion regulation. He has over 20 years of experience in meditative practice and began researching emotion regulation and mindfulness as an undergraduate student. He developed the Personal Factors that Influence Academic Behaviors Assessment (PIABs) which aims to further bring the fields of mindfulness, emotion regulation, and postsecondary education together to help enrich the lives and successes of college and college-bound students. He also teaches mindfulness and emotion regulation strategies to children, adolescents, and adults in his clinical practice and provides Dialectical Behavior Therapy, a mindfulness-based treatment to adolescents and adults.

List of Figures

Fig. 5.1   Adaptation of PVEST to induce full self-acknowledgment
          (physiognomy to ontology) as a factor in normal human
          development   46
Fig. 6.1   Components of mindfulness as proposed by the authors and
          adapted from the works of Baer, Kabat-Zinn, and Linehan   56
Fig. 6.2   (**a**) First and second folds of the snow in summer mindfulness
          activity. The arrow indicates the center of the paper. (**b**) Third fold
          of the mindfulness activity and first shape cutout. (**c**) Additional
          shape sample cutouts   67
Fig. 6.3   Completed sample snowflake when opened. Adding more folds
          will increase the complexity of the snowflake   68
Fig. 6.4   (**a**) First eight folds of the origami lotus flower mindfulness
          activity. The arrow indicates the center of the paper. (**b**) Beginning
          fold for the next two layers of petals and the first of the back folds.
          (**c**) Final folds and the finished lotus flower   69
Fig. 8.1   Factors influencing moral choices of secondary school
          students   96
Fig. 9.1   Mind of the learner and use of silent sitting or visualization   103
Fig. 11.1 Framework of factors causing teachers' problems and
          contributing to their coping ability   130
Fig. 11.2 Teacher problems addressed in this investigation   133

List of Tables

Table 2.1   Five universal values and sub-values 8
Table 2.2   Summary of the multiple purposes of silent sitting/visualization and how the strategy is used to address them 14
Table 5.1   PVEST operational grid (see Talley et al. 2015 for more details) 49
Table 10.1 Brookfield's (1995, 1998, 2017) four lenses for critically reflective practice 115
Table 10.2 Silent sitting diary 122
Table 11.1 Independent samples t-test to compare mean ratings before and after the intervention 135
Table 12.1 Emergent categories and frequency counts of teachers' responses (Emergent themes and respective categories are from Teddlie and Tashakkori 2009) 156
Table 12.2 Emergent themes and their categories in teachers' narratives about the use of silent sitting and visualization. Emergent themes and respective categories are from Teddlie and Tashakkori (2009) 157
Table 13.1 Students' responses by Krathwohl's taxonomy levels 169

Chapter 1
Introduction: Why Do We Need Education in Human Values?

Margaret Taplin and Suma Parahakaran

In today's world, with moral decline, breakdowns in family structures, inappropriate use of money and natural resources, misuse and abuse of drugs, lack of individual peace and loss of culture, individuals are suffering increasingly from physical, mental, social, and emotional disease. There is an urgent need to address these deficiencies. Governments worldwide are calling for schools to institute holistic education that encourages not only intellectual but also physical, social, mental, emotional, moral, and spiritual well-being (Lovat et al. 2011).

This idea was introduced as long as 25 years ago in *The Report of UNESCO Commission on Education for the twenty-first Century* (1995), which describes the four pillars of education critical for an economically productive and socially rich life:

1. Learning to be: the right to self-identification, self-definition, self-esteem, etc.
2. Learning to know: the right to self-knowledge, learning to learn, etc.
3. Learning to do: the right to self-development, employment, etc.
4. Learning to live together: the right to self-determination, to work in groups and teams, to resolve conflicts, etc.

Despite the importance of this type of holistic health, teachers are still challenged today to move beyond the goals of "learning to know" and "learning to do." Encompassing "learning to be" and "learning to live together" into their teaching programs could help their students cope with potentially being overwhelmed by life and help them gain some sense of control and well-being.

Visiting scholar at time of research.

M. Taplin
Centre for Research and Development in Values Education, South China Normal University, Guangzhou, China
e-mail: info@ssehv.org

S. Parahakaran (✉)
American University of Sovereign Nations, Sacaton, AZ, USA

© Springer Nature Singapore Pte Ltd. 2021
S. Parahakaran, S. Scherer (eds.), *A Human Values Pathway for Teachers*,
https://doi.org/10.1007/978-981-16-0200-9_1

Positive psychology and mindfulness are two techniques that have skyrocketed in popularity in recent years as a response to this challenge. The educators who have contributed to this book are experienced in various aspects of these techniques, within the context of a holistic education in a human values program called Sathya Sai Education in Human Values (SSEHV). A particularly useful tool used in SSEHV that embodies components of these popular techniques is silent sitting and creative visualization. This tool is easy to use and does not take up too much classroom time, but the effects can be powerful for teachers and for students. The authors have written this book because they want to share their experiences and, in doing so, to encourage teachers to think about using this technique as a regular part of their classroom practice and to reflect for themselves on the benefits. This book is a sharing of experiences by people who have used silent sitting and visualization in different ways, on different continents.

The book is intended for a varied readership. It is envisaged as a resource for teachers because of the range of hands-on approaches designed to contribute to character development. For new teachers, this book offers practical ideas that can help to establish routines for classroom management and coping with the transition to the teaching profession. For experienced teachers, it suggests a way of thinking that can help to maintain or renew enthusiasm for teaching (e.g., Chap. 11), improve students' attitudes and enhance their learning (e.g., Chaps. 6, 8, and 13), and help them to develop self-control and self-understanding (e.g., Chaps. 6 and 8). For teacher educators and higher-education teachers, it shows examples of techniques that can enhance students' transition to university learning (e.g., Chaps. 5 and 8) and shares a model of professional development that can support teachers to learn how to use this tool (e.g., Chap. 10).

1.1 How to Use this Book

As explained above, the purpose of this book is to focus on silent sitting and visualization and, in some cases, the popular concept of mindfulness as one component of the multiple SSEHV strategies. It is a compilation of cases and other studies, with research data reported where appropriate and practical strategies that practitioners can use. Its purpose is to give a broad overview of ways in which silent sitting, visualization, and mindfulness can be used with a range of audiences for a range of purposes, without placing too many demands on practitioners' already busy schedules.

For readers who would like to find out more about SSEHV, Chap. 2 gives an overview of this program and then goes on to introduce silent sitting and visualization.

The next two chapters provide more specific examples of silent sitting and visualization. In Chap. 3, Margaret Taplin draws on strategies used by busy teachers around the world to integrate the guided visualization aspect of silent sitting into subject curricula. These strategies support the cognitive understanding of the subject topic and reflect on affective aspects and values messages suggested by the topic.

Taplin presents examples of visualization scripts that can be used to achieve this purpose.

In Chap. 4, Lalini Reddy draws on Nelson Mandela's experience of silence while imprisoned and how his relationship with silence helped him to change the world. She then goes on to discuss the role of silence in coming to an understanding of "Who am I?" and quotes examples from teachers about their students' experiences of silence. She also describes some teachers' and students' experiences of different types of silent sitting, including the light meditation (a technique fundamental to SSEHV), word repetition, and centering practices.

The next six chapters (Chaps. 5–10) share cases and examples of the use of silent sitting and visualization, along with other aspects of mindfulness and positive psychology in a range of different contexts, with advice about how to introduce the technique. In Chap. 5, Cheryl Talley, Stephen Scherer and Oliver Hill describe a program at Virginia State University in the USA for a group of first-year university students from challenging backgrounds not conducive to academic success. The students were introduced to a daily mindfulness practice that was held at the beginning of each class session. The authors suggest that techniques associated with mindfulness can provide the access to introspective ability that many students need and can possibly lead to significant improvements in academic performance. While this chapter is of particular interest to higher-education teachers and those looking for some theory underlying the SSEHV practices, the ideas can be applied to school students as well, particularly those from disadvantaged backgrounds. To get the full picture, the reader needs to follow this with Chap. 6 by the same authors (Scherer, Talley, and Hill), in which they describe a range of silent sitting techniques and strategies to help hone students' attention and focus and model creative uses of these activities to increase opportunities for mindfulness in the classroom. This chapter, along with Chap. 7 by Kevin Francis, suggests some useful approaches for teachers and counselors. In Chap. 7, Francis provides an overview of his use of silent sitting, incorporating positive affirmations and cognitive rehearsal, which he used effectively in both his teaching and counseling practices in state and private schools in Australia. He offers a number of successfully used practices for the reader to use, both personally and with secondary or tertiary students.

In Chap. 8, Vishalache Balakrishnan presents a different viewpoint on the concept of silent sitting. Balakrishnan talks about the specific subject of moral education and how students' understanding can be enhanced through the use of silent reflection. She illustrates how silent reflection and visualization enable students to see all sides of a moral dilemma before making the decision on how to act. Balakrishnan describes the silent way, whereby students are given space to reflect on and make their own decisions about their moral dilemmas. Teachers at all levels may find it interesting to explore the use of this technique.

In Chap. 9, Suma Parahakaran gives another perspective on the use of silent sitting and visualization in the context of environmental care. Drawing primarily on successful water education programs, she provides examples of silent sitting and visualization as an integral part of classroom teaching to create a sense of connection between students and the environment. These ideas are based on Cornell's (1989) Flow Learning concept for sharing the joy of nature.

In Chap. 10, Margaret Taplin addresses teacher professional development, with an example of a model for facilitating teachers to become adept at and willing to use silent sitting and visualization in their practices. Taplin uses Brookfield's (1995, 1998) critical lenses of reflective practice as a framework for this model. The model creates opportunities for participants to see the benefits for themselves and their students, take ownership of its implementation, and develop their skills and knowledge to use it through ongoing collegial discussions in a community of practice.

In the final part of the book, the authors share evidence from some evaluations of silent sitting and visualization initiatives, adding to the evidence of beneficial effects described in Chaps. 5, 6, and 7. In Chap. 11, Margaret Taplin and Li Lingli illustrate that silent sitting is not only for students—it is beneficial for teachers too. They describe positive impacts on teachers' perceived abilities to cope with their professional and even personal problems. This chapter is a must-read for all teachers, whether they are beginners experiencing the stress of a new career, experienced teachers who may be feeling burned out, or those who simply want to enhance the quality of the teacher–student relationships. The teachers in this project indicated that the use of silent sitting in their classrooms helped to reduce some of the problems associated with student behavior, which reduced their feelings of not coping. Meanwhile, their personal use of the technique helped them to look at their problems in a more positive light and therefore enabled them to approach situations more calmly and lovingly.

In Chap. 12, Suma Parahakaran describes comments made by teachers in a school in Malaysia during a professional development program to introduce them to the techniques of silent sitting and visualization for use in their classrooms. She describes the approaches the teachers liked to use, the challenges they faced as they learned to use them, and their awareness of the effects the training had on them personally.

In Chap. 13, Parahakaran reports comments collected from students about their acceptance of the technique and their perceptions of how it influenced them affectively. She has used the responses of her findings and linked them to Krathwohl's hierarchy of affective domain taxonomy.

The authors hope that everyone who reads this book takes away the ideas that work the best for their particular contexts and develop them in their own ways. The beauty of the SSEHV model overall, and the silent sitting and visualization technique in particular, is that there is no one-size-fits-all approach; as the cases described in this book suggest, silent sitting and visualization can be adapted to fit many contexts in varied cultures. The authors trust that this is the beginning of a satisfying and fulfilling journey for readers and their students.

References

Brookfield, S. (1995). *Becoming a critically reflective teacher.* San Francisco: Jossey-Bass.

Brookfield, S. (1998). Critically reflective practice. *The Journal of Continuing Education in the Health Professions, 18,* 197–205.

Cornell, J. (1989). *Sharing the joy of nature: Nature activities for all ages.* Nevada City, CA: Dawn Publications.

Lovat, T., Dally, K., Clement, N., & Toomey, R. (2011). Values pedagogy and teacher education: Re-conceiving the foundations. *Australian Journal of Teacher Education, 36*(7), 31–44. https://doi.org/10.14221/ajte.2011v36n7.3.

Chapter 2
An Overview of Sathya Sai Education in Human Values and Silent Sitting/Visualization

Margaret Taplin and Suma Parahakaran

2.1 The Sathya Sai Education in Human Values Model

The Sathya Sai Education in Human Values (SSEHV) was founded in India by educator and philanthropist Sathya Sai Baba (Jumsai 1997). SSEHV now operates successfully in more than 160 countries and is supported by national education department policies in several of these. SSEHV is a secular program concerned with putting character development and values back into education and developing all domains of the student's personality: cognitive, physical, mental, emotional and, particularly, spiritual. Specifically, its goals are as follows:

1. To bring out human excellence at all levels (character, academic, and "being").
2. To develop the students all around (the heart, the head, and the hands).
3. To help students to know who they are.
4. To help students to realize their full potential.
5. To develop attitudes of selfless service.

SSEHV is based on five human values of truth, right conduct, peace, love, and non-violence that are universal and interdependent (Bhargava 2015) and is concerned with eliciting these values that are already inherent in all of us. Love is, in fact, considered to be the basis of character and encompasses all of the other values: "Love in thought is truth, love in feeling is peace, love in understanding is non-violence, and love in action is right action" (Jumsai 1997, p. 103).

M. Taplin (✉)
Centre for Research and Development in Values Education, South China Normal University, Guangzhou, China

S. Parahakaran
American University of Sovereign Nations, Sacaton, AZ, USA

© Springer Nature Singapore Pte Ltd. 2021
S. Parahakaran, S. Scherer (eds.), *A Human Values Pathway for Teachers*,
https://doi.org/10.1007/978-981-16-0200-9_2

Table 2.1 Five universal values and sub-values

Truth	Accuracy, curiosity, discrimination, honesty, human understanding, integrity, self-reflection, sincerity
Right action	Courage, dependability, determination, efficiency, endurance, healthy living, independence, initiative, perseverance
Peace	Calmness, concentration, contentment, equanimity, optimism, self-acceptance, self-discipline, self-esteem
Love	Compassion, consideration, forgiveness, humaneness, interdependence, selflessness, tolerance
Non-violence	Benevolence, cooperation, concern for ecological balance, respect for diversity, respect for life, respect for property

Table 2.1 gives an example of some of the values encompassed in these five categories, although SSEHV respects and utilizes values of the respective communities in which it is conducted.

The fundamental principle of SSEHV is that all teaching is based on the concept of *love all, serve all* and that the teacher's example in living the values is the most critical component of values education. Successful implementation of this model depends on the teachers valuing the values themselves and making efforts to make them a part of their own daily lives—then the values permeate all aspects of the school culture.

SSEHV is not a program in the sense that it follows set protocols or procedures, or even any kind of linear curriculum. Rather, it offers a set of values, concepts, and teaching approaches that can be utilized in various combinations as appropriate. The intention of SSEHV is that the values and strategies can be adapted to local cultures and implemented in any tradition or local conditions. Its uniqueness is that what matters is the teacher–student relationship.

The teaching approaches are not new. They have been used for generations to convey the values of societies. The main five approaches advocated in SSEHV are silent sitting and visualization, inspiring quotations, storytelling, music, and group activities. While all of these strategies are discussed in more detail below (see Sect. 2.1.3), this book explores and explains the use of only one teaching pedagogy—silent sitting and visualization. Some reference is also made in this book to mindfulness since this is currently popular in school systems worldwide as a means of decreasing negative emotions (Vickery and Dorjee 2016), reducing stress, developing social cohesion, and promoting a state of general well-being, which in turn influences academic achievement (Schonert-Reichl et al. 2015). Practicing mindfulness involves intentionally focusing the mind in a way that helps to regulate mental and emotional processes. Habitual mindfulness practice causes a shift in awareness over time, allowing for improved ability to monitor the continuous flow of thoughts from moment to moment (Roeser and Peck 2009). Mindfulness-based cognitive therapy has also shown positive developments related to social and emotional resilience (Semple et al. 2010). The authors who have used mindfulness practices have been invited to share their experiences in this book so that they can be practiced in conjunction with other SSEHV activities.

2.1.1   SSEHV Philosophy and Pedagogy

The term educare has been adopted from the Latin *educaré* as the philosophy underpinning SSEHV. The word *educaré* means "to bring out that which is within." When students develop the principle of love and follow the path of truth, according to Sathya Sai Baba, then it is true education.

> Human values are hidden in every human being. One cannot acquire them from outside; they have to be elicited from within. But as man has forgotten his innate human values, he is unable to manifest them. Educare means to bring out human values. To bring out means to translate them into action. (Sathya Sai Baba, 2000, p.183)

The educare method does not mean that teachers just inform students about the five values, but rather they strive to bring a personal meaning to these values through questioning and leading students through a process of reflection on their own lives. This process helps to arouse students' awareness of their inner selves and their inner potentials as they practice the five human values. The learning outcomes include listening to the voice of the conscience, taking care of the environment, and controlling desires that bring about wastage of time, money, energy, food, or other resources.

> Values integration does not mean quoting a value and discussing it. It is leading the students to see a personal meaning in which teachers teach in the classroom. This is the dimension that is often neglected in the learning process. (United Nations Human Settlements Programme [UN-Habitat] and Southeast Asian Ministers of Education Organization [SEAMEO] 2007, p. 26)

In educare, students are encouraged to do the following:

- Appreciate the five basic human values of truth, right action, peace, love, and non-violence as essential to the development of character.
- Learn the cultures, customs, and religions of other people along with their own, in order to appreciate the brotherhood of man.
- Acquire decision-making skills, which help to facilitate development of moral learning.
- Develop a sense of responsibility for the consequences of their actions and act with regard for the rights, life, and dignity of all persons.
- Develop self-discipline and self-confidence necessary to promote the fulfillment of their potential by enhancing their moral, physical, social, and academic achievements.
- Develop value skills needed for personal, family, community, national, and world harmony.
- Develop a caring attitude towards all forms of life and learn to value the need for preservation, conservation, and general care of the environment.

To bring out these qualities, teachers are constantly examining all of their activities and interactions with their students by reflecting on the following questions:

- Does it go to the student's heart?
- Does it have practical application?
- Does it help the student transform?

Students are taught two important ingredients for life. One is that whatever thoughts come into their heads, they think about and examine in their hearts before they act. This is referred to as 3 HV, the harmony of head, heart, and hands. This harmony can also be interpreted as a head that can discriminate, have vision, and possess a strong sense of clarity; a heart that is compassionate, kind, and connected; and hands that serve society. The other ingredient is concentration and inner stillness.

Not all the outcomes of SSEHV can be measured easily because the transformations that come about in students are often very subtle and do not emerge until the students have left school and entered into adult life. Even as adults, like the rest of us, they will probably still make mistakes. But the big gift given to children by SSEHV is that they can pick themselves up from their mistakes and move on.

2.1.2   Direct and Indirect Approaches

Commonly, SSEHV activities are presented either as a direct approach, which is useful for reflecting on one specific value in a designated SSEHV lesson, or as an indirect approach, by integrating the principles, the messages underpinning the values, and the teaching strategies into existing curriculum subjects. The indirect approach empowers all teachers, irrespective of their subject specializations, to be teachers of human values. When these activities and strategies permeate the whole-school environment, students come to understand that values are for all aspects of life and not just for the moral education classroom.

Another way in which the SSEHV model can be incorporated into existing school practices is by addressing contemporary issues that exist in schools, such as discipline problems, students refusing to work, bullying, and lack of respect for authority. The SSEHV approach intends to empower teachers to examine themselves and to think about how they might be able to reflect the major human values in their own behavior, particularly their interactions with students and colleagues. In so doing, teachers enhance their own mental health and well-being, their resilience to cope with the stresses of teaching, and the ways in which their pupils respond to them.

2.1.3 Five Main Teaching Approaches for Drawing out Inherent Values

As mentioned above, five main teaching approaches are particularly useful in drawing out the values inherent within all of us. *Silent sitting and visualization* has been selected as the focus of this book, so it is discussed in more detail below.

The use of *inspiring quotations and positive affirmation* is considered to be an important component of the SSEHV model on the assumption that children's thinking can be influenced by regular exposure to positive statements. The teacher can select quotations that are relevant for the students' age, interests, and culture. Quotations can be displayed every day and used as a basis for discussion and other language activities or can simply be left for the students to read for themselves.

Teachers are encouraged to utilize opportunities to tell *stories and anecdotes* about famous people, heroes, and ordinary people who have demonstrated the relevant values. By regular exposure to stories of such people, the students will come to value the good qualities described and to use them as a framework to draw on when the need arises.

Music and song are valuable ways of promoting inner peace and emphasizing positive values. These days, with concerns that young people are exposed to many negative values, this needs to be counter-balanced by the use of music and songs that promote positive feelings and celebrate healthy values.

Group activities refer to activities in which students are not just sitting together in a group but are truly interdependent, with each making a contribution that is an essential component of the outcome to promote the understanding of the notion of strength in unity. In addition to the fact that current research about teaching suggests that pupils can come to better understanding if they have the chance to work together in pairs or small groups (Dobao 2012, 2014; Dobao and Blum 2013; Kozar 2010), this methodology allows for the development of unity, cooperation, mutual regard, and creative conflict resolution, which are essential if people are going to be able to live together in peace and harmony.

2.1.4 Supplementary Teaching Strategies

Other components of SSEHV are used to supplement the five main strategies described above. The first component is called Ceiling on Desires, which develops self-control in students. This strategy advocates that they make the best use of their time, money, and food, thus targeting that one uses only what is needed.

The second component is W.A.T.C.H. This is an acronym for "watch your words; watch your actions; watch your thoughts; watch your character; watch your heart" (Hall 2010). It provides a simple but powerful structure for reminding us about these important components of a values-based life, particularly in conflict resolution, and it has been reported as having positive impacts on troubled adolescents (Hall 2010).

The third component is mind mapping. This strategy is designed to facilitate students' cognitive understanding of the concept of any given value, through reflecting on a series of questions: *What is it? What does it look like? How does it make me feel? How does it make others feel? What are the limits of the value? What is the opposite of the value? What are related values? What are the obstacles to practicing the value? What are the benefits?* After reflecting on these questions and creating a mind map, students are led in a guided visualization that enables them to focus on the feelings invoked by practicing it.

The fourth component is selfless service. This component is in alignment with the current popularity of community service learning, which combines learning objectives with community service (Sigmon 1979). In SSEHV, selfless service is offered as a form of love, in the form of compassion and empathy for the recipients.

2.1.5 Silent Sitting and Visualization

While all five teaching approaches are equally important, one has been selected for focus in this book, namely silent sitting. This approach has been chosen because it is a simple tool that educators can adapt and use easily, but one that leads to relatively quick and impactful results. This technique also has close links to the concept of mindfulness, which is currently receiving a lot of attention in schools.

Silent sitting refers to encouraging pupils to sit quietly and allow their minds to relax for a few minutes, often at the beginning of a lesson, to make them feel more focused and peaceful. Often, this time is used to listen to soft, relaxing music.

Visualization refers to imagining, or visualizing, a scenario while sitting comfortably and preferably with eyes closed to reduce distractions. In SSEHV, this usually takes the form of guided visualization in which the teacher describes a scenario for the students to imagine. Visualization is based on the premise that the subconscious mind is constantly and often creatively sending messages to our physical, mental, and emotional bodies and that it is possible to help pupils to develop strategies for programming their subconscious minds in positive, constructive ways through visualization (Jumsai 1997).

Visualization is a technique that is used in sport (for example, Singh 2014; Smith et al. 2007) and alternative medicine (for example, Perez-De-Albeniz and Holmes 2000; Zgierska et al. 2016). Several reports show that visualization techniques have been used successfully in values education programs in schools (Arweck et al. 2005). These techniques can be used with the whole class, small groups, or individuals to introduce, reflect on, or consolidate curriculum topics; to reflect on feelings or behaviors (Parahakaran et al. 2019); to prepare students to tackle problems or examinations; or to settle them down after being active.

The SSEHV model encompasses multiple ways of using silent sitting and visualization in classrooms, as summarized in Table 2.1. Used in these ways, it is possible to impact upon the conscious, subconscious, and superconscious levels of the mind (Jumsai 1997). Jumsai proposed a theory about how this impact occurs.

Through the five senses, the conscious mind receives and processes information from the environment in order to create awareness and understanding. The subconscious stores the memories of everything that is experienced and feeds these memories to the conscious mind to control the individual's thoughts and actions and even to color our perceptions of events that happen around us. The superconscious mind is the source of our wisdom, knowledge, conscience, and higher consciousness. In a holistically balanced person, these three levels of the mind interact to contribute to the individual's cognitive, physical, mental, emotional, and spiritual well-being. Jumsai (1997) suggested that two important components are needed for this healthy interaction to occur. The first is to free the mind from extraneous chatter to enable enhanced concentration and memory. The second is to ensure that the information that is stored in the various levels of the mind is clean, positive, and constructive, since its retrieval has such a significant effect on the individual's thoughts and actions, which can, in turn, contribute to the presence or absence of holistic well-being.

Silent sitting and visualization, as advocated in the SSEHV model, is a multifaceted strategy that can be used at different times during the school day for different purposes and to target all three levels of the mind (Table 2.2).

2.1.5.1 The Light Meditation

One particularly effective form of a guided visualization is to invite pupils to visualize the effects of a pure, cleansing light, burning out their negative thoughts and actions, and leaving only room for the positive. The light is symbolic of purity, warmth, and growth (Jumsai 1997, 2001). This technique is beneficial in silencing the mind's extraneous chatter to improve concentration and problem-solving and in enabling the children to go deeply within their own consciousness to tap into the latent values. The light meditation is an exercise in concentration on various parts of the body and then expanding to include other people and all of nature. A sample guided script for the light meditation is presented below.

> Sit with your back straight. Breathe in and out deeply.
> Let us now imagine a light in front of you. Bring this light to your forehead.
> Let your head be filled with light.
> Whenever there is light there can be no darkness. You are filled with good thoughts.
> Your thoughts are filled with love.
> Bring the light down to your heart. Imagine a flower in your heart.
> When the light reaches the flower, it opens petal by petal, until it is a beautiful flower.
> Your heart becomes pure. Your heart is filled with love.
> Bring the light to your arms, to your hands. Both your hands are filled with light.
> Say to yourself, "I will do good, serve everyone. I will form my actions with love."
> Bring the light down to your legs, to your feet. Both your legs are filled with light.
> You will walk forward bravely, with self-confidence towards the goals of your life.
> Take the light up through your body, all the way to your mouth and tongue. Let your mouth and tongue be filled with light.
> Say to yourself, "I speak the truth, I speak only what is good and useful."
> Take the light to your ears. Let your ears be filled with light.

Table 2.2 Summary of the multiple purposes of silent sitting/visualization and how the strategy is used to address them

Purpose of silent sitting and visualization	How the strategy is used
Conscious mind	
Control how teachers and students take in information through the senses (how they see things, how they hear things)	Guided visualization to "see good, hear good" Light meditation Personal visualization by teachers to envisage classroom environment and students in positive, loving ways Focus on breathing
Create an environment of "clean" positive stimuli (reflecting the five values)	Guided visualization to introduce a lesson topic and create suitable ethos and related values environment
Cognitive understanding of the five values (in conjunction with mind maps)	Guided visualization to consolidate mind mapping activity
Use of the light as a metaphor for goodness, purity, and wisdom (divinity)	Light meditation
Focus attention, concentration, mindfulness, and awareness of present moment	Focus on breathing
Subconscious mind	
Program in positive way (five values) so that when a crisis occurs they are able to retrieve calm, still, peaceful responses (creative visualization)	Guided visualization to envisage themselves in values-rich situations Guided visualization or self-reflection on positive affirmations
Feeling the values and establishing them in programmed memory (in conjunction with mind maps)	Guided visualization to consolidate mind mapping activity Guided visualization to link values to explore the affective domain to a lesson topic Guided visualization or self-reflection on changing negative emotions or inappropriate behaviors Silent reflection at the end of a lesson to feel and consolidate the values conveyed during the lesson
Use of the light metaphor to program divine thoughts, words, and actions	Light meditation
Superconscious mind	
Tap into inner depths to solve problems	Guided visualization and silent reflection in class before taking exams or tackling problem-solving tasks
Tap into inner depths to open their hearts, understand themselves better	Light meditation Guided visualization on mind maps or values message in lesson topic
Stilling the external chatter (sitting in silence, listening to music)	Use at the beginning of a lesson, particularly after an active session, or when there is a need to settle down
Use of the light metaphor to connect to their own inner divinity	Light meditation

Say to yourself, "I listen to good things. I hear good things. I listen to everyone with love."

Now take the light to your eyes. Both of your eyes are filled with light.

With your eyes full of light, you see good in everyone and in all things.

Now take the light up to your head once again. Let your head be filled with light.

Let the light increase in intensity and start to expand outwards until it covers all of us in this room, until we become one with the same light.

Now take the light to your parents, to your teachers, to your friends and relatives.

Imagine you are sending the light especially to people who are unkind to you or who you perceive are being unkind.

Now send the light to all the people of the world, all the animals, and all of nature.

Continue to expand the light until it covers every corner of the universe.

Say to yourself:

"Let the whole world be filled with light.

Let the whole world be filled with love.

Let the whole world be filled with peace.

And let me be the source."

Then imagine yourself filled with light, and say to yourself:

"I am in the light.

The light is in me.

I am the light."

And now bring the light back to your heart. Install this light in your heart. Whatever you do, wherever you go, you will have this light in your heart, guiding you, helping you, and protecting you all the time. You may now open your eyes.

References

Arweck, E., Nesbitt, E., & Jackson, R. (2005). Common values for the common school? Using two values education programmes to promote 'spiritual and moral development'. *Journal of Moral Education, 34*(3), 325–342.

Bhargava, D. (2015). *Transforming humanity*. Gurgaon, India: Zorba Books.

Dobao, A. (2012). Collaborative writing tasks in the L2 classroom: Comparing group, pair, and individual work. *Journal of Second Language Writing, 21*(1), 40–58. https://doi.org/10.1177/1362168813519730.

Dobao, A. (2014). Vocabulary learning in collaborative tasks: A comparison of pair and small group work. *Language Teaching Research, 18*(4), 497–520. https://doi.org/10.1177/1362168813519730.

Dobao, A., & Blum, A. (2013). Collaborative writing in pairs and small groups: Learners' attitudes and perceptions. *System, 41*(2), 365–378. https://doi.org/10.1016/j.system.2013.02.002.

Hall, D. (2010). *W.A.T.C.H. – for good living*. Queensland, Australia: D. Hall.

Jumsai, A. (1997). *The five human values and human excellence*. Bangkok: International Institute of Sathya Sai Education.

Jumsai, A. (2001, September). *Significance of light meditation* [conference presentation]. Northern California & Nevada Regional Annual Conference, Los Angeles, CA:Sathya Sai Baba Center.

Kozar, O. (2010). Towards better group work: Seeing the difference between cooperation and collaboration. *English Teaching Forum, 48*(2), 16–23.

Parahakaran, S., Eak, A., & Ng, K. (2019, October 16–17). Human values-based teaching: Higher order thinking skills using the Dhall & Tehseen model [Conference presentation]. *10th Annual International Symposium of Foreign Language Learning (AISOFOLL)*, Bogor, Indonesia: SEAMEO

Perez-De-Albeniz, A., & Holmes, J. (2000). Meditation: Concepts, effects and uses in therapy. *International Journal of Psychotherapy, 5*(1), 49–58.

Roeser, R., & Peck, S. (2009). An education in awareness: Self, motivation, and self-regulated learning in contemplative perspective. *Educational Psychologist, 44*(2), 119–136. https://doi.org/10.1080/00461520902832376.

Sai Baba, S. (2000). *The source and the centre of values*. Discourse 17, Sri Sathya Sai Speaks, 33, 176–187.

Schonert-Reichl, K., Oberle, E., Lawlor, M., Abbott, D., Thomson, K., Oberlander, T., & Diamond, A. (2015). Enhancing cognitive and social-emotional development through a simple-to-administer mindfulness-based school program for elementary school children: A randomized controlled trial. *Developmental Psychology, 51*(1), 52–66. https://doi.org/10.1037/a0038454.

Semple, R., Lee, J., Rosa, D., & Miller, L. (2010). A randomized trial of mindfulness-based cognitive therapy for children: Promoting mindful attention to enhance social-emotional resiliency in children. *Journal of Child and Family Studies, 19*, 218–229.

Sigmon, R. (1979). Service-learning: Three principles. *Synergist, 8*(1), 9–11.

Singh, R. (2014). Personality, spiritual exercise and cognitive-behavioural interventions in enhancing sports performance. *Indian Journal of Positive Psychology, 5*(3), 301–309.

Smith, D., Wright, C., Allsopp, A., & Westhead, H. (2007). It's all in the mind: PETTLEP-based imagery and sports performance. *Journal of Applied Sport Psychology, 19*(1), 80–92.

United Nations Human Settlements Programme (UN-Habitat) & Southeast Asian Ministers of Education Organization (SEAMEO). (2007). In P. Pannen, T. Ng, J. Ikhsan, & D. Mustafa (Eds.), *SEAMEO resource package: Human values-based water, Sanitation and hygiene education (HVWSHE)*. Indonesia: SEAMEO Regional Open Learning Centre (SEAMOLEC) and United Nations Centre for Human Settlements (UN-Habitat).

Vickery, C., & Dorjee, D. (2016). Mindfulness training in primary schools decreases negative affect and increases meta-cognition in children. *Frontiers in Psychology, 6*, 2025.

Zgierska, A., Burzinski, C., Cox, J., Kloke, J., Stegner, A., Cook, D., Singles, J., Mirgain, S., Coe, C., & Bačkonja, M. (2016). Mindfulness meditation and cognitive behavioral therapy intervention reduces pain severity and sensitivity in opioid-treated chronic low back pain: Pilot findings from a randomized controlled trial. *Pain Medicine, 17*(10), 1865–1881.

Chapter 3
Guided Visualizations for Integrating Education in Human Values into Curriculum Subjects

Margaret Taplin

Abstract As a tool, the guided visualization aspect of silent sitting can be introduced into subjects across the curriculum relatively easily, without taking up too much lesson time. This chapter contributes some sample guided visualization scripts designed to integrate education in human values into curriculum subjects, using science, information technology, mathematics, and English/history topics as examples. In line with Taplin's extension of a model of holistic education that was developed originally by Buchanan and Hyde, these scripts are designed to achieve three aims: to reinforce and consolidate the cognitive subject knowledge; to address the affective aspects of the topic; and to create an opportunity to reflect on a values message that underpins the topic.

Keywords Guided visualization · Cross-curricular integration

3.1 Introduction

The purpose of this chapter is to offer some examples to illustrate how silent sitting, and particularly guided visualization, can be integrated into curriculum subjects to achieve the dual purpose of consolidating or enhancing the subject knowledge while also addressing the affective (feelings and attitudes) and spiritual dimensions.

In the past decade schools have needed to go beyond focusing only on cognitive development. They are also expected to provide effective preventative and intervention strategies to address the academic, social, and emotional needs of the children they serve (Van Acker and Mayer 2008). This expectation means an emerging focus on the relationships between cognition, emotion, and socialization, which are no longer seen as separate outcomes (Lovat et al. 2011). Terms such as "non-cognitive skills," "21st century competencies," "personal qualities," "social and emotional skills," and "soft skills" are now common vocabulary (Joksimović et al. 2018).

M. Taplin (✉)
Institute of Sathya Sai Education, Kowloon, Hong Kong
e-mail: mtaplin@hotkey.net.au

© Springer Nature Singapore Pte Ltd. 2021
S. Parahakaran, S. Scherer (eds.), *A Human Values Pathway for Teachers*,
https://doi.org/10.1007/978-981-16-0200-9_3

In other words, the call is for a holistic education that not only includes the above-mentioned dimensions but also develops a vocabulary, conceptualization, and reflective experience of the values that are inherent in developing the whole person. Thus, teaching needs to become a "cultivating of hearts as well as minds across the curriculum" (Mustakova-Possardt 2004, p. 261), essential for promoting connectedness, meaning, and empathy (De Souza 2004).

Nevertheless, while educators generally agree about the importance of this type of values pedagogy, there are challenges associated with implementing it. Teachers are not always equipped sufficiently with the skills to promote a pedagogy that addresses all aspects of a student's development (Lovat et al. 2011), and many teachers think that values education is a subject to be taught by specialists, having little to do with their own subjects (Hill 2004). Additionally, teachers are prone to feeling stretched beyond their means when implementing a values-based pedagogy:

> Educators are beyond weary as they face the added demands . . . calling for greater academic accountability . . . they cannot be all things to the children and communities they serve. There is no "free energy" available to tap into efforts to promote the delivery of needed mental health services within schools. (Van Acker and Mayer 2008, p. 101)

Hence the problem remains that there is a tendency, especially in secular education systems, to focus mostly on the cognitive aspect of development (Buchanan and Hyde 2008). Without emotional development it is difficult for such systems to nurture the human spirit (Semetsky 2009). Clearly, if any kind of affective and/or spirit nurturing is to be achieved within a system of education, it needs to be done in a way that will not add pressure to students or teachers.

To address this gap between what is required of teachers and what they are equipped to do, and particularly to illustrate a way in which holistic education can be integrated seamlessly into school curricula, Taplin (2014) drew on the work of Buchanan and Hyde (2008), in which they called for "students in schools not only to achieve the cognitive competencies that comprise any given curriculum area, but engage in the type of learning experiences which have the power to be transformative," and for learning to go "beyond the surface and touch the soul of the student" (Buchanan and Hyde 2008, p. 318). Taplin's (2014) version of the model refers to a holistic type of education that combines cognitive, affective, and spiritual dimensions. The first of these refers to cognitive knowledge of the curriculum topic, direct teacher-talk about the values message embedded in the topic. The affective dimension refers to creating a classroom environment that encourages teachers to use words and body language that model the values important to them in order to contribute to positive mental health, emotions, self-esteem, collaboration, etc. The spiritual dimension involves encouraging students' reflection on the values message in daily life and what it means to themselves and others if this value is put into practice. Examples of learning outcomes for these three dimensions include define, describe, or recall (cognitive); show awareness of, experience, accept or appreciate (affective); and empathize with, reflect inwardly on, contemplate or accept responsibility for (spiritual) (De Souza 2004).

There is no one-size-fits-all approach to meditation and visualization, but a large body of recent research, including neuroscience studies of effects on the brain, has provided evidence of various types having positive effects on different aspects of the practitioners that include cognitive, affective, and spiritual dimensions. A brief overview below of some of this research illustrates the potential of silent sitting and visualization-type practices.

At the cognitive level, research on various types of meditation activities has identified evidence of positive effects on the parts of the brain that relate to cognitive performance. One such effect is enhanced attention and memory consolidation, which may be explained by activation of the hippocampus (Basso et al. 2019; Tomasino et al. 2014). Others have reported activation in regions involved in the voluntary regulation of thought and action (inferior frontal gyrus, posterior dorso-lateral prefrontal cortex/pre-motor cortex, and dorsal anterior cingulate cortex/pre-supplementary motor area), as well as activation in the insula (Buckner et al. 2008; Spreng and Grady 2010; Vincent et al. 2008). These areas of the brain are associated with cognitive control, self-reflection, and the processing of internally and externally produced information.

At the affective level, there is evidence of meditative techniques having positive effects on mood and emotional regulation (Basso et al. 2019). In particular, loving-kindness and compassion meditations have been found to cultivate positive emotions, such as joy and compassion, as well as such social skills and tendencies as empathic concern and altruistic behavior. In this type of activity, the focus is on active "mentalizing" in the form of taking the perspectives of others and imagining their emotional experiences. A growing body of research suggests that these strategies can be effective in increasing empathy and prosocial behavior toward others (Condon et al. 2013; Kang et al. 2013; Leiberg et al. 2011; Lim et al. 2015; Weng et al. 2013).

One of the tools of silent sitting is guided visualization, in which the imagination is used to create mental visual images of suggestions and goals (Khare 2013). According to Khare, "a suggestion can be direct or indirect; a direct suggestion addresses the problem or the desired goal in clear, overt and explicit terms; whereas an indirect suggestion addresses a problem in a disguised manner" (p. 378). These creative mental images can have an effect on programming the subconscious mind which, in turn, "empowers people to discover and develop strengths in themselves they didn't know they had" (Jaloba 2011, p. 18). Programming of the subconscious mind can lead to significant positive effects on self-concept (de Vos and Louw 2009). Teachers can use this type of visualization to foster development of the cognitive, affective, and spiritual domains. Depending on the nature of the prompts they use, teachers may help students recall what they have learned (cognitive), focus on feelings and emotions associated with the lesson topic and/or its values message (affective), and look deeply within themselves to reflect on their own lives, in relation to the lesson topic or the values message (spiritual).

Another reason why silent sitting can be a useful tool in promoting holistic education is that it can be done in just a few minutes of class time and can have the added benefit of settling the class down or giving them a "brain break" before or during a lesson. However, despite the argument that this is an effective way to achieve multiple goals in curriculum subjects, it can be challenging for teachers to develop suitable visualization scripts that can enhance the subject learning and encourage students to reflect on values messages at the same time. The next section of this chapter offers some examples, with some discussion of how they have been designed to meet the dual purpose of subject learning and reflection on values. Taplin's (2014) model has been used as a framework to illustrate how silent sitting, and particularly guided visualization, can be integrated into curriculum subjects to achieve the dual purpose of consolidating or enhancing the subject knowledge while also addressing the affective and spiritual dimensions.

3.2 Examples of Visualization Scripts Integrating Values Messages and Subject Topics

3.2.1 Science[1]

Topic: Body Systems (Digestive System, Nervous Systems, Skeletal Systems, etc.)

Imagine a bright light entering your head and filling your head and your heart … Now imagine the light moving through your [insert name of the body system you are working on] … Let the light fill your [one by one go through the parts of the system. The teacher might need to remind the students which part of the body each is in] … Let the light join each system part together so they can work together in harmony for your health … Now imagine that you are sending the light to the person sitting on your right hand side. From there it goes to the next person … and so on until you have sent light to every person in the room … Imagine the light connecting everyone in the room to everyone else. Say to yourself, "Just like the parts of the [body system], we are all a team, and we support each other to be the best that we can be, so that the team can be healthy.

This visualization begins with an affective task of imagining the bright light, which in SSEHV represents purity and wisdom. It then goes on to give a cognitive revision of the components of the body system, as the light is imagined moving to each one. As students imagine the light joining each component of the system so they will work in harmony, there is an overlap between the cognitive scientific fact of the inter-dependence of the system parts and the values message that we too are healthiest and most effective when we work together in harmony. The visualization finishes with an overt affirmation of this values message.

Topic: Atoms

Do a shortened version of the Light Meditation (see Sect. 2.1.5.1) but concentrate particularly on the part where the students are asked to send light to people who are being unkind to

[1]The examples in this section were contributed by Gita Singh, a teacher in the Sathya Sai College, Australia.

them or who they perceive to be unkind. Ask them to imagine that they are sending the light in the form of bright stars from their hearts to deflect the negative thoughts or words coming their way.

The cognitive message here is that atoms are made up of subatomic particles: neutrons, electrons, and protons. The teacher can reinforce the values message by sharing stories about a time when you have used this technique successfully to improve a situation with somebody who has been sending negative thoughts to you.

For homework, you can challenge the students to choose somebody who they think is negative towards them and to practice this activity every day for 1 week. Suggest a timeframe, such as 2 min per day, to focus on sending the stars from their hearts. Remind them every day to do this. At the end of the week, ask students to share any success stories. To encourage students to do the activity and report on their experiences, you could display stars on the wall with the names of the students who report a success story.

Topic: Photosynthesis

This cognitive message is that plants carry out the process of photosynthesis—using the sun's energy to produce food and giving out oxygen. The message then moves to the affective dimension, concentrating on the feeling of strength that students can invoke in themselves and the values message that they can learn from nature's photosynthesis process about sharing and uplifting others. This visualization can be used at the end of the lesson for consolidation.

> Recall and consolidate the process of photosynthesis, step by step. This will help students to transfer the information to their long-term memories. Then ask the students to imagine they are like a tree, drawing in the sun's energy, filling their bodies and minds, giving them strength . . . then to imagine that, like the trees, they are sharing their strength with their friends, with their family members, with their school, with the community, and with the whole country and whole world.

As a homework challenge, having established how important trees are to sustaining life, challenge students to practice the habit of not wasting time, energy or money; by not spending their money on something that they do not really need, they can save some that can be used to buy trees that they can plant and nurture.

Topic: Neutralization Reactions

> Imagine yourself as a piece of litmus paper. You can choose whether you are blue or red. Imagine some of the things that can make us feel negative emotions . . . Imagine something that has made you feel angry recently, and then watch as you manage to stay the same blue or red that you have chosen to be. Now think of something that has made you feel jealous recently—and again imagine that this has not affected you and you are still able to hold your blue or your red color. Now think of a time when you have felt disappointed. Once again imagine that this disappointment is not able to affect you at all and that your litmus paper still keeps its original blue or red color. Before you open your eyes, make a promise to yourself that you will not change your color whatever negative things might happen around you— you will still continue to keep your blue or your red balance.

In this visualization, there is a brief revision of the role of litmus paper, which changes color according to the acid or alkaline balance of the liquid being tested or remains the same if this balance is neutral. The next part is affective, inviting the students to focus on negative emotions they may have felt recently and to link to the notion of remaining neutral rather than being affected by these feelings. It finishes with a values message reminder to keep this equilibrium in daily life, no matter what happens around them.

As with many silent sitting activities, this one can be followed up with a homework task that can take the students' reflections on the values message to a deeper level. Individuals can be asked to write down one negative emotion and to think of a positive thing that they could think, say or do to balance it. To encourage students to do this activity, they could be divided into groups to see which group could come up with the best set of ideas. Here you can talk to them about strength in unity and how the group working together can come up with better results than individuals working alone.

Topic: Cells Organelles make up the subunits of a cell. There are numerous each with their own function.

> Just like the organelles, each one of us has something special and unique about us, and we have a responsibility to discover what ours is and how we can use it to make ourselves and others happier. Imagine that you are very, very tiny, and you are walking inside the brain. It looks like a library, with lots of shelves and books. Inside the books are all the things you have ever learned. You walk along the shelves until suddenly you find what you are looking for. It is a big book on a very high shelf. You take it off the shelf and look at the cover. On the cover it has your name, and it is called *My Book of Special Strengths*. Imagine that you open the book. On the first page is a list of all the special strengths that you have and all the things that you are good at. It might be words, or it might be a picture, or it might be like a movie. If you can't see anything, don't worry because it will pop into your mind later. Have a good look at what is on the page and make sure you take careful notice of the information that is given to you. When you are ready, close the book and put it back on the shelf.

The values message in this visualization is concerned with inter-dependent team-work—that everyone has a unique and special strength and if each contributes their strength to the team, the result can be more effective than individuals working alone. The opening cognitive message reinforces the concepts of organelles having unique functions, then the script goes into a reflection on the students' own unique qualities.

3.2.2   Social Media

Topic: Unhealthy Addiction to Social Media

> Close your eyes and take some deep breaths to relax ... Now in your mind's eye imagine your mobile phone. Imagine how it looks, how it feels ... As you look at it, you hear a *ping* as a message arrives ... How do you feel when you hear a message arriving? Where in your body do you feel the sensation? Is it a good feeling, a bad one or a neutral one? ... Now imagine that you send a message to a friend or friends. You can see that they are online. Your

message was important, and you are excited to get their reply. You wait and wait and wait . . . but no reply comes. All day and that night, still no reply comes. How do you feel about your friends not answering? Where in your body do you feel this feeling? What do you do? What do you feel about yourself because your friends have not answered you? What are the thoughts going through your mind? Take a moment to listen to the thoughts going through your head . . . Let yourself feel any of the feelings that these thoughts bring up . . . Now imagine that you have a bright light shining in your heart. Let the light get bigger and bigger until it fills your whole body. Imagine that it is especially bright and strong in the parts of the body where you felt reactions to your friends not answering your messages. Allow the warmth of the light to burn away any bad feelings, until you feel strong and powerful . . . Then when you are ready, open your eyes.

This visualization focuses primarily on the affective dimension although it uses the social media context as the catalyst for this reflection on the topic. The cognitive reminder is the actual psychostimulant effect that can be aroused by social media. The values message is: Are we drawing our happiness and self-validation from our social media or from inside ourselves? This visualization can lead to some useful discussion:

- Invite two or three students who are willing to share what they felt during the visualization.
- Hopefully some students will talk about annoyance or impatience when their friends failed to reply instantly. They might have had thoughts like, "I know they are online, but they are not answering. Why? Are they angry with me? Have I said something to upset them? Have they unfriended me? Should I unfriend them?"
- Social media are about "different places/different times" (that is, the people are in different places, and the person receiving the message might read it at a different time from when it was sent). But using social media has caused us to expect "different places/same time." So when we do not get a reply in the "same time," especially when we know the other person is online, we have doubts and ask questions about ourselves and whether they like us, etc. Also, when we hear the *ping* of a message coming in, the chemical dopamine is released, which makes us feel good, so we start to get addicted to this feeling and want more and more messages to *ping* into our inboxes.
- Discuss how students felt when they allowed the good feelings to come from inside their own hearts instead of from the social media.
- What advice does this activity give us about our happiness? What, if anything, can we do in our lives to put this into practice?

3.2.3 Mathematics

Topic: Problem Solving.
In mathematical problem solving, silent sitting can help students to connect to their own "inner computers," the deeper levels of their minds where creative solutions can often be found. This helps to reinforce some key ideas:

- We all have the deep inner resources to solve problems—this is an extremely powerful tool.
- We all need to learn to be dependent on our own inner strength rather than relying only on other people and things around us for our strength and happiness.
- To tap into our inner computer, it is important to do silent sitting so we silence the chatter in the outer parts of our minds.

In the curriculum, there are many occasions when students are required to solve problems. Teach them that silent sitting for 30 s to 1 min before trying to solve a problem or doing these activities will help them to do the work better and more quickly.

At the cognitive level, the following two visualizations give a reminder that we all have this inner wisdom to solve problems. The visualizations create the opportunity, at the affective level, for students to experience the positive emotions associated with solving a problem successfully. The values message is reinforced that in life, as in class, using silent sitting can empower students to solve their own problems.

Visualization 1

First read the problem. Then put it aside. Close your eyes and just listen to the inner silence of your mind for a few moments. Focus your concentration on the back of your closed eyelids at the point where your eyebrows meet. Don't try to think about anything—just allow your mind to be still and empty, and concentrate on the blankness behind your eyes. When you feel that your mind is completely still, think for a moment about the problem you need to solve. You can either repeat the whole question in your mind, or you can simply say, "I need to find the solution to the problem I am about to tackle." Once you have asked this question, return your attention to focusing on the silent, blank emptiness of your mind behind your closed eyelids for a few more minutes. Then visualize your subconscious mind working like a computer. First it sorts the knowledge you already have to solve the problem. Then it sorts out what else you need to know. Next, it puts this knowledge together in a logical way. Finally, it sends the output into your conscious mind so it can work on the problem. Take three slow, deep breaths, then open your eyes and start to work on the problem.

Visualization 2

Take three deep, slow breaths. Each time you breathe out, let go of any frustration or anxiety. Each time you breathe in, breathe in inspiration. You can decide what this might look like—a light that lights up your mind like a bulb, a color, or a shape. Just keep drawing it in each time you breathe. Now imagine that your mind has gone completely blank—as if the power has been cut and it has been plunged into darkness. Sit there for a few moments in the total blackness. If any thoughts or images come into your head, just let them go and return to thinking about the darkness.

Now imagine that you are going down a long, dark tunnel, right into the deepest part of your mind. This tunnel leads you to your inner mathematician, deep inside your brain. This is the place where you have all the answers and all the techniques you need to solve the problem. All you need to do is unlock the door behind which the inner mathematician is sitting. The door is golden, and in the lock is a big golden key. Slowly turn the key, open the door, and all the knowledge you need can be seen right there. As you return along the tunnel, imagine that you are dragging the knowledge along behind you, bringing it closer and closer to the front of your conscious mind, where you can put it to good use. Now open your eyes. Don't worry if the inspiration isn't there immediately, as it will come.

Topic: The Pyramid.

Prior to this visualization, you can show some pictures of pyramids made from blocks, such as the pyramids in Egypt. The following visualization can be used to tell the history of the Egyptian pyramids and provide some information about their significance:

> Close your eyes and imagine that you are inside a pyramid. Imagine the base. What is its shape? How many angles does it have? What kind of angles are they? Now imagine each side. How many are there? What is their shape? Imagine the pyramid opened out flat. If you need to find the areas of these shapes, what formulae will you need to know?
>
> A pyramid is extremely stable even during its building. No earthquake can destroy it. Repairs to parts already built are seldom required, and the builder can work efficiently on the construction of the pyramid. Take a moment to imagine yourself as a pyramid, so strong and stable that nothing can upset you.
>
> The pyramid represents the sense of harmony and unity within ourselves and with our environment. The individual building blocks of the pyramid are lessons we have already successfully completed about ourselves. Take a moment to think about some of the things you have already learned about yourself . . . Now think about the things that you would still like to improve about yourself . . . As soon as the top of our pyramid has been built to the necessary height, we can then be in harmony with ourselves and our environment. Now take a moment to think about how it will feel when you are in full harmony with yourself and your environment. When you are ready, open your eyes and bring your full attention into the classroom to continue the lesson about the pyramid.

This visualization allows for cognitive consolidation of the properties of the pyramid—particularly by imagining it opened out flat—as well as some historical information about why this shape has been used in buildings since ancient times. Affectively, students are given the chance to focus on feelings of strength and stability invoked by the pyramid. The values message is clearly the positive effects of being in harmony with ourselves and our environment.

Topic: Sphere.

The purpose of this visualization is to be cognitively aware of the properties of a sphere and, affectively, to think about how this shape can be used to help us to achieve the kind of inner peace that is not disturbed by whatever goes on around us in our lives. The image of the golden sphere, or ball, can be used to represent security and purity. The visualization also demonstrates that, in our daily lives, we encounter other people and enjoy "traveling" with them for a while but that we need to respect their boundaries of their golden spheres, just as we need to respect our own.

> Imagine that you are inside a golden sphere. You are floating around in the sphere, very safe and happy. The other children are in their spheres too. Sometimes you bump gently against each other, but you are inside your own sphere and nobody else can come in. Your golden sphere is your own special space where you can go whenever you like.

Topic: Subtraction.

Start the lesson with the following visualization:

> Close your eyes and take some slow, deep breaths to relax … Now imagine that you are looking at yourself in a mirror, so you can see yourself as other people see you. Imagine that you can see a big minus sign above your head in the mirror. Minus means taking away from something, or making something smaller. Look closely at yourself in the mirror and look at your own bad qualities that make you unhappy or you would like to be rid of. These are the things that take away from you being the best that you can be. As you look at your own bad qualities, one by one tell them to go away and imagine that they are leaving you. See your unhappiness growing smaller and smaller each time one of your bad qualities is subtracted … Feel your happiness growing as you subtract the bad things.

The cognitive message here is the reminder that subtraction means to make something smaller. The affective focus is on happiness and the idea that unhappiness can become smaller as we systematically take away the "bad qualities" that can cause unhappiness. While some reflective discussion is valuable in all silent sitting activities, it would be particularly important after doing this visualization to discuss the kinds of qualities that can cause unhappiness if they are not discarded; this is where the values message in this visualization can be strengthened.

Topic: Place Value

Visualization 1 (From Sathya Sai Vidya Vahini Project, India)

> We just learned that every digit in a number has a face value and a place value. The actual value of the number is the face value, and the place value depends on its place, or position, in the number.

> For example, in number 59, though 5 is smaller than 9, its place value is higher than 9, due to its position on the left side of 9. If 5 is placed instead, to the right of 9 the place value of 5 decreases, even though the number 95 becomes greater.

> Similarly, in this world, people initially get respect, fame and popularity due to being rich monetarily. A person's money is the face value of that person. If the same wealth is used only for selfish purposes and not for helping the needy, the person's place value in the society decreases. It also decreases if they are proud of their assets or wealth and look down upon other people.

> Famous personalities like [insert name of appropriate local people] are loved even today because they used their personal wealth to help the poor and needy by establishing many charities. Their place value in the society will always be greater.

> The possession of material things does not make persons great; it is their good nature that makes them stand out in society.

> Think about your own life. Are you more concerned about your face value or your place value? Think about a time when you really did have place value, such as when you put aside your need for fame or success and instead used your unique talents to give value to somebody else. Think about how this made you feel. How did it make others feel?

This visualization can be expanded to think about face value not only as money but as fame, success, what others think of us, etc., and place value not only as what we do with our money but how we "add value" to others by making the best use of our own special, unique strengths, and talents.

After revising the concept of place value, this visualization provides a useful parallel values message about our own "place value" in life. Some questions can be asked to get the students to reflect on how effectively they are applying the values message to their own lives.

To reinforce the values message, a homework activity could be to try to add place value rather than face value during the following week and report back on how it affected themselves and others. Discussion can incorporate the following points:

- Just like the numbers, we all have a place in the world. We all have something that is special about us.

  - John is good at playing music.
  - Susie is good at math.
  - Mary is good at making unhappy friends feel better.
  - Anne has a beautiful smile that makes everyone feel good.

- Think about what your special place value is and tell your groupmates.
- How can you use your special place value to be valuable and to help others—that is, to find and make good use of it?

Visualization 2.

While reinforcing the concept that adding zeros changes the place value, this alternative visualization conveys a values message of self-love or self-worth. It also conveys the message of strength in unity, that if we work together and support each other we can become bigger and stronger. The students are asked to reflect on the feeling of strength that this can create.

> Imagine one small unit number, all alone . . . Then another one joins it, and there are two . . . then another and another until there are 10. They join hands and stand in a line. Now they are much bigger and stronger than when they were alone. Now you see other lines of 10 coming along and joining together. Soon there are 10 of them, and they have made a big, fat, strong 100 . . .
>
> Next, think about the number 8. It is a very small number, all alone. Along comes a 0 and stands beside it. Now with the help of the 0, the 8 has become 80. It is 10 times bigger than it was before. Then along comes another 0 and stands beside the first one. Now the 80 has turned into 800, with the help of the two zeros. What a big and powerful number it is now. Watch the number get bigger and bigger as more and more zeros come to stand beside it.
>
> Now imagine yourself all alone. Then imagine others come to stand beside you and help you to grow bigger and stronger. Feel how big and strong you become. Say thank you to the helpers. Now imagine you are standing beside your friend and helping him or her to grow bigger and stronger. How do you feel when you are helping your friend in this way?

A follow-up to the values message underlying this visualization could be to put a photo of each child (or his or her name) on the wall. Underneath each photo, write the thing that is special about this child that adds value to himself or herself and to others.

3.2.4 English/History

In English (or other first language classes) or history, there are many opportunities to read stories or accounts that have values messages embedded. Two examples have been included here to illustrate how visualizations can be utilized to draw out students' awareness of the key issues in the text and to reflect on these issues in relation to their own lives, through introducing an affective component.

Topic: Story with a Moral Conflict

Close your eyes and imagine yourself all alone where nobody can see you. Think about your inner diamond, your conscience, your inner voice that tells you what is right and what is wrong. What does this feel like? Where in your body do you have this feeling? Have you ever had a time when you have listened to your conscience and made a good choice because of it? Try to remember how this made you feel. Have you ever had a time when you have done the wrong thing, knowing that it was wrong, just because you knew you would never get caught? Try to remember the feeling it gave you, deep inside your conscience.

Now think about the characters in the story you have just read. Try to put yourself in their position. Imagine you are experiencing . . . [insert key incidents in the story that influence the development of the moral conflict, one by one, allowing time for reflection]. How does this incident make you feel? Now connect to your conscience just like you did a few moments ago. If you were this character, what choice would you make in this situation? How do you feel now that you have made this choice?

[The teacher may wish to extend this visualization script by adding some further scenarios, such as those below.]

Imagine that you are alone in the classroom, and you see your classmate's iPhone that he has left behind. You know it would be very easy to take it, and nobody would know. Ask your inner voice to tell you what you should do. Ask your inner voice to say, "I should do this" or "I should not do this."

Now imagine that you are hurrying to play at your friend's house, and you see your old neighbor carrying her groceries home from the market. They are very heavy, and she is struggling. If you help her, you will be late to your friend's house. Will you help her? Ask your inner voice to say, "I should do this" or "I should not do this."

[Continue with this pattern, adding in another two or three actions that are relevant to the children in the class or relevant to the story under consideration.]

The values message here is clearly concerned with encouraging students to be aware of and listen to their consciences. This script starts with an affective focus, inviting students to reflect on the concept of a conscience and to experience the feelings of acting according to or against their consciences. It then continues with a cognitive task, reminding the students of the key incidents involved in the story that led to the moral conflict and the eventual resolution—but at the same time asking them to tune in to their own consciences before making their decisions about how they might have acted if they were the character(s) involved.

Topic: Story about a Natural Disaster (e.g., an Earthquake).
This visualization was developed for a story about a devastating earthquake that occurred in the Tibetan town of Yushu in 2010. After reading the story, the students worked in groups to suggest ideas for helping the people who were affected.

> Close your eyes and listen to the beautiful music.
>
> Imagine that you are in Yushu. Imagine you are standing in front of some children there. Now think about what you suggested in your group that you could do for them or give them. Imagine that you are really doing this now for the Yushu children standing in front of you. As you do it, feel love in your heart for them. They say thank you and go away.
>
> Now think about how it makes you feel in your heart to have helped the Yushu children. Think about the feeling in your heart that comes from helping somebody in trouble. When you open your eyes, try to hold this feeling in your heart for the rest of the day.

In this example, the teacher started by asking the class to listen to some relaxing music, which helped to settle them down after the group activity and to get into the right frame of mind for the visualization. The affective aspect is to experience the feelings of love, compassion, and happiness that come from helping others. The values message implied here is "love all, serve all."

Topic: Grammar (Present Tense)

> During this lesson, we have done some exercises to correct the use of the present tense in sentences. Close your eyes and listen while I read aloud the correct sentences. As you listen, try to appreciate the sense of balance in these correct sentences. [Read aloud as appropriate.] Now, while your eyes are closed, think about a time in your life when you have been worried or agitated about something that is going to happen in your future. Think about the way you felt; whether it was a pleasant or unpleasant feeling; whether it caused any distress in any part of your body. Now think about a time when you were upset about something that happened in the past. Again, think about the way you felt; whether it was a pleasant or unpleasant feeling; whether it caused any distress in any part of your body. Now bring your attention back into the room. Feel the chair underneath you, the floor beneath your feet, the table if you are leaning on it. Be aware of any sounds you can hear in the room . . . or sounds outside the room. Be aware of the temperature in the room. Be aware of the smells in the room. Now think about your breathing. Breathe in and out gently, just watching your breath as it flows in and out. [Allow 30 seconds to one minute for this breathing exercise.] Think about how you feel now, after focusing all of your attention on being in the present. How is it different from when you were worrying about the future or holding onto something from the past? Allow yourself to feel the balance of being in your own present tense. The breath is always with you as a refocusing tool to bring you back to the present moment.

The revision of the class exercises on present tense was used to open this visualization, as a means of reinforcing the cognitive aspect of what was covered in the lesson. It then moves on to exploring how students can be affected if they allow themselves to move away from their own present tense by worrying about the past or future, then appreciating the calmness of being in the present moment.

3.3 Discussion and Conclusion

This chapter has presented some examples of the silent sitting tool of guided visualization that can be used as a means of integrating education in human values into subject topics by combining cognitive subject knowledge, affective experiences, and reflection on a values message embedded in the topic. While silent sitting is not the only way to achieve this type of integration, it is an effective one because it is relatively easy to use and does not take up too much of the lesson time. Of course, this type of visualization should not be done in every lesson, as to do so would be to reduce its impact if students become too familiar with the approach. That said, silent sitting should be used regularly so that students realize its effectiveness. To this end, from time to time, discuss with students the effectiveness of silent sitting as a tool for cognitive understanding of both the subject topic and the underpinning values message, for evoking affective aspects, and for reflecting on the values message in relation to their own lives.

While only a few selected subjects have been included here, it is hoped that these will be sufficient as examples for teachers to develop their own scripts for other topics.

References

Basso, J., McHale, A., Ende, V., Oberlin, D., & Suzuki, W. (2019). Brief, daily meditation enhances attention, memory, mood, and emotional regulation in non-experienced meditators. *Behavioural Brain Research, 356,* 208–220.

Buchanan, M., & Hyde, B. (2008). Learning beyond the surface: Engaging the cognitive, affective and spiritual dimensions within the curriculum. *International Journal of Children's Spirituality, 13*(4), 309–320.

Buckner, R., Andrews-Hanna, J., & Schacter, D. (2008). The brain's default network: Anatomy, function, and relevance to disease. In A. Kingstone & M. B. Miller (Eds.), *The year in cognitive neuroscience 2008: Annals of the new York Academy of Sciences* (Vol. 1124, pp. 1–38). New York: Blackwell Publishing.

Condon, P., Desbordes, G., Miller, W., & DeSteno, D. (2013). Meditation increases compassionate responses to suffering. *Psychological Science, 24*(10), 2125–2127.

De Souza, M. (2004). Teaching for effective learning in religious education: A discussion of the perceiving, thinking, feeling and intuiting elements in the learning process. *Journal of Religious Education, 52*(3), 22–30.

de Vos, H., & Louw, D. (2009). Hypnosis-induced mental training programmes as a strategy to improve the self-concept of students. *Higher Education, 57*(2), 141–154.

Hill, B. (2004, April 28–29). *Values education in schools: Issues and challenges.* Melbourne, Australia: National Values Education Forum.

Jaloba, A. (2011). Change of mind. *Nursing Standard, 25*(50), 18–19.

Joksimović, S., Wang, E., San Pedro, M., Way, J., Siemens, G. (2018). Beyond cognitive ability: Enabling assessment of 21st century skills through learning analytics - call for papers. *Journal of Learning Analytics.* Retrieved from https://epress.lib.uts.edu.au/journals/index.php/JLA/announcement/view/138

Kang, Y., Gray, J., & Dovidio, J. (2013). The nondiscriminating heart: Loving kindness meditation training decreases implicit intergroup bias. *Journal of Experimental Psychology: General, 143* (3), 1306–1313. https://doi.org/10.1037/a0034150.

Khare, S. (2013). Dealing life hassles' with hypnotherapy: Case studies. *Indian Journal of Health and Wellbeing, 4*(2), 376–381.

Leiberg, S., Klimecki, O., & Singer, T. (2011). Short-term compassion training increases prosocial behavior in a newly developed prosocial game. *PLoS One, 6*(3), e17798. https://doi.org/10. 1371/journal.pone.0017798.

Lim, D., Condon, P., & DeSteno, D. (2015). Mindfulness and compassion: An examination of mechanism and scalability. *PLoS One, 10*(2), e0118221. https://doi.org/10.1371/journal.pone. 0118221.

Lovat, T., Dally, K., Clement, N., & Toomey, R. (2011). Values pedagogy and teacher education: Re-conceiving the foundations. *Australian Journal of Teacher Education, 36*(7), 31–44. https:// doi.org/10.14221/ajte.2011v36n7.3.

Mustakova-Possardt, E. (2004). Education for critical moral consciousness. *Journal of Moral Education, 33*(3), 245–269.

Semetsky, I. (2009). Transforming ourselves/transforming curriculum: Spiritual education and tarot symbolism. *International Journal of Children's Spirituality, 14*(2), 105–120.

Spreng, R., & Grady, C. (2010). Patterns of brain activity supporting autobiographical memory, prospection, and theory-of-mind and their relationship to the default mode network. *Journal of Cognitive Neuroscience, 22,* 1112–1123.

Taplin, M. (2014). A model for integrating spiritual education into secular curricula. *International Journal of Children's Spirituality, 19*(1), 4–16.

Tomasino, B., Chiesa, A., & Fabbro, F. (2014). Disentangling the neural mechanisms involved in Hinduism- and Buddhism-related meditations. *Brain and Cognition, 90,* 32–40.

Van Acker, R., & Mayer, M. (2008). Cognitive-behavioral interventions and the social context of the school: A stranger in a strange land. In M. Mayer, R. Van Acker, J. Lochman, & F. Gresham (Eds.), *Cognitive-behavioral interventions for emotional and behavioral disorders: School-based practice* (pp. 82–110). Washington, DC: Guilford Press.

Vincent, J., Kahn, I., Snyder, A., Raichle, M., & Buckner, R. (2008). Evidence for a frontoparietal control system revealed by intrinsic functional connectivity. *Journal of Neurophysiology, 100,* 3328–3342.

Weng, H., Fox, A., Shackman, A., Stodola, D., Caldwell, J., Olson, M., Rogers, G., & Davidson, R. (2013). Compassion training alters altruism and neural responses to suffering. *Psychological Science, 24*(7), 1171–1180.

Chapter 4
Light Meditation and Other Silent Sitting Techniques

Lalini Reddy

Abstract Our instructional system of education may be in need of changes if we are to meet the 2030 Sustainable Development Goal (SDG) deadline set by the United Nations Educational, Scientific and Cultural Organization (UNESCO 2016). According to the UNESCO Director-General, Irina Bokova:

> A fundamental change is needed in the way we think about education's role in global development, because it has a catalytic impact on the well-being of individuals and the future of our planet... Now, more than ever, education has a responsibility to be in gear with twenty-first century challenges and aspirations, and foster the right types of values and skills that will lead to sustainable and inclusive growth, and peaceful living together.

As teachers, we should not merely impart knowledge but rather the skill of how to acquire knowledge. Research has shown that students who are exposed to silent sitting or meditation develop improved holistic health and cognitive abilities. Various types of silent sitting and meditation techniques are recommended for various age groups of childhood and adolescence. This chapter offers a selection of techniques ranging from visualizations to music and repetition of words. The chapter also describes some cases of the impacts of these methods on students' performances and characters. One such impact is that the use of music or guided visualizations helped to lead students gradually inward, increasing awareness of their inner selves.

Keywords Silent sitting · One-pointed focus · Light meditation · Guided visualization

L. Reddy (✉)
Department Biotechnology and Consumer Science, Cape Peninsula University of Technology, Cape Town, South Africa
e-mail: reddyl@cput.ac.za

© Springer Nature Singapore Pte Ltd. 2021
S. Parahakaran, S. Scherer (eds.), *A Human Values Pathway for Teachers*,
https://doi.org/10.1007/978-981-16-0200-9_4

4.1   Introduction

Silent sitting is a way to transcend boundaries of race, color, or nationality. This was my personal experience. Silent sitting is a journey taking one to the core of one's being where there are no differences, just oneness. Born in South Africa and having traveled to many other countries in Africa to promote values-based education, I have seen it as a gifted opportunity to have witnessed the awesome power of silent sitting practiced by people across various races and nationalities. I have seen that it has a calming and healing effect and grants peace, joy and a sense of unity among us as citizens of the world.

During the apartheid era in South Africa, we experienced explicitly the effects of racial differences, having being subjected to restrictions and separateness. This stirred up many dilemmas in children, adolescents, and adults as to the questions of "Who am I?" and "Are we really different from each other?" The senses were perceiving diversity and incongruences all around. There were tensions in the students trying to educate themselves in the ways of the world. There was a cry for peace of mind and unity among all. Political rallies and student unrest were the norm of the era before the iconic President Nelson Mandela ushered in a democracy for the South African people.

Mandela spoke of what it was like to spend so many years alone and in silence while confined to his 6.4 by 5.4–meter prison cell. After his release, he told an interviewer that he was able to connect with his soul in that silence. And in the period of silence, he became committed to the path of forgiveness and reconciliation for all peoples (Montclair Presbyterian Church 2013). Nelson Mandela was an example of somebody who was able to change the world by first starting with himself, in silence.

Most students of today have to bear enormous challenges in order to achieve high academic standards. They are distracted by the various social and technological influences prevalent in modern society. The importance of education has become clouded. Events such as wars, natural disasters, and pandemics are causing young people to be stressed about the current and future status of their lives, of mankind and of planet Earth as a whole.

The education systems seem to be in need of rejuvenation to improve performance. In addition to academic achievement, the education system should also develop character in the youth of today, the future leaders of society. The education system needs to help them realize their potential by developing skills for lifelong learning. It is said that education is not merely for living but for life.

Transformative techniques in education may therefore be the need of the hour. It seems poignant for us to return to the age-old traditions and practices of our forefathers. Silent sitting is one such significant ancient technique that is rapidly becoming popular. Those experienced in the use of silent sitting and similar techniques have reported that it can help reduce stress, boost immunity, increase concentration, and improve sleep quality—all of which are beneficial to highly successful people (Natale 2018).

4.2 The Significance of Silent Sitting

The physical, emotional, psychological, and spiritual benefits of various silent sitting or meditation techniques might include higher levels of energy, creativity, and spontaneity; lower blood pressure; increased exercise tolerance; better concentration; decreased stress, depression and anxiety; fewer cravings for alcohol and cigarettes; increased job satisfaction; and better relationships with others (Black et al. 2009).

Meditation is a mental discipline by which one attempts to get beyond the thinking mind into a deeper state of awareness. The word meditation comes through the Latin *meditatio*, which originally indicated any type of physical or intellectual exercise. In the context of this chapter, the word meditation is used interchangeably with the words silent sitting or silencing the mind.

Meditation is not mere attention, relaxation, concentration, contemplation, or reflection. It is also not intended to control or develop willpower but rather to develop a connection with your true (inner) self. It may be said that your own inner voice is only heard in the depths of silence.

Silent sitting is presented as a powerful set of teaching or transformation techniques that can inspire children from a young age toward both academic and character excellence. The techniques may be used as standalone direct methods or may be integrated into various lessons. Silent sitting is meant to decrease the fleeting thoughts that occupy our minds. One needs to have control of the mind. We need to be conscious of our thoughts and differentiate between good and bad ones because thoughts determine our words, and our words determine our actions. We should W. A.T.C.H. our words, actions, thoughts, characters, and hearts (see Sect. 2.1.4 for further elaboration of this acronym). This control results in nurturing children with desirable characters. Their thoughts, words, and actions will be pure and in harmony.

The noise present in our day-to-day lives keeps most people from experiencing the oneness of all things. Sitting in silence helps us to know the oneness of all things not just mentally, through thoughts and ideas, but also spiritually, through direct contact and experience with our own inner nature and potential.

Silent sitting is a technique that is suitable for people of all ages, even very young children. The following section presents examples of techniques that are suitable for different age groups.

4.3 Examples of Silent Sitting for Different Age Groups

For all visualization scripts below, the dots represent the amount of time you have allotted for the children to stay silent.

4.3.1   Four- to Six-Year-Olds

Two simple examples appropriate for this age group to relax the body and mind are described below.

Example 1

> Sit comfortably with your back straight. Take a deep breath in, and now slowly let it out again. Close your eyes. You are sitting on a garden seat looking at the flowers. The flowers are many colours. Some are red; some are yellow. What other colours can you see? Now they are gently swaying in the breeze. You are enjoying looking at all the different colours of the flowers ... Now it's time to open your eyes. You are back in your room.

Example 2

> Sit comfortably with your back straight. Take a deep breath in, and now slowly let it out again. Close your eyes. Repeat the breathing nine times. Feel how relaxed your whole body now is. Now slowly open your eyes.

4.3.2   Seven- to Nine-Year-Olds

Children in this age group are usually quite energetic. In order to calm and settle them for their lessons, music may be played. This process of *tuning in* may put children in touch with their own inner feelings and help their emotional growth.

While light, peaceful music plays, the teacher instructs as follows (Robinson 2013):

> Sit comfortably with your back straight. Take a deep breath in, and now slowly let it out again. Close your eyes and listen to the music. Listen for when it plays a little louder. Listen for when it plays a little quieter. Feel quiet and peaceful while you are listening ... When the music stops playing, slowly open your eyes and sit quietly.

Another example enjoyed by this age group is the narration of a fun-filled journey to the beach or park:

> Sit comfortably with your back straight. Take a deep breath in, and now slowly let it out again. Close your eyes. Children, today we are going on a journey to the beach. Gather your sunhats, and let's walk to the yellow mini-bus parked in the school ground. As you climb in, don't forget to check that all your classmates are in the bus. The bus starts, and we begin our journey to the beach. Look through the window and admire the trees and flowers and enjoy the wind blowing on your face. There we are, children. We have arrived at the beach. Get down from the bus and walk to the picnic spot with your teachers. Oh, what a beautiful sunny day and with a cool breeze. Feel the soft, warm sand under your feet. Dip your toes in the water and feel how cool it is. You play a little longer and then have your snack ... By now, you must be tired. It's time for us to head back to school. Your parents will be waiting ... We have arrived. Look, your parents are waiting for you. I hope you had a wonderful time. Now slowly open your eyes.

4.3.3   Ten- to Twelve-Year-Olds

A simplified version of the light meditation visualization in Sect. 2.1.5.1 can be used with younger children, but this age group is one that particularly enjoys it. Meditation is recommended to be practiced either in the morning or in the evening in peaceful surroundings and preferably always sitting in the same place so the mind settles more easily.

A light, such as a candle, is used as the focal point. The flame never diminishes in luster. Light symbolizes wisdom and purity. We can use the metaphor that we can light up many others by shining our light on them, but our own inner light still remains shining in all its splendor.

4.3.4   Thirteen- to Fifteen-Year-Olds

Various techniques appeal to this age group. They enjoy narrations, sound recordings, videos, or audiovisual media comprising music and/or verbal instructions.

To sensitize students to conserving and appreciating nature, one may use nature pictures or videos as indicated below:

> Sit comfortably with your back straight. Take a deep breath in, and now slowly let it out again. Close your eyes and listen to your breath as you inhale and exhale three times. Now open your eyes and look at the picture of nature. What a beautiful serene sight. How clean and pure the water looks. The trees and shrubs are abundant. The sky is clear, and the air looks pure. The sunlight brightens up everything. Appreciate the perfect splendor of creation. Think about what you can do to help to preserve this beautiful world.

4.3.5   Sixteen- to Eighteen-Year-Olds

This group of youth may be exposed to light meditation, music, videos, and other stimulating foci to control the sensory input, purify the mind, and refine the intellect.

Meditating after listening to classical music, such as Beethoven's classics, or watching an inspiring video on a topic such as service to humanity after a disaster may alter their brainwaves or trigger mindset shifts, allowing their human values to unfold.

4.3.6   Nineteen-Year-Olds and above (E.G., University Students)

> The following is an example of a visualization to encourage students to think about their roles and responsibility in caring for the environment.

As with all groups of students, silent sitting starts with physical calming.

> Sit comfortably with your back straight. Take a deep breath in, and now slowly let it out again. Close your eyes and listen to your breath as you inhale and exhale three times. Just as rhythmic breathing is essential for our survival, our stock markets [or our environment, society or health] is constantly subjected to ups and downs. We should experience this sense of equanimity irrespective of happenings in the external world. Tuning in and experiencing the inner vision should provide you with great resilience to become mindful and competent citizens.

4.4   Impact of Light Meditation on Teachers and Students in Africa

This section gives a brief description of the experiences of a group of African teachers who were taught to use the Light Meditation technique. The objective was for them to gain inner peace for themselves and for the students with whom they subsequently used it. Teachers and students who were engaged in silent sitting gave personal testimonies.

The teachers reported that students in their classes claimed that they "chose to stay silent, instead of having continuous meaningless chatter and noise in the classroom which distracts from their work; I could concentrate on the task at hand; I felt empowered." The students relished the calming effect of the process. Silence seems to have the opposite effect for the brain compared to noise. While noise may cause stress and tension, silence releases tension in the brain and body. Bernardi et al. (2006) suggested that two minutes of silence can prove to be even more relaxing than listening to relaxing music.

These findings were similar to those of a study with Chinese learners, who experienced high demands from their parents. The parents held high expectations for their children's academic success and eventual admission into college or university. The parents were obsessed and often did not consider the price their children had to pay for this pressure. The stress placed on children can be overwhelming and have the opposite of the intended effect on their performances. In such situations, silent sitting was recommended to avoid stress and to increase brain potential and intellectual capacity (Lin and Chen 1995).

The African teachers found that silent sitting served to motivate students by affording them "a new experience." Word repetition during the silent sitting was found to be a favorite for children. This may have been a word such as "peace" or an inspiring quotation such as, "I am content at this moment." The important thing was that the word or phrase had a meaning for the students, offered hope, redirected their focus from negative to positive, or even drowned out chatter in the mind. The words may have been spoken aloud or repeated silently. Word repetition is an effective way to utilize the SSEHV technique of positive affirmations and quotations (see Sect. 2. 1.3). A further discussion of the use of word or quotation repetition is given in Chap. 6 and 7.

In spite of the repetition of words or chanting, repeated breathing and sitting in a precise body posture, the children did not find this boring. In fact, they looked forward to the time when the teacher began a silent sitting session. Gradually, even the mischievous children began to calm down.

One teacher reported that, in summer, she took her students outside to lie on the grass and look at the endless sky, and the students experienced clarity and felt serenity. Teachers reported that they experienced clarity and serenity as well. This is another example of an approach to using silent sitting in nature to experience the peace of inner silence.

The teachers found that when their students spoke less, their mental abilities appeared to be sharper and their performances on their academic tasks improved. One teacher explained, "When I became more silent in the class, the students followed suit gradually." When one becomes silent oneself, silence is induced in others. If we are able to carry with us an atmosphere of quiet contemplation, we can induce calmness in others. The students indicated they felt calm and composed and had more energy to tackle the work at hand. They were not easily agitated by others around them.

Another teacher declared that she had been struggling with anger with her family and students and even with road rage. After 2 months of practicing silent sitting, her anger subsided.

4.5 Conclusion

You need not escape into a forest to gain silence and to experience uninterrupted spiritual practice. "You can make the place where you are a citadel of silence; shut off the senses, let them not run after objects" (Sathya Sai Baba).

"Silence is the first step ... It promotes self-control; it lessens chances of anger, hate, malice, greed, pride" (Sathya Sai Baba). Silence is certainly a tonic for transforming young people's characters.

References

Bernardi, L., Porta, C., & Sleight, P. (2006). Cardiovascular, cerebrovascular, and respiratory changes induced by different types of music in musicians and non-musicians: The importance of silence. *Heart, 92*(4), 445–452.

Black, D. S., Milam, J., & Sussman, S. (2009). Sitting-meditation interventions among youth: A review of treatment efficacy. *Pediatrics, 124*(3), e532–e541.

Lin, J., & Chen, Q. (1995). Academic pressure and impact on students' development in China. *McGill Journal of Education, 30*(2), 149–168.

Montclair Presbyterian Church. (2013). *Mandela and the power of silence.* Retrieved May 17, 2020, from https://mpcfamily.org/2013/12/06/mandela-power-silence/

Natale, N. (2018). 8 highly successful CEOs and celebrities who practice meditation. *Everday health*. Retrieved May 17, 2020, from https://www.everydayhealth.com/meditation/highly-successful-ceos-celebrities-who-practice-meditation/

Robinson, J. (2013). *A manual for integrating human values into children's education*. Perth, Australia: Jacqui Robinson.

United Nations Educational, Scientific and cultural organization (UNESCO). (2016). Education needs to change fundamentally to meet global development goals. *UNESCO*. http://www.unesco.org/new/en/media-services/single-view/news/education_needs_to_change_fundamentally_to_meet_global_devel/

Chapter 5
A Conceptual Framework for a Mindfulness Intervention

Cheryl Talley, Stephen Scherer, and Oliver Hill

Abstract A significant number of students reside in high stress, high risk, and under-resourced communities in the USA. Social and cultural factors are often reported to contribute to low educational outcomes in distressed communities. However, students attending under-resourced schools demonstrate a great deal of positive traits that are conducive to high academic achievement. For those students from challenging backgrounds, a constellation of traits contributes to academic success. Grouped together, they come under the term resilience. How is resilience impacted by values education? What specific components of Sathya Sai Education in Human Values (SSEHV) are most effective in helping students become better students? What role does a conceptual theory play in replicating the effects of SSEHV? After providing evidence for a sound theoretical framework, we seek to answer these questions using an illustrative form of a knowledge case study.

Keywords Mindfulness · PVEST · Teaching · Pedagogy · Human values · School · Stress

5.1 PVEST as a Theoretical Framework

Transformative learning is an emerging body of work from adult learning theory and is defined as a process of perspective transformation with three dimensions: psychological (changes in understanding of the self), convictional (revisions of belief systems), and behavioral (changes in life style) (Mezirow 1991). Transformative learning, therefore, is the expansion of worldview and specific capacities of the self. Adult learners typically engage in this type of learning following a "disorienting

C. Talley · O. Hill
Virginia State University, Petersburg, VA, USA

S. Scherer (✉)
Virginia State University, Petersburg, VA, USA

R.I.S.E. Psychological Services, White Plains, NY, USA
e-mail: sscherer@jdam.org

© Springer Nature Singapore Pte Ltd. 2021   41
S. Parahakaran, S. Scherer (eds.), *A Human Values Pathway for Teachers*,
https://doi.org/10.1007/978-981-16-0200-9_5

dilemma," a life crisis or major life transition. An example of a life crisis is a change of job or loss of a spouse, significant life events that become more likely as one gets older (Mezirow 1997).

In this chapter, we posit that Sathya Sai Education in Human Values (SSEHV) is a type of transformative learning, developed originally for but not limited to children (Alderman 1988, 1996; Kaliannan 2010). We begin with the premise that SSEHV causes changes in a child's understanding of the self, which lead to revisions of their belief systems. These together result in a change in behavior. Children experience their own versions of major life transitions and disorienting dilemmas. This is particularly true of children of marginalized groups (Coakley 2003; Harper 2008; Palmer et al. 2009). However, children are not likely to be able to express the expansion of worldview and enhanced capacities of the self as transformative learning theory would posit. Hence, while SSEHV may contribute to transformative learning, the transformative learning theory may not be appropriate to investigate transformative experiences in children.

A theoretical framework contains multiple theories that appear to be interrelated. We posit here that transformative learning theory should be combined with a theory developed for children and adolescents. The two theories together provide a framework that would be useful in investigating the efficacy of SSEHV.

Interventions need to have theoretical underpinnings since the theory helps define the specific constructs that are impacted by the intervention. In addition, a sound theory enables future researchers to build upon the knowledge of the constructs with reliable and valid assessments. Finally, following understanding and measurement, researchers are able to further the knowledge gains by predicting when an intervention is likely to be most effective; identifying what components are absolutely essential no matter the context; and most importantly, explaining why the intervention works in the first place.

Understanding the theoretical framework for SSEHV would ensure that the impressive improvement in educational outcomes seen in India and other parts of the world by SSEHV programs can be copied with fidelity regardless of the cultural setting. In most of the reported success cases with SSEHV, the targeted populations were children from non-Western parts of the world, and some of the interventions were provided to children who attended poor schools or no school at all (Farmer and Farmer 2015; Kaliannan 2010; Majmudar 1998; Taplin 2014; Yust 2016). SSEHV has also been used successfully with "troubled" children in Australia and with children orphaned due to AIDS in Nigeria (Farmer and Farmer 2015; Ogada n.d.).

In this chapter, we report on an SSEHV-inspired program targeting African American college students, most of whom were educated in urban schools in the USA. With this case in mind, we utilized another learning theory, one that is specifically designed for children at risk but that also considers the constellation of positive traits these students bring to their learning experience. The knowledge case study approach is used here in order to illustrate how the theoretical framework was used in describing the essential components of the intervention.

The Phenomenological Variant of the Ecological Systems Theory (PVEST) uses a resilience-based approach to investigate youth development (Spencer et al. 1997).

In this chapter, we consider PVEST as a theoretical framework to illustrate an academic intervention that focuses on values education for college freshmen. The students who participated in the intervention attended a historically Black college/university (HBCU) where nearly 98% of the student body qualified for federal financial aid. Societal norms regarding race and class distinctions are often reflected in educational outcomes in American public schools (Klein 2011). Therefore, less-privileged students are far more likely to attend under-resourced public schools that routinely score in the bottom quartile of mandated standardized tests. In order to succeed in college, these students must undergo the psychological, convictional, and behavioral changes needed to succeed in an entirely different context from their previous school experience. According to the PVEST model, students that are able to make these changes must utilize resilience.

PVEST uses a systems-oriented human development perspective to maximize our understanding of not only resilience but also vulnerability and risk factors often experienced by marginalized youth. This focus on risk and resilience is also linked to normative developmental processes that occur regardless of social context. PVEST rests on the premise that challenges are an inherent part of normal development and negotiating solutions to challenges demonstrates a degree of competence or skill, independent of the circumstances. Risk, therefore, must be conceptualized as a normal and expected part of development.

However, PVEST acknowledges not only personal challenges inherent in normal development but also personal challenges exacerbated by broad sociopolitical processes such as racism, sexism, or poverty. (Gallay and Flanagan 2000). In other words, overcoming personal as well as socially derived challenges provides the basis for a "disorienting dilemma" from which an identity is formed. According to Spencer (1995), the central task for all adolescents is successful identity formation. Therefore, the central task for racial and ethnic minority adolescents is successful identity formation within the context of being a member of a disfavored group.

Spencer's (1995) work was developed using a multidisciplinary perspective and drew from sociology, anthropology, and developmental psychology. The primary psychological theories were from Bronfenbrenner (1979) and Erickson (1968), who Spencer felt best explained the "ontogeny of self." Aspects of ethnicity and ethnic identity have profound implications for the ongoing experiences of marginalized youths, especially during puberty. Adolescence is the stage of human development in which insecurity of the self is the normative state. For individuals in disenfranchised groups (those physically distinct from the majority culture and/or disfavored by social grouping), the qualitative experiences have particularly important implications for the formation of identity.

According to Spencer (2018), the vast majority of academic interventions primarily focus on the skills needed in the school setting and in the building of an individual's academic competencies. While these individual skills and competencies are necessary, they are not sufficient to ensure long-term successful educational outcomes and a meaningful, well-lived life that contributes to the larger community. For that, it is necessary to have not only cognitive competence but also emotional, social and, we argue, *intra*personal competencies.

SSEHV focuses on aspects of social emotional learning and is often delivered to students in regular classrooms. Some researchers have shown that training in being cooperative, fair, or compassionate, for example, when delivered to children as a "stand-alone" or "added-on" program is far less effective than when embedded in regular classroom teaching (Lovat et al. 2010). Embedding social emotional learning is also known as values-based education.

Values-based education is an approach to teaching that includes values and, in so doing, focuses on developing children's social, emotional, and relational skills, along with cognitive abilities. In a values-based curriculum, such skills as honesty, compassion, and generosity would be honed by learning activities utilizing emotional and, some would argue, spiritual components.

For instance, one of the primary teaching techniques utilized in SSEHV is a meditative technique called silent sitting. The ability to be in the present moment and observe the inner landscape of the mind is an important competency that helps hone creativity, concentration, and focus. Of course, meditation or any other metacognitive skill can be taught only by experience. Traditionally, trained classroom teachers rarely have the time or inclination to provide opportunities to teach or perhaps learn skills such as these. This is true despite business leaders calling for graduates to have experience with teamwork, creativity, and even ethical behavior, as these skills are much needed for the workers of the twenty-first century (Radermacher and Walia 2013).

A recently published meta-analysis of over 200 public schools showed that social and emotional learning (SEL) has a direct impact on achievement outcomes, as well as life outcomes (Durlak et al. 2011). SEL is defined as follows:

> ... the process through which children and adults acquire and effectively apply the knowledge, attitudes, and skills necessary to understand and manage emotions; set and achieve positive goals; feel and show empathy for others; establish and maintain positive relationships and make responsible decisions. (Collaborative for Academic, Social, and Emotional Learning [CASEL] 2005)

The PVEST model fundamentally incorporates SEL's stated goals. The proximal goals of SEL programs are to foster the development of cognitive, affective, and behavioral competencies: self-awareness, self-management, social awareness, relationship skills, and responsible decision making (CASEL 2005). However, the incorporation of identity formation along with emotional development from the PVEST model allows for a more nuanced understanding of what is needed for successful interventions to actually acknowledge the social aspect of social and emotional learning.

Ultimately, according to PVEST, a young person's emergent identity is impacted by the coping processes they have developed in order to navigate the stresses they encounter. Of course, some students experience more stress than others, as well as different emotional vulnerabilities. However, all students create strategies for dealing with their environment in ways dictated by their stage of development and affirmed or accepted by their community. When those strategies lead to positive outcomes for the child, that is known as resilience.

5.2 PVEST and Resilience

As mentioned earlier, a primary goal of a sound theoretical framework is its ability to identify and define important constructs that are deemed crucial to the intervention. After examining hundreds of research studies, the American Psychological Association's (APA's) Task Force on Resilience and Strength in Black Children and Adolescents (APA 2008) used PVEST to define resilience as the interaction between traits (critical mindedness, agency, flexibility, and communalism) across several developmental domains (identity, emotional, cognitive, social, and physical). Within an educational context, optimal resilience requires competencies in all of these areas, which intersect and interact with each other.

According to the task force report (APA 2008), enhancing resilience in African American students must be considered a primary goal. However, the following limitations of this goal are evident, as the report acknowledges that resilience is not easy to assess.

1. Resilience is a fluid process that is not easily encompassed by a list of protective factors; rather, it is the interaction of strength, resources, and risk factors within a context and across space and time.
2. Resilience is a dynamic, multidimensional construct that incorporates the bidirectional interaction between individuals and their environments within contexts (family, peer, school, immediate community, and society).
3. Resilience occurs in the presence of real or perceived risk or adversity and includes more than merely surviving but also encompasses the ability to be empowered to live life fully.

The difficulty in defining (and therefore assessing) resilience might be one reason for its absence in educational outcomes in most published work. In addition, few educational studies and fewer educational policies acknowledge how cultural or race-related factors influence adaptive behaviors in school. Just as resilience is difficult to assess, so are the psychological and convictional values that precede the adaptive behaviors of overcoming challenges.

Behaviors that reflect resilience can go unrecognized or are misinterpreted as disciplinary problems within educational settings. The result is that vulnerable youths are often denied the recognition of their accomplishments obtained by demonstrating agency and success in adverse living conditions. Thus, the potential and positive protective factors are ignored instead of acknowledged. The ramifications of being socialized as pathological or deviant impacts identify formation. Thus labeled, an individual's perception of self and future opportunities is affected along with the imposed expectations and stereotypes from others (Spencer et al. 2015).

The challenge of developing a positive self-concept in light of negative societal norms is not unique to African Americans. This challenge was also likely to be present for the Dalits (i.e., the lower caste in rural India, where SSEHV originated) and for children who have been classified as "different" in schools in Nigeria (orphans due to AIDS) and Australia (troubled boys). However, SSEHV as a regular

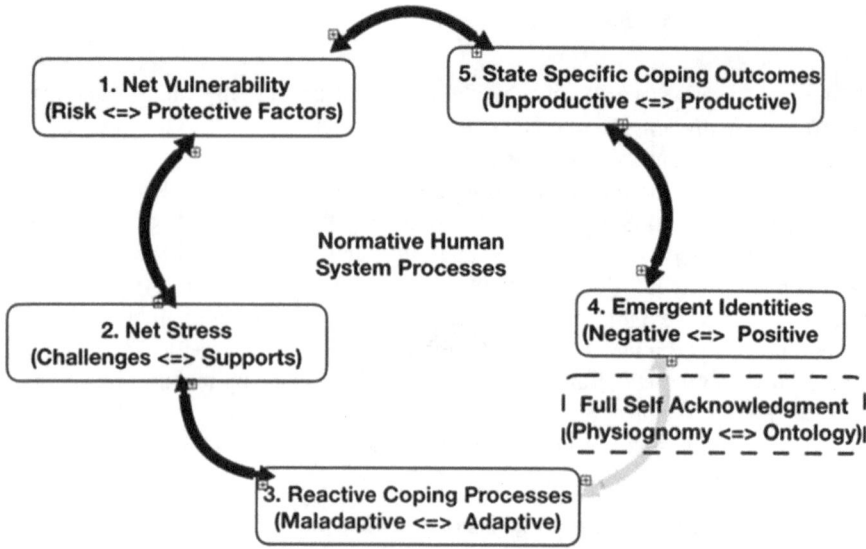

Fig. 5.1 Adaptation of PVEST to induce full self-acknowledgment (physiognomy to ontology) as a factor in normal human development

school offering has been slow to take root in the West. Perhaps this can be changed by framing SSEHV as an effective intervention that is data driven and based on a strong conceptual foundation and learning theory.

An effective intervention requires measurement. Once interventions are assessed, then iterative changes can be made as indicated by the results. Usually, the assessment is developed from a theory that then drives the creation of the intervention. This is what is known as a data driven and conceptually based approach. However, in real life, the theory does not always drive the research. Sometimes, the intervention has proven successful and then attempts are made to retrofit it onto a theory. Fortunately, PVEST is also resilient as a theory and can be used to dissect interventions into foundational components. Those components, once accurately identified, can then be individually assessed. One tool that has proven useful in fitting the components of an intervention or creating an assessment instrument consistent with the PVEST framework is an adaptation of the model developed by Spencer et al. (1997) (see Fig. 5.1).

The Spencer model moves counterclockwise around the circle of the normative human system processes of identity formation. Dichotomous outcomes are associated with each of five boxes:

1. Net vulnerability.
2. Net stress.
3. Reactive coping processes.
4. Emergent identities.
5. Stage-specific coping outcomes.

In this adaptation, a sixth box is inserted between reactive coping processes and emergent identities. This factor, called full self-acknowledgement, recognizes the potential for growth in the area of knowledge of one's self across the broad spectrum of a human being's inner experience. Within the PVEST theory, full self-acknowledgment provides a space for emerging self-discovery and the potential to impact both reactive coping and identity formation. This can be done without denying or downplaying the impact of cultural and societal forces on development. History has provided myriad examples of individuals who rose above the gender, racial, or class roles thrust upon them to create a powerful persona of their own choosing. A common feature of such accounts is introspection, self-reflection, or spiritual inquiry.

According to Spencer et al. (1997), the five boxes of her theory influence each other serially like train cars on a track or snarled traffic: if one breaks down, the cars behind are affected. The boxes can also be represented as building blocks, where the sequence is stacked. Those blocks coming before serve as foundation for the ones after. The insertion of full self-acknowledgement presumes that each of the numbered boxes is also affected by growth in ontological considerations, such that alternative meanings can be given to stress, vulnerability, coping and, eventually, to one's own identity.

In the original model and in this adaptation, the entire enterprise is moving along a developmental trajectory, from birth to early adulthood. Thus, as identities are formed and reformed in each stage of life, they are built upon the strengths and weaknesses, stressors and coping methods, meaning and framing that were learned during the preceding stages.

In the next section, we show how an academic intervention was created based on the premise that behavioral transformation was possible and would occur when students were provided a means of full self-acknowledgment through an adaptation of SSEHV that included a mindfulness practice.

5.3   Project Knowledge at Virginia State University (VSU)

Research conducted at Virginia State University (VSU) has demonstrated the effects of building resilience through a values-based intervention. The findings show that strategies that encourage student academic motivation are more effective when based on the strengths that the students recognize in themselves and have already demonstrated in some capacity. The academic intervention aimed at revealing this capacity in a group of incoming first-year college students was called Project Knowledge (2013). Project Knowledge was funded by the National Science Foundation (Fife et al. 2015; Talley et al. 2016). This academic intervention did not include any academic content, remediation, or tutoring but was solely focused on affective, sometimes called non-cognitive, factors. The idea behind Project Knowledge was that self-knowledge was the most important knowledge to be obtained by a college education. In this section, we examine Project Knowledge as a knowledge case study. We also illustrate the use of PVEST as a theoretical framework for an academic intervention adapted from SSEHV.

The first phase of the three phases of Project Knowledge was called Transition to College (T2C) and occurred the week before freshmen orientation. Entering students with an intent to major in a field associated with science, technology, engineering or math (STEM) were paired with other STEM freshmen who had been accepted into the university honors program. The program began 1 week before all other freshmen arrived on campus, and so this first group of around 40 students was not aware who was in the honors program and who was not. The program was inferred to be for elite, successful students so that the non-honors students would begin to identify themselves as successful, even before classes started. This tactic took advantage of the Pygmalion effect, as described by Rosenthal and Jacobson (1968), in which the expectation of a teacher influences how students may view themselves in terms of academic ability.

The students were grouped with academic mentors in a 1:5 ratio. The mentors had all been trained in the Project Knowledge mentoring pedagogy, which included components derived from servant leadership, expectancy task value, and critical race theory (Delgado and Stefancic 2012; Dennis et al. 2010; Eccles 2005). Since the entering freshmen had previously stated their intention of pursuing a STEM major (e.g., computer science, civil engineering, or mathematics), they were placed with a mentor who was pursuing that same major. The use of near-peer academic mentors was based on a substantial body of literature that shows the profound effect of vertical mentoring on retention of college students, particularly African American college freshmen retention (Booker and Brevard 2017; Kendricks et al. 2013; Riggs et al. 2014).

The first phase of the program contained nearly 80 h of programming. Eventually, up to 75 students were engaged in some planned activity from 9:00 a.m. until 10:00 p.m. for 6 days. The instructors (principal investigators and graduate students) facilitated the bulk of classroom instruction that occurred during the day. However, as many as 15 undergraduate mentors (under the supervision of three graduate students) provided the programming in the evenings. Every activity, other than outcomes assessment, was tied to the operational grid of the PVEST theory (see Table 5.1).

Three of the T2C activities are relevant to this discussion. The first activity focused on reflection and introspection and helped to answer the question of why the students decided to come to college. This activity was adapted from the work of Simon Sinek (2009). The second activity was in-class discussion on what virtues were necessary to succeed in college and resulted in the students identifying those virtues as themes for future classes. The third activity was the introduction, for the majority of the students, to a daily meditation practice that was held at the beginning of each class session. As stated earlier, mindfulness has been associated with many positive benefits, including higher academic achievement with college students in STEM (Hall 1999; Nidich et al. 2011; Scherer et al. 2017; Talley and Scherer 2013). A more in-depth discussion of mindfulness is provided in Chap. 6 of this book by the same authors.

Table 5.1 PVEST operational grid (see Talley et al. 2015 for more details)

	1. Critical mindedness	2. Active engagement	3. Flexibility	4. Communalism
A. Identity development	A.1	A.2	A.3	A.4
B. Emotional development	B.1	B.2	B.3	B.4
C. Social development	C.1	C.2	C.3	C.4
D. Cognitive development	D.1	D.2	D.3	D.4

During the one-week intensive portion of the intervention, the classroom sessions that took place Monday through Friday were modified from the SSEHV curriculum (Alderman 1988). The sessions utilized what are known as the five teaching techniques. These techniques, although developed for younger children, were easily adapted for incoming college freshmen. Each class session included the reciting of an affirmation, a group song, a narrative or story that featured a particular virtue, an action game, and a mindfulness practice.

The second phase of the intervention, known as Straight to the Top, occurred over the course of the entire freshmen year during weekly one-hour sessions. For 12 weeks each semester, the information that was first introduced during T2C was repeated and reinforced. The sessions contained lessons and activities that utilized the five teaching techniques and focused on a virtue that had been previously identified as important to college success by the participants themselves. The weekly sessions also emphasized study techniques and encouraged the development of sound academic habits.

The third phase of the intervention was the recruitment and training of mentors for the following academic year. The research showed that the students who excelled in the program were more likely to excel in their coursework. These very students were often motivated to become mentors themselves. The mentoring phase of the intervention also served as the mechanism for sustaining the program after the funding period.

By 2017, the first freshmen cohort who started in 2013 had persisted in their STEM discipline with a graduation rate of 69%, which is higher than the national average in STEM (50%). In addition, qualitative findings show that participants in Project Knowledge retained the skills from freshman year and utilized them for the remainder of their time in college.

The Project Knowledge graduates often stated that their relationship with a mentor was the most important aspect of the program. Therefore, the training of Project Knowledge mentors was considered key to the program's effectiveness. The most important quality a mentor possessed, as stated by the mentees, was a strong ability to provide empathy. In fact, the most successful mentors were those who scored higher on an assessment of servant leadership qualities (Howard et al. 2018).

Increasing retention and graduation rates among African American STEM students is an important accomplishment for a college-based intervention. The program was successful in not only providing what the STEM students needed but also providing training and resources for non-participants on and off campus. One example is the online modules on study skills, adapted from the book *How to Become a Straight-A Student* (Newport 2007). This resource has been viewed over 140,000 times (Project Knowledge 2013). However, the data regarding the mindfulness practice has provided the best insight as to why the intervention was effective.

Mindfulness has been implicated in a number of analyses. A path analysis revealed a positive relationship between mindfulness and cognitive-emotional regulation and a negative association between mindfulness and self-handicapping behaviors (self-defeating actions that are used as an ego-protecting device) and a negative outlook on one's own ability (Scherer et al. 2017; Tope-Banjoko 2018). In other words, as students increase their mindfulness practice, their ability to regulate their emotions increases, and conversely, their self-handicapping behavior decreases. These results support previous findings from our program that show that self-regulation is positively associated with grade point average (GPA) (Scherer et al. 2017). A prior study also indicated that African American students were more likely to utilize self-handicapping behaviors (Pearson 2013). Therefore, an intervention that decreases the need for self-handicapping and increases self-regulation is likely to increase academic achievement with African American students.

Our most recent findings confirm the relationship between self-regulation and GPA. Freshmen were given an affective assessment (Personal Factors that Influence Academic Behavior, or PIAB III) at the beginning and end of their freshmen year. The findings show an association with self-regulation and grades during the first semester, but by the second semester, self-efficacy became associated with grades. With further analysis, we expect to see that a mindfulness practice is useful in the beginning to help students remain in school, and once they are retained, they become more successful in regulating negative emotions that interfere with academic success.

Taken together, these findings provide support for academic enrichment programs that include a metacognitive or mindfulness component and elucidate variables that contribute to their effectiveness, like self-regulation. Considering these results within the PVEST conceptual framework suggests that metacognitive activities such as mindfulness may serve as a mediator between reactive coping and a student identifying themselves as high performing. Further work in this area will increase our understanding of the role of resilience and help to inform academic enrichment programs anywhere in the world.

5.4   Conclusion

Project Knowledge is an example of how PVEST was used in the design, implementation, and assessment of an academic intervention aimed at college freshmen. Project Knowledge was modeled after the SSEHV program. One primary goal of

Project Knowledge was to influence the habits, behaviors, attitudes, and affective factors of entering college students. The researchers assumed that no significant change occurred in the academic habits of students in the 3 months between graduation from high school (Grade 12) and their first year of college (Grade 13). By training mentors in the Project Knowledge mentoring pedagogy, the intervention ultimately had the potential to reach students from kindergarten through the last year of college (Grades K–16).

The focus on PVEST-identified concepts as primary targets of the intervention allowed for the creation of an assessment battery to measure targeted constructs and provide quantitative data analysis. Combining this methodology with qualitative methods, such as focus groups, enabled us to address two questions: "Did the intervention work?" and, just as crucial, "Why did it work?"

According to Spencer (2018), the question of why the intervention worked is the more important. As SSEHV becomes more mainstream, more empirical studies will be needed to elucidate the underlying mechanisms necessary for replication efforts. This present study has provided some clues as to what drives success in SSEHV programs. The qualitative data suggests that the psychological, convictional, and behavioral changes would not have occurred without the aid of near-peer academic mentors providing a trusting relationship (Howard et al. 2018). The quantitative data clearly shows a relationship between self-regulation and GPA. Continuing students who had higher grades exhibited more self-regulation (Davis et al. 2018). There was also a positive association between self-regulation and mindfulness (Scherer et al. 2017). Additional study is needed to further elucidate a causal relationship, if one exists, between mindfulness and higher grades.

The mindfulness practice was taught as part of a voluntary extracurricular activity held once per week. Quite probably, the effects on self-regulation could be magnified if the techniques were used in the classroom setting every day with younger children.

The intrapersonal skill of monitoring one's own thoughts and feelings was not included in the original PVEST model. However, in this adaptation, the notion of full self-acknowledgment recognizes personal epistemology as a useful academic competency. Many students in low-performing school districts have little or no opportunity for self-reflection or quiet inner experience. Techniques associated with mindfulness can provide the access to introspective ability that many students need and may lead to significant improvements in academic performance. Additional evidence supports this view. For example, Ramirez and Beilock (2011) found that reflective writing by students about their fears and anxieties right before a test produced significant improvement in performance. Additionally, Lutz et al. (2008) demonstrated that a few minutes of mindfully putting the attention on a region of the body shifts neural activation from the medial frontal cortex, which is associated with rumination and negative self-talk, to more lateral areas associated with relaxed states. In Chap. 6 by the same authors, a more detailed description of incorporating mindful teaching approaches in the primary and secondary classroom is provided.

In conclusion, we are just beginning to answer the question of why a non-academic intervention based on values would work. The answers are not completely clear, but our experience with Project Knowledge suggests that a values-based intervention, such as SSEHV, depends on the fact that, while values are malleable, they cannot be taught in the traditional sense. Instead, a values-based intervention requires close bonding relationships in order to create the context (trust and vulnerability) for the modeling and then adoption and sustaining of academic behaviors associated with successful outcomes.

The findings from our research suggest that self-regulation is an important competency in terms of academic achievement and that self-regulation is enhanced with a mindfulness practice. The identification of such crucial components of the intervention along with the development of a reliable assessment instrument provides support for PVEST serving as an effective theoretical framework.

The modeling and training in the values taught in the SSEHV curriculum lead to transformative learning. Students altered their beliefs about themselves, acted on their convictions, and adopted and maintained sound academic habits. Our hope is that in promoting values, we are providing our students the tools for a transformative life.

Acknowledgments This research was partially supported by National Science Foundation (NSF) grants HRD-1533563 and DRL-1621416 to Oliver Hill.

References

Alderman, C. (1988). *Education in human values*. East Sussex, UK: Sathya Sai Education in Human Values of the UK.

Alderman, C. (1996). *Sathya Sai education in human values, book 1, ages 6–9*. East Sussex, UK: Sathya Sai Education in Human Values of the UK.

American Psychological Association (APA). (2008). Task force on resilience and strength in black children and adolescents. In *Resilience in African American children and adolescents: A vision for optimal development*. Washington, DC: American Psychological Association.

Booker, K., & Brevard, E., Jr. (2017). Why mentoring matters: African-American students and the transition to college. *Mentor: An Academic Advising Journal, 19*, 1–9. https://doi.org/10.26209/MJ1961245.

Bronfenbrenner, U. (1979). *The ecology of human development*. Cambridge, UK: Harvard University Press.

Coakley, K. (2003). What do we know about the motivation of African American students? Challenging the "anti-intellectual" myth. *Harvard Educational Review, 73*(4), 524–558.

Collaborative for Academic, Social, and Emotional Learning (CASEL). (2005). Retrieved August 3, 2018 from, https://casel.org/what-is-sel/

Davis, V., Morrison, K., Tope-Banjoko, T., Fife, J., & Talley, C. P. (2018). *Project knowledge: An effective non-academic academic intervention* (In preparation).

Delgado, R., & Stefancic, J. (2012). *Critical race theory: An introduction*. New York: New York University Press.

Dennis, R. S., Kinzler-Norheim, L., & Bocarnea, M. (2010). Servant leadership theory. In *Servant leadership* (pp. 169–179). London, UK: Palgrave Macmillan.

Durlak, J. A., Weissberg, R. P., Dymnicki, A. B., Taylor, R. D., & Schellinger, K. B. (2011). The impact of enhancing students' social and emotional learning: A meta-analysis of school-based universal interventions. *Child Development, 82*(1), 405–432.

Eccles, J. S. (2005). Subjective task value and the Eccles et al. model of achievement-related choices. In A. J. Elliot & C. S. Dweck (Eds.), *Handbook of competence and motivation* (pp. 105–121). New York: Guilford Press.

Erickson, E. (1968). *Identity, youth and crisis*. New York: W. W. Norton.

Farmer, R., & Farmer, S. (2015). *Handbook for teachers in human values education*. Beenleigh, Australia: Dr. Ron and Suwanti Farmer.

Fife, J. E., Talley, C. P., & Hill, O. (2015). *Reducing stereotype threat by enhancing emotional regulation: A role for mindful awareness practice for STEM majors*. (Unpublished manuscript).

Gallay, L. S., & Flanagan, C. A. (2000). The well-being of children in a changing economy: Time for a new social contract in America. In R. D. Taylor & M. C. Wang (Eds.), *Resilience across contexts: Family, work, culture, and community* (pp. 3–33). Mahwah, NJ: Lawrence Erlbaum Associates Publishers.

Hall, P. D. (1999). The effect of meditation on the academic performance of African American college students. *Journal of Black Studies, 29*(3), 408–415.

Harper, S. R. (2008). Realizing the intended outcomes of brown: High-achieving African American male undergraduates and social capital. *American Behavioral Scientist, 51*(7), 1030–1053.

Howard, S., Morrison, K., Davis, V., & Talley, C. P. (2018). *Emotional intelligence and servant leadership* (unpublished manuscript).

Kaliannan, M. (2010). Education in human values (EHV): Alternative approach for a holistic teaching. *Educational Research and Reviews, 5*(12), 802–807.

Kendricks, K. D., Nedunuri, K. V., & Arment, A. R. (2013). Minority student perceptions of the impact of mentoring to enhance academic performance in STEM disciplines. *Journal of STEM Education: Innovations and Research, 14*(2), 38–46.

Klein, J. (2011). The failure of American schools. *The Atlantic, 307*(5), 66–77.

Lovat, T., Toomey, R., & Clement, N. (Eds.). (2010). *International research handbook on values education and student wellbeing*. Dordrecht, Netherlands: Springer. Academic Publishers.

Lutz, A., Slagter, H. A., Dunne, J. D., & Davidson, R. J. (2008). Attention regulation and monitoring in meditation. *Trends in Cognitive Sciences, 12*(4), 163–169.

Majmudar, M. (1998). *Sathya Sai education in human values (SSEHV): Theory and practice*. Scotland: Majmudar.

Mezirow, J. (1991). *Transformative dimensions of adult learning*. San Francisco, CA: Jossey-Bass.

Mezirow, J. (1997). Transformative learning: Theory to practice. *New Directions for Adult and Continuing Education, 1997*(74), 5–12.

Newport, C. (2007). *How to become a straight-a student: The unconventional strategies real college students use to score high while studying less*. New York: Three Rivers Press.

Nidich, S., Mjasiri, S., Nidich, R., Rainforth, M., Grant, J., Valosek, L., Chang, W., & Zigler, R. L. (2011). Academic achievement and transcendental meditation: A study with at-risk urban middle school students. *Education, 131*(3), 556–564.

Ogada, C. (n.d.). *Spiritan self awareness initiative*. https://www.joyvillages.org/the-founder/r

Palmer, R. T., Davis, R. J., & Hilton, A. A. (2009). Exploring challenges that threaten to impede the academic success of academically underprepared black males at an HBCU. *Journal of College Student Development, 50*(4), 429–445.

Pearson, B. (2013). *Motivation during academic uncertainty in STEM: A temporal approach to understanding STEM students' behavioral and emotional responses to academic performance decline*. Petersburg, VA: Virginia State University.

Radermacher, A., & Walia, G. (2013). Gaps between industry expectations and the abilities of graduates. In *Proceeding of the 44th ACM technical symposium on computer science education* (pp. 525–530). Denver: ACM.

Ramirez, G., & Beilock, S. L. (2011). Writing about testing worries boosts exam performance in the classroom. *Science, 331*(6014), 211–213.

Riggs, S. A., Musewe, L., & Harvey, J. P. (2014). Mentoring and academic performance of black and under-resourced urban middle grade students. *Negro Educational Review, 65*(1–4), 64.

Rosenthal, R., & Jacobson, L. (1968). Pygmalion in the classroom. *The Urban Review, 3*(1), 16–20.

Scherer, S., Talley, C. P., & Fife, J. E. (2017). How personal factors influence academic behavior and GPA in African American STEM students. *SAGE Open, 7*(2), 1–14. https://doi.org/10.1177/2158244017704686.

Sinek, S. (2009). *Start with why: How great leaders inspire everyone to take action.* New York: Penguin.

Spencer, M. B. (1995). Old issues and new theorizing about African American youth: A phenomenological variant of ecological systems theory. In R. L. Taylor (Ed.), *Black youth: Perspectives on their status in the United States.* Westport: Praeger.

Spencer, M. B. (2018). *Ghosts of Brown v. Board of Education 1954... Still fighting for "human status" and social justice: Developmental insights about diverse children's identity.*

Spencer, M. B., Dupree, D., & Hartman, T. (1997). A phenomenological variant of ecological systems theory (PVEST): A self-organization perspective in context. *Development and Psychopathology, 9.4*(1997), 817–833. https://doi.org/10.1017/S0954579497001454.

Spencer, M. B., Harpalani, V., Cassidy, E., Jacobs, C. Y., Donde, S., Goss, T. N., Muñoz-Miller, M., Charles, N., & Wilson, S. (2015). Understanding vulnerability and resilience from a normative developmental perspective: Implications for racially and ethnically diverse youth. In D. Cicchetti & D. J. Cohen (Eds.), *Developmental psychopathology: Theory and method* (Vol. 1, pp. 627–672). Hoboken, NJ: Wiley.

Talley, C., Fife, J., Harris, T., & Hill, O. (2015). Increasing achievement by strengthening resilience: An ecologically-based intervention for African American students. In L. Dowdell-Drakeford (Ed.), *The race controversy in American education* (pp. 163–190). Westport, CT: Praeger.

Talley, C. P., Fife, J. E., Harris, T. S., & Gambrell-Boone, L. (2016). *Targeted infusion project: Using evidence-based programming to inform a living-learning community* (Unpublished manuscript).

Talley, C. P., & Scherer, S. (2013). The enhanced flipped classroom: Increasing academic performance with student-recorded lectures and practice testing in a "flipped" STEM course. *The Journal of Negro Education, 82*(3), 339–347.

Taplin, M. (2014). A model for integrating spiritual education into secular curricula. *International Journal of Children's Spirituality, 19*(1), 4–16.

The Project Knowledge. (2013, July 1). Studying through active recall (video). *YouTube.* Retrieved from https://www.youtube.com/watch?v=eL0QFTwgEgQ

Tope-Banjoko, T. (2018). *The role of cognitive-emotional regulation, self-handicapping, and mindfulness on academic success in African American STEM students* (unpublished master's thesis, Virginia State University).

Yust, K. M. (2016). Adolescent spirituality and education. In M. de Souza, J. Bone, & J. Watson (Eds.), *Spirituality across disciplines: Research and practice* (pp. 81–93). Dordrecht, Netherlands: Springer Academic Publishers.

Chapter 6
Mindfulness and Silent Sitting in the Classroom

Stephen Scherer, Cheryl Talley, and Oliver Hill

Abstract Resilience and the application of the Sathya Sai Education in Human Values Program (SSEHV) to the phenomenological variant of ecological systems theory (PVEST) were discussed at length in Chap. 5. In this chapter, we examine the concept of mindfulness as a type of silent sitting and provide practical tools and resources for creatively integrating mindfulness into Grades K–12 and college classrooms. The purpose of this chapter is to provide specific techniques to help hone students' attention and focus and to model creative use of activities to increase opportunities for mindfulness in the classroom.

Keywords Mindfulness · Silent sitting · Classroom · Self-care · PVEST

6.1 What is Mindfulness?

Resilience and the application of the Sathya Sai Education in Human Values Program (SSEHV) to the phenomenological variant of ecological systems theory (PVEST) were discussed at length in Chap. 5. In this chapter, we examine the concept of mindfulness as a type of silent sitting and provide practical tools and resources for creatively integrating mindfulness into Grades K–12 and college classrooms. The purpose of this chapter is to provide specific techniques to help hone students' attention and focus and to model creative use of activities to increase opportunities for mindfulness in the classroom.

S. Scherer (✉)
Virginia State University, Petersburg, VA, USA

R.I.S.E. Psychological Services, White Plains, NY, USA
e-mail: sscherer@jdam.org

C. Talley · O. Hill
Virginia State University, Petersburg, VA, USA

S. Parahakaran, S. Scherer (eds.), *A Human Values Pathway for Teachers*,
https://doi.org/10.1007/978-981-16-0200-9_6

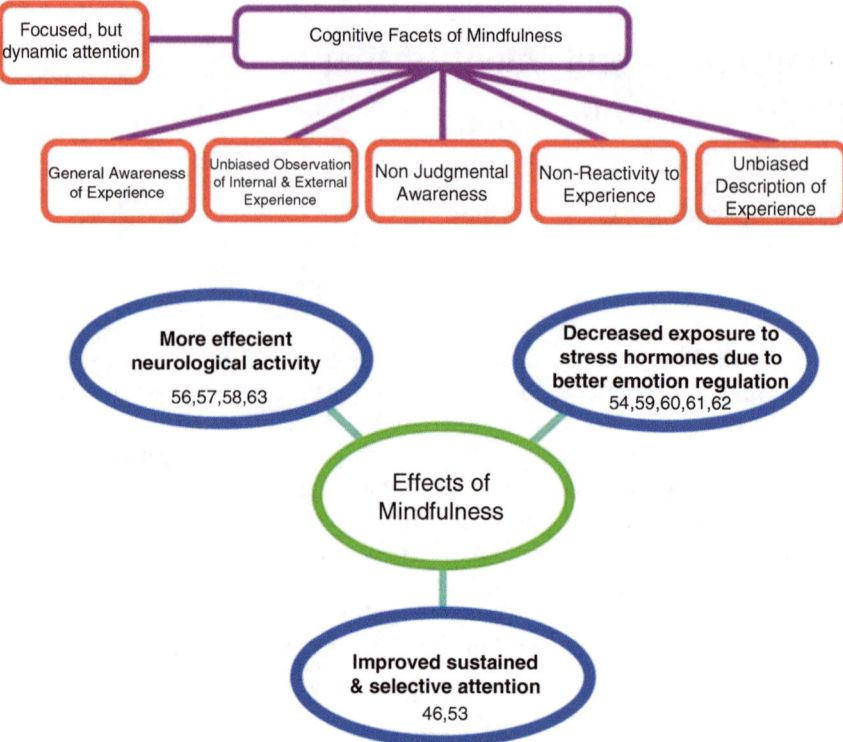

Fig. 6.1 Components of mindfulness as proposed by the authors and adapted from the works of Baer, Kabat-Zinn, and Linehan (Scherer et al. 2017)

Silent sitting, like mindfulness, is a secular, cross-cultural technique that focuses an individual's awareness on the present moment through the five senses (Taplin 2011).

Mindfulness, often defined as intentional and nonjudgmental awareness of one's own experience in the present moment, is a simple yet extraordinarily effective act that aids in the identification, regulation, and alteration or enhancement of an individual's cognitive-emotional experience and is quite similar to the concept of silent sitting in SSEHV (Baer 2003; Kabat-Zinn 2011; Linehan 1993; Taplin 2011). Although simple in practice, mindfulness, as it applies to silent sitting, is a complex technique that comprises a wide range of aspects of present-mindedness. These facets include awareness of one's own actions, observing internal and external stimuli, describing those stimuli, nonjudgmental awareness of thoughts and experiences, and non-reactivity to thoughts and experiences (see Fig. 6.1) (Baer et al. 2008; Brown and Ryan 2003; Linehan 1993). For the purpose of this chapter, we discuss the mindfulness aspect of silent sitting.

The areas of awareness that are enhanced by mindfulness are well documented in neurocognitive research (Cahn and Polich 2006; Davidson et al. 2003; Farb et al.

2007; Hölzel et al. 2011; Treadway and Lazar 2009). A growing body of literature supports the hypothesis that students who are disorganized in managing their work, are unaware of their experiences, or have a heavy bias toward making negative judgments also struggle to manage stress. This is particularly the case for those coming from under-resourced communities. These individuals are also often at risk of poor academic outcomes (Mello and Worrell 2004; Parker et al. 2004; Perkins et al. 2015; Scherer et al. 2017).

One of the essential factors of mindful awareness in the regulation of emotion is nonjudgment (Gu et al. 2015; Hölzel et al. 2011; Kabat-Zinn 2011; Linehan 1993; Scherer et al. 2017). Nonjudgment can be a difficult concept for those new to mindfulness. It is not necessarily being completely neutral, denying emotional experiences, or removing labels. Nonjudgment in the scope of mindfulness is simply seeing what is going on around you as separate from your emotional experience but not denying your emotional experience (Kabat-Zinn 2011; Linehan 1993; Ramel et al. 2004).

For example, if you are driving to school and you see construction ahead with all kinds of detour signs and no one directing traffic, you might feel anxiety or worry rise in your mind and body. "This is terrible." "I can't do this right now." "Of all days to do this, why do they have to pick today?" These might be thoughts that initially come to mind. These thoughts, although natural responses, are laden with judgment. A nonjudgmental thought that clarifies what we actually experience in the moment may be something like, "I feel myself getting worried because I believe this construction will make me late to school" or "Last time I drove through a construction zone I got a flat tire, and I'm worried about that now" or possibly "I feel confused and overwhelmed by all of the activities that are going on around me right now. I need to take a moment to stop and reorient myself." Nonjudgment clarifies what is actually going on around us and clearly identifies how we are responding to our environment. Nonjudgment is not passivity, or intellectual or emotional detachment. It is a state that allows proper assessment of situations, which can then lead to appropriate action.

For example, teenage students often respond to others almost reflexively, with implicit assumptive judgments. Jumping to conclusions ("He stole my pencil!") or projecting motives onto others ("She was making fun of me!") are examples of how a student's emotion-filled assumptions can cause them to take impulsive action in situations in which implicit assumptions may not necessarily be true—such as starting a fight with a peer because of a perceived disrespect or challenge to their person. These minor infractions by other students can quickly escalate into severe episodes of emotional and behavioral dysregulation that may lead to high levels of distractibility in class, a low tolerance for emotional distress, suspension, or even expulsion from school.

The answer may seem obvious at this point, but why is mindfulness important in education? Over time, mindfulness causes a shift in the perspective a person takes in everyday events, especially how a person interprets events based on their mood (Linehan 1993; van der Velden et al. 2015). When a mindful perspective is adopted, major shifts occur in how the world is perceived. When applying this to a classroom, one might be surprised by how those around them react to this worldview shift. Teachers who take small moments of mindfulness throughout the day and who are aware of their own internal experiences are seen as safe and peaceful people from whom the students can draw their own calm and inner peace. This environment helps the students learn how to self-regulate and develop resilience in the school setting. Over time, this learned behavior may be generalized to the home and social environment (McCloskey 2015; Rechtschaffen 2016).

As people become more proficient in the act of being mindful or aware of themselves throughout their lives, they develop a unique ability to willingly shift how they perceive events, which leads to an increase in resilience. For instance, a person who suffers from depression often views events through internal experiences. Small events feel overwhelming and lead to feelings of failure or low self-confidence. This negative and judgmental perspective can lead to feelings of low self-esteem and low self-worth due to a negative attribution bias toward taking responsibility for negative events and attributing positive events to external factors.

As people become more aware of themselves and their thoughts, they can begin to modify automatic thoughts that sustain negative moods (Beck 1991). An individual who is making a conscious effort to increase positive emotions actively identifies and changes negative thoughts to more closely reflect what is really happening in that moment. For this to occur, however, the individual must first recognize the automatic thought (observe), label the impact it has on the emotions (describe) without any self-judgment for having it (nonjudgment and non-reactivity), and then restructure the negative thought (act with awareness) (Baer et al. 2008; Linehan 1993).

An example might be a student who forgot to turn in a homework assignment and thinks, "I'm such an idiot, I'm always forgetting things and I'm going to fail this class because I can't remember what I have to do." If the student adopts a mindful perspective toward their own experience, they may be able to reframe similar thoughts to something more akin to, "I forgot to write down the assignment again. I need to come up with a new way to remember what's due in class so my grade doesn't go down."

6.2   Mindfulness as a Protective Factor

In the Buddhist tradition, from which mindfulness was originally derived, mindfulness practice is considered to be a regular activity that serves to protect the individual from emotional and spiritual turmoil (Fronsdal 2006). Supporting this assumption, mindfulness has been examined thoroughly under the lens of clinical psychology as a method of reducing suffering and symptoms associated with depressive disorders, anxiety disorders, trauma, chronic pain, and eating disorders, among other attitudes and behaviors, which can overwhelm a student's ability to attend to important tasks, such as studying or other academic work (Cristea et al. 2017; Godfrey et al. 2015;

Khoury et al. 2013). Often, the following conditions directly impact a student's functioning in school:

- Anxiety (e.g., test anxiety, social anxiety, intrusive thoughts that impact attention and awareness, etc.).
- Depression (e.g., low motivation, difficulty sleeping, concentration issues, day-time fatigue, memory impairment, isolation from others, etc.).
- Trauma (intrusive thoughts of worry, paranoia, or fear for safety; flashbacks; difficulty concentrating; etc.).
- Chronic illnesses (PTSD, psychosomatic disorders).

These barriers can lead to poor achievement, burnout, and even dropping out of school, especially if the individual does not have the skills to cope with whatever he or she is facing (Allen et al. 2008; DeBerard et al. 2004; Durlak et al. 2011; Gumora and Arsenio 2002; Mega et al. 2014; Ramirez and Beilock 2011). Researchers have shown that mindfulness in the school setting can in fact decrease the above symptoms and improve students' and teachers' ability to learn and teach (Gouda et al. 2016). Mindfulness training can also help students control impulsive behaviors, such as those associated with in-the-moment decisions to engage in behaviors contrary to academic success (Davidson et al. 2003; Lutz et al. 2008).

Researchers in education have already begun applying mindfulness techniques in K–12 education and have demonstrated the importance of integrating mindfulness into the classroom. Many schools do not have an abundance of resources to help students manage overwhelming emotions, send teachers to expensive training, make rapid changes in teaching curricula, or add new services to support learning. All this adds greatly to teacher stress (Montgomery and Rupp 2005). Mindfulness is a cost-effective and beneficial skill to add to the classroom on a daily basis. Not only do teachers benefit, but students also see positive gains in their executive abilities, such as managing strong emotions such as anger and anxiety, regulating impulsive behavior, sustaining and intentionally shifting attention, and improving problem-solving ability (Chan et al. 2008; Davidson et al. 2003; Ramsburg and Youmans 2014; Semple and Lee 2014; Singh et al. 2012; van der Velden et al. 2015).

6.3   Creating the Mindful Classroom

Several researchers have documented the successful integration of mindfulness into the classroom (Meiklejohn et al. 2012). According to Meiklejohn et al., teachers can integrate mindfulness into the classroom indirectly by developing their own mindfulness practice and modeling it for students, directly by teaching the techniques to students or by both indirect and direct methods. When educators practice mindfulness and become more aware of their own thoughts and emotions, they also become more aware of their environment. This allows teachers to show students how to apply mindfulness in their day-to-day routines. Meiklejohn et al. (2012) argued that this is the most important aspect of a successful integration of mindfulness in the classroom.

Several programs exist which train teachers in mindfulness and help them include it in their classrooms, such as Mindfulness-Based Wellness Education (MBWE), Cultivating Awareness and Resilience in Education (CARE), and Stress Management and Relaxation Techniques in Education (SMART). These three programs focus primarily on the teacher's role in the classroom and aim to reduce stress and burnout. They also address increasing awareness of emotions, improving concentration and attention, and increasing empathy and compassion. The programs improve the teacher's ability to influence the classroom indirectly by their presence in the room in addition to providing concrete skills in empathy, emotional understanding, and compassion. Other popular programs include Wellness Works, Learning to BREATHE, and Mindful Schools (Jennings et al. 2012). More information regarding these specific programs can be found in Appendix 6.1.

Through cultivating their own practice in mindfulness, teachers can impact the classroom environment indirectly. In order to support this practice, several activities are provided at the end of this chapter to aid in the development of a mindfulness practice and the teaching of mindfulness and self-awareness to students. However, developing mindfulness requires consistent practice and requires the instructor to begin to embody a mindful perspective (Meiklejohn et al. 2012). This embodiment is the key factor in effectively bringing mindfulness to the classroom. Through the use of techniques that focus on bringing awareness to sensory experiences, thoughts, emotions, movement and loving-kindness practices, both students and teachers can shift their overall perspective to embody a mindful approach to learning.

Many educators may feel the burden of integrating yet another thing into their classrooms. Fortunately, brief, consistent, and daily mindfulness practice has been shown to result in powerful and positive changes in the brain (Davidson et al. 2003; Kabat-Zinn 2011; Kaunhoven and Dorjee 2017; Linehan 1993).

6.4   A Mindful Case Study

In this section we discuss a case study of an individual student who attended individual therapy for disruptive behaviors in school, during which mindfulness was the primary clinical intervention.

At the time of treatment, Joey (real name changed to protect his identity) was an 11-year-old boy living in the USA. Joey's parents brought him to the clinic because he was experiencing inattention, hyperactivity, emotional dysregulation, and aggression at school and in his home. He often got out of his seat and engaged in talking and other disruptive behaviors in class. He would get into fights during recess because he perceived others to be bullying him, and that was the only way he felt comfortable making bullies stop teasing him. He had difficulty following directions in the classroom and often became confused with lengthy instructions or forgot them quickly. At times he would even get lost in his own thoughts and not hear people speaking to him.

Joey, like many active kids his age, was not interested in sitting down and practicing a silent sitting or mindful breathing exercise. In order for him to gain the skills he needed to self-regulate his impulses and emotions, a creative or, as we've come to describe it, a "covert" approach to mindfulness was needed. Children often respond positively to laid-back fun tasks, and Joey was no exception. He was engaged in games and activities that focused on self, and environmental awareness was key to his success.

For example, to introduce the task of slow breathing (inhale regularly, then exhale slowly and with a small amount of force), Joey was introduced to blowing bubbles—very, very big bubbles. Joey enthusiastically attempted to blow a bubble the size of a cantaloupe, but when he found he could not succeed, he became frustrated and called the activity "dumb." With a little encouragement, he was able to slow down enough over time that he mastered the breathing and could attend to himself more regularly. To achieve this took an incredible awareness of the breath and of his own thoughts and impulses.

Another activity he responded well to, and actively sought out, was the mindful mintz activity (see Sect. 6.5.5). Using a soft mint candy to emulate Kabat-Zinn's (2011) mindfulness-based stress reduction raisin activity, Joey was able to gain a stronger sense of body awareness using all of his senses. Below is a general script that can be used to guide students through the activity:

> Hear the sound of the mint's wrapper before you open it. Can you smell the mint through the wrapper? Feel the pressure it takes to open the plastic. Feel the texture of the mint. If I could not see, how would you describe all the details of this candy to me? [Often this becomes a drawing activity where one person describes the mint and the other draws it.] Now that the wrapper is open, don't eat the mint yet! Smell the mint; what smells do you observe? Do you notice anything about the smell or how it makes your nose feel? Now take a small taste; what does it taste like? Is it sour, savory, bitter, sweet? Now you can put the mint in your mouth, but don't chew it! Try to feel what the shape of the mint is, the texture of it also; make a picture in your mind of the mint. What do you notice? Has the mint changed at all? What is it doing? What is the flavor like now? Take one, super slow-motion bite and notice when the mint actually breaks, then pay attention to what these new shapes feel like and make a new image of the mint in your mind.

As the frequency and intensity of the mindfulness activities increased, which sometimes included movement exercises to notice how his body shifted in response to weight changing, Joey was able to generalize self-awareness to other tasks through the use of games. Often Joey or the first author would say the word "freeze" at random times during the therapy sessions. This word "freeze" became shorthand for "time for a brief mindfulness break; take three slow calm breaths and pay attention to the feelings of your body." As his treatment progressed, he began to call for these freeze breaks during therapeutic activities without prompting.

At one point, Joey became in charge of the mindfulness activities of the therapy session. Essentially, he was able to check in with himself more and more often and soon became able to do so in school when he felt he was being bullied or when he felt he needed to get out of his chair or talk to others. He gained the ability to monitor himself and wait for permission to let out his energy in a constructive way.

His parents also noticed a change at home: Joey was able to follow directions more often without repeated prompting, he got into far fewer arguments with his siblings, and he seemed overall much happier being himself. Joey completed treatment and has successfully managed impulsive urges associated with ADHD in addition to improving his focus in class and his ability to stay organized as a result.

6.5   Mindfulness Activities for the Classroom

A general rule of thumb is, "If you can do it, you can be mindful of it." Although true, this statement can be difficult to apply to activities that engage students in mindfulness. Mindfulness can be incorporated into the day-to-day activities of the classroom in an infinite number of ways. Below is a list of activities. Brief descriptions of each appear after the list. This is by no means all inclusive; rather, this list serves to provide a starting point for the development of additional activities in the classroom:

1. Mindfulness of Breathing
2. Dialectical Behavior Therapy (DBT) TIPP Skills
3. Mindfulness of Balance
4. Mindful Bubble Breathing
5. Mindful Mintz
6. Zip-Zap-Zop
7. Feelings Charades
8. Body Scan
9. Mindful Slime
10. Slow-Mo Bodies
11. Snow in Summer (or whichever season it is)
12. Origami Lotus Flowers
13. Yoga

6.5.1   Mindfulness of Breathing

Mindfulness of breathing is a foundational activity that is taught in many Eastern traditions to help cultivate awareness of body sensations and increase attentional awareness. Participants sit in a comfortable, upright posture and inhale and exhale slowly. Each breath is counted up to ten, then the count is reset to one and continued for several minutes.

6.5.2 Dialectical Behavior Therapy (DBT) TIPP Skills

The DBT TIPP skills are great for helping students manage difficult emotions while being mindful of what their experiences are. According to Marsha Linehan (2015), the DBT TIPP skills are meant for managing emotional crises. These skills tap into the observing, describing, nonjudgment, and non-reactivity elements of mindfulness practice.

The T skill in TIPP stands for "tip the temperature" and involves using an ice pack over the eyes and forehead or using a bowl of cool water to dip the eyes and forehead in for 20 s while holding one's breath. This skill not only is soothing because of the temperature but also initiates what is known as the "dive reflex" that causes a rapid reduction of blood pressure and heart rate that reduces anxiety and emotional dysregulation (Linehan 2015).

The I skill is "intense exercise" and can include any moderately strenuous activity, such as yoga, running, brisk walking or cycling, weight lifting, or playing a sport. This activity increases mindful participation, helps reduce built-up energy, and is particularly helpful for increased motor movement due to ADHD or anxiety (Linehan 2015).

The first P stands for "paced breathing" and involves slow and controlled breathing into the belly. Inflating the belly like a balloon, the student takes one breath approximately every 12 s. They breathe in slowly for a count of 5 s and breathe out for a count of 7 s. The most important part of this technique is breathing out longer than breathing in (Linehan 2015).

The second P stands for "paired muscle relaxation" and involves slow belly breathing, noticing the sensation of tension in the body, tensing while breathing in and releasing while breathing out. Students can start with tensing both hands, moving to the lower then upper arms, shoulders, forehead (furrowing the brow), chest, back, lower abdomen, buttocks, upper legs, calves, ankles, and finally feet (Linehan 2015).

6.5.3 Mindfulness of Balance

Mindfulness of balance helps students gain more awareness of their bodies, which is commonly a good way to notice shifts in emotion as changes in the way the body feels. This technique involves closing the eyes and standing behind a chair with both feet together. Students keep one hand resting gently on the chair to prevent them from falling over during the exercise.

First, ask the students to move their weight from one foot to the other in slow motion and to pay attention to the weight they feel on the bottoms of their feet. Next, ask students to stand as stiff as a board and lift one arm to the side without moving. Most students begin to tip over as they are not compensating for the increased weight out to the side. It is helpful to stand next to the students to make sure they do not fall over completely, or it can be made into a team-building activity with groups. Next, you can have students relax and bring their weight to center on both feet. Have them lift one arm at a time while noticing how their weight naturally shifts between their feet and how their torsos will move to maintain balance. Have students practice lifting the left and right arms out to the side, then both arms forward.

6.5.4 Mindful Bubble Breathing

The mindful bubble breathing technique is great for younger children as it helps them master slow breathing and the mindfulness skills of observe and participate. This technique involves using the DBT TIPP paced breathing skill to blow bubbles. The idea is to make the bubble as large as possible and, once the bubble is released from the bubble wand, for the student to see how many objects in the room they can name in the reflection of the bubble. Students can become competitive to see who can name the most objects or blow the largest bubble, and younger kids and even teens have a lot of fun once they see the instructor blow very large bubbles.

6.5.5 Mindful Mintz

The mindful mintz exercise was adapted from Jon Kabat-Zinn's (2011) mindfulness-based stress reduction introductory activity of eating a raisin mindfully. This very engaging sensory activity calls the student to observe and then describe their experience.

Using soft peppermints, students are first instructed to listen to the crinkle sounds of the mint's wrapper and to describe it as specifically as they can. Next, they are asked to try to smell and describe the smell of the mint through the wrapper without using the word "mint." They are then asked to pay attention to how much force they need to use to slowly open the wrapper and describe the texture of the mint. Afterward they are asked to describe what the mint looks like with as many details as possible. The instructor can also attempt to draw the mint based solely on the student's description of it, which is another activity described below called "drawing without seeing." Next, the instructor tells the student to smell the mint and describe it, and then the student can put the mint in their mouth without chewing. The instructor asks the student to describe the texture and try to visualize the mint in their mind by using their sense of touch. After a few moments, the mint starts to disintegrate, and the instructor asks the student to describe what is happening to the mint and to visualize the new shape of the mint.

6.5.6   Zip-Zap-Zop

The Zip-Zap-Zop game is played in groups and focuses on spontaneous and mindful participation. In order to play, individuals must be attentive to their environment and the other participants around them. The idea of the game is to send a group member a *zip, zap,* or *zop* by saying the word and pointing to the person they want to send it to. The person who receives the word quickly chooses a new word to send to another group member.

For example, person one says zap to person two, who then says zip to person three, who then says zap to person 4, who then says zop to person two.

The words do not need to be sent in a set order, and students often want to send the words faster over time. This game can be made more difficult by asking students to send sounds toward each other instead of *zip, zap,* or *zop* and can be sped up as group members get into a natural pace. This helps students maintain focus through mindful participation in the activity.

6.5.7   Feelings Charades

Feelings charades is a mindfulness of emotional expression game that students can play in teams or pairs. Several cards representing different emotions are developed or printed out from images online and are shuffled. Students pick a card and try to act out the emotion listed on the card. Group members must be present and attentive to the expressions of others in order to identify the correct emotion, which helps them to develop mindfulness of others. Several basic example cards of emotions are provided in Appendix 6.2.

6.5.8   Body Scan

Body scan is a classic mindfulness activity that helps students and adults practice attending to different sensations in the body in a set manner. Many times, the body scan starts at the head or feet, and awareness is guided to the temperature, tension, or physical feeling of that body part (clammy, tingly, itchy, etc.). This activity helps students gain awareness of their own body sensations and allows them to observe nonjudgmentally and with non-reactivity. The activity can also allow students to take steps to reduce tension (such as before a test) by releasing the tension they experience or using paired muscle relaxation. There are many variations of body scan meditation. An adapted autogenic training script, originally developed by Schultz in the late 1920s, for a body scan that can be effective for reducing test anxiety is provided in Appendix 6.3 (Schultz and Luthe 1959).

6.5.9 Mindful Slime

Mindful slime is a popular activity with children and young teens. This activity involves the creation of slime by combining common household ingredients with beads, glitter, or other small objects of various shapes in order to create a unique tactile experience. Making slime involves combining the following ingredients:

- 6 oz. of white glue
- ½ tbsp of baking soda
- 1 tbsp of contact lens solution (must contain boric acid and sodium borate)
- Food dye (optional)

Stir this mixture with a spoon. Before it completely congeals, the student can add beads of various shapes, glitter, small toys, or other objects to create a more engaging tactile experience. The ingredients can be mixed in small plastic bags, such as sandwich or snack bags, to minimize clean up and allow the students to manipulate the slime without having to wash their hands afterward. The instructor slowly guides students through the mixing process and prompts them to notice the sensations they experience and to describe the sensations, thoughts, and emotions at various stages of the process.

6.5.10 Slow-Mo Bodies

The slow-mo bodies activity is a mindfulness of movement exercise that draws attention to the physical experience of the student. The instructor can make this a Simon Says-type activity for younger children, have students act a scene from a play or movie in slow motion, or ask students to make their own scene. This activity helps students gain awareness of their bodies in space as they move around and can be helpful if students are feeling restless.

6.5.11 Snow in Summer

The snow in summer activity involves using an 8 in. × 8 in. piece of common printer paper (cut the excess off to make a perfect square; see Fig. 6.2a) and folding it in a way that students can cut different shapes and designs to make unique snowflakes. This activity is both a nonjudgment and a participation activity. Students learn through trial and error how to make snowflakes of different patterns by cutting the paper in various ways.

Students start off by folding the paper into a triangle (Fig. 6.2a), then folding that triangle into a smaller triangle, and once more into another smaller triangle (Fig. 6.2b). Students must keep folding from the center of the paper, which is the

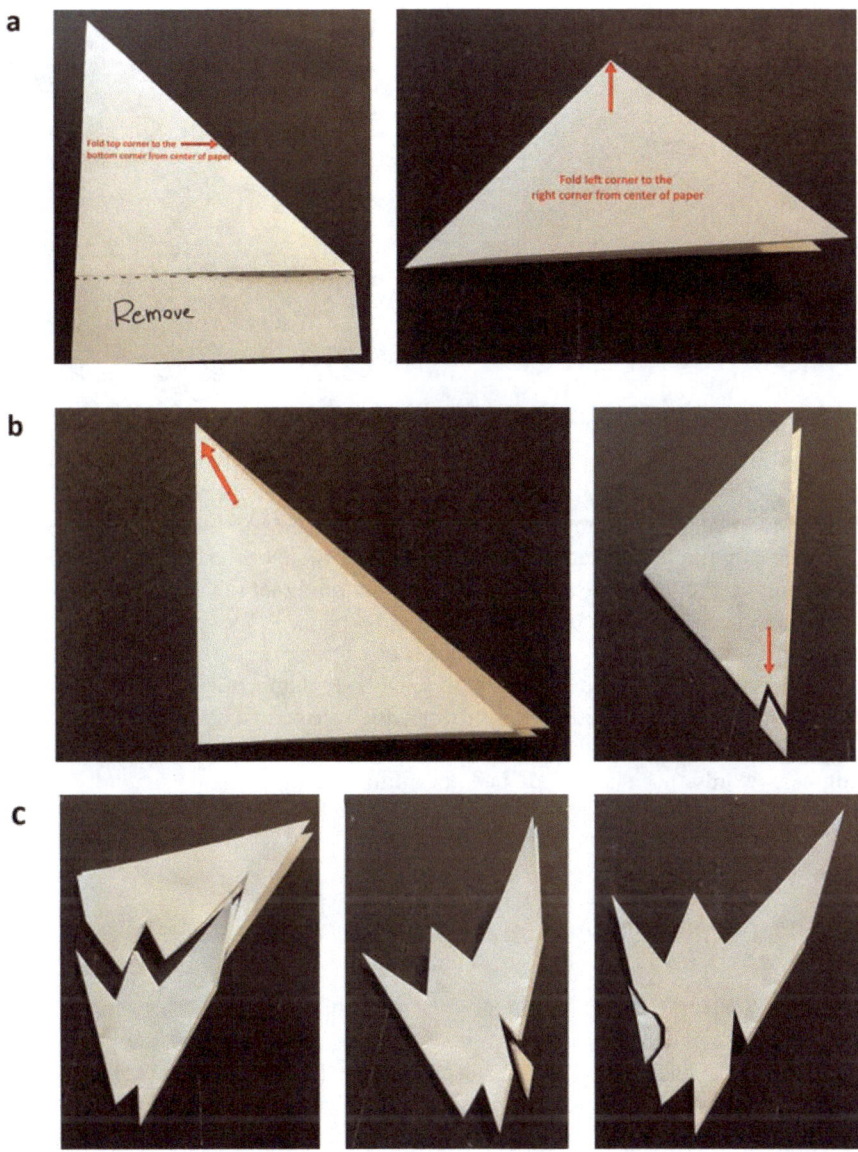

Fig. 6.2 (**a**) First and second folds of the snow in summer mindfulness activity. The arrow indicates the center of the paper. (**b**) Third fold of the mindfulness activity and first shape cutout. (**c**) Additional shape sample cutouts

corner that doesn't allow the paper to be opened. As students are cutting, they must be mindful of each side in that they leave some of it intact; otherwise, the snowflake will fall apart (Fig. 6.2c). Prompts to enhance this activity may include, "Notice how much pressure you need in order to fold the paper," "Feel the texture of the paper as

Fig. 6.3 Completed sample
snowflake when opened.
Adding more folds will
increase the complexity of
the snowflake

you are folding it," "How much pressure do you need to cut the paper?" and "What does it feel like and what sounds do you hear when you open the paper back up?" See Fig. 6.3 for a completed snowflake.

At the end, prompt students to be aware of their thoughts and feelings once they have completed cutting out the snowflake, and remind them that each snowflake is unique and beautiful in its own way. If students begin to judge the snowflakes as good or bad, reorient them to the purpose of the exercise: being present-minded and observing what they are doing in a new way, without judgment. Teachers can ask the students if they can tell which cutouts made which shape in their snowflakes. It may also help students to ask them if they can describe the snowflake without using judgment words, such as good, bad, beautiful, or ugly. Help students see the uniqueness of each snowflake.

6.5.12 Origami Lotus Flowers

Similar in concept to snow in summer, the origami lotus flowers activity is about nonjudgment and focused participation. This activity is easiest to complete using origami paper that is square in shape but can also be done with 8 in. × 8 in. computer paper if assistance is provided to make the final folds.

Students fold the paper in half both ways and then diagonally both ways to make a "+" shape and an "x" shape in the paper (Fig. 6.4a images 1–5). Next, they fold each corner to touch the center of the paper (Fig. 6.4a images 6–8).

The folding pattern above is repeated two more times (Fig. 6.4b images 1–4). Then the students flip the paper over and fold the corners to the midpoint one more time, then ¾ of the way back (Fig. 6.4b images 5–8). Next, they turn the folded paper back over and bend the "petals" back so they stand up (Fig. 6.4c images 1–3). Students must be careful during this step, as the paper can easily tear.

Once all three layers of petals are folded back, the student sees their completed lotus flower (Fig. 6.4c images 4–5). Students can work together to create a lotus

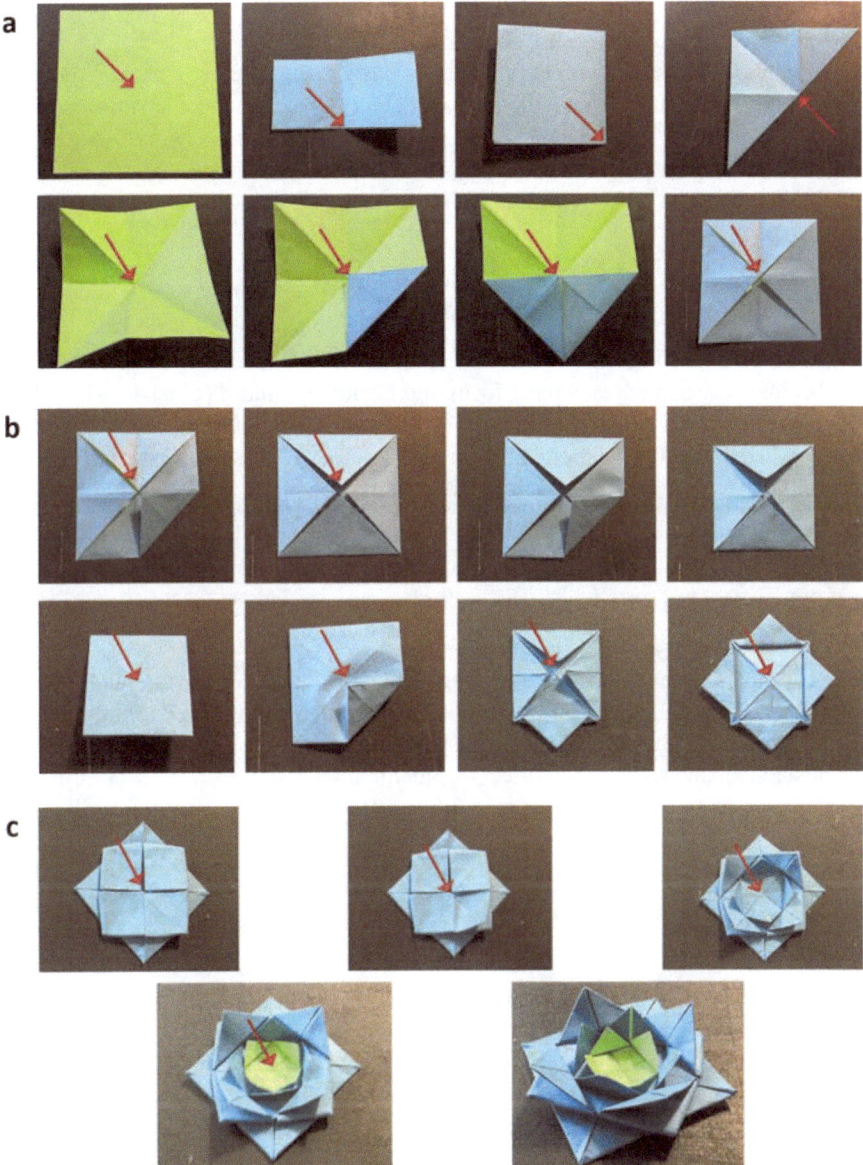

Fig. 6.4 (**a**) First eight folds of the origami lotus flower mindfulness activity. The arrow indicates the center of the paper. (**b**) Beginning fold for the next two layers of petals and the first of the back folds. (**c**) Final folds and the finished lotus flower

flower garden by taping their flowers to blue pieces of construction paper and drawing or cutting out green lily pads around them.

Throughout the task, prompt students to pay careful attention to how they are folding the paper, the texture of the paper, and the weight of the flower and to describe the flower without using judgment words. If students begin to judge their lotus flowers, remind them that each flower is unique.

6.5.13 Yoga

As described in the TIPP skill, yoga is a great way to help students use excess energy in a healthy way and to teach them focus and breathing control (Linehan 2015). It is recommended that a trained instructor be present during activities; however, simple exercises can be done without a trained instructor, such as cat pose, tree pose, mountain pose, sailboat pose, warrior pose, and elephant pose.

6.5.14 Silent Sitting

Silent sitting is a technique that helps to generate a sense of inner peace and focused awareness. One of the most powerful elements of silent sitting is mindful awareness of the experience. One simple technique is to follow the breath with attention as you inhale and exhale and to gently direct the attention back to the breath every time the mind wanders.

6.6 Conclusion

As teachers shift to incorporate mindfulness in the classroom, students begin to benefit from the rewards of a mindful classroom. Developing a regular mindfulness practice of a few seconds to a few minutes each day can help develop and strengthen a mindful perspective. Simply attending to a task, grading papers, reading over teaching notes, eating lunch, noticing what it feels like to drink a cool beverage, mindfully walking with your class from one room to another, attending to the feeling of chalk on the chalkboard while teaching a lesson, and noticing the faces of students and their expressions during a lesson all are opportunities for mindful practice. The more a teacher or instructor can model what it is to live mindfully, the easier it will be for students to shift their perspectives and manage day-to-day challenges (Felver et al. 2016; Meiklejohn et al. 2012; Rechtschaffen 2016; Taplin 2011).

Again, the purpose of this chapter is to help educators identify creative ways to increase mindfulness in the classroom. After a mindfulness activity, one may consider opening up discussion among the students to further solidify the impact of the exercise. Appendix 6.4 contains sample discussion questions that continue to facilitate growth of a mindful perspective for students.

Mindfulness, in and of itself, can serve to increase resilience and inner peace in students from all backgrounds (Fronsdal 2006). Twenty years of empirical studies have validated its impact in the classroom. It is important for teachers to gain familiarity with this tool as one method to help bridge the achievement gap and one necessary element in providing quality education to all students.

Acknowledgments This research was partially supported by National Science Foundation (NSF) grants HRD-1533563 and DRL-1621416 to Oliver Hill.

Appendix 6.1 Mindfulness Programs Resource Guide

Program	Website	Training locations	Description
Cultivating awareness and resilience in education (CARE)		USA	Cultivating awareness and resilience in education (CARE) is a unique professional development program that helps teachers handle the stresses and rediscover the joys of teaching. CARE has been carefully studied in a series of randomized trials showing its effectiveness in boosting teacher's mental capacities, performance, and social and emotional functioning, which results in more rewarding personal and professional experiences. CARE workshops for teachers can be provided in a variety of ways to meet the needs of different educator audiences
Learning to BREATHE	https://learning2breathe.org/	USA	From this website: "This curriculum is intended to strengthen attention and emotion regulation, cultivate wholesome emotions like gratitude and compassion, expand the repertoire of stress management skills, and help participants integrate mindfulness into daily life. Each lesson includes

(continued)

Program	Website	Training locations	Description
			age-appropriate discussion, activities, and opportunities to practice mindfulness in a group setting"
Mindful schools	www.mindfulschools. org	USA/inter-national (online)	From this website: "Our courses and curricula are designed for under-resourced public schools facing high turnover rates and toxic stress. We offer educators practical skills for self-care, facilitation, and connecting with youth, providing simple, effective mindfulness practices that can be integrated into the school day and adapted for diverse environments"
Wellness works	http://www. wellnessworksinschools. com/about.html	USA/inter-national (online)	Wellness works offers three unique curricula that focus on increasing emotional and social awareness, the impact of emotions on behavior and interpersonal relationships, and integra-tion of mindfulness skills into the classroom. Well-ness works curricula also provide tools and videos to help encourage and support teachers in sustaining the practices and skills pro-vided in each curriculum

Appendix 6.2 Feelings Charades Sample Cards

Appendix 6.3 Autogenic Training Script

Autogenic training (AT) is designed to help individuals focus on various parts of their body to facilitate awareness of the self and elicit a sense of relaxation. The full guided session can take up to 20 minutes to complete and results in a very profound state of calm awareness when successfully completed. Autogenic training was developed by Johannes Schultz during the 1920s and formally published in the 1930s. See Sadigh and Montero (2001) if you would like to delve into the therapeutic applications a bit further

The version of AT below is one that the authors modified and updated for use in academic research with good results. Different scripts are used for different concerns; the following script reflects a progressive muscle relaxation approach to reducing general anxiety. Notice the mindfulness orientation throughout the exercise and at the end. As you go through the exercise, prompt your students to refocus on the breathing and imagery by restating the task and visualization of the sun, warmth, etc. Occasionally bring their awareness to the pulse of their heartbeat as they attend to various areas of the body (specifically hands and again for legs)

The adapted autogenic training script is as follows (Scherer 2012):

To start off, let's sit with a relaxed posture, our hands in our laps and our legs uncrossed. Sit with your back against the chair. Close your eyes. I want you to imagine yourself sitting comfortably in your favorite spot outside. I want you to see the sun and the shade from nearby trees. Now I want you to gently breathe in and bring the air down into your stomach. Feel the rise and fall of your stomach as you gently breathe in and slowly exhale

Imagine the sun, beaming down onto your hand, pleasantly warming it

As you breathe in, I want you to say to yourself, "My right hand …"

As you breathe out, I want you to say, "… is heavy and warm"

[Have them repeat five times]

Now I want you to shift your attention to your left hand

As you breathe in, I want you to say to yourself, "My left hand …"

As you breathe out, I want you to say, "… is heavy and warm"

See the sun pleasantly warming your hand

[Have them repeat five times]

Now as you breathe in, say, "My arms …"

As you breathe out, say, "… are heavy and warm"

See the sun, pleasantly warming your arms. Feel the relaxation from your shoulders all the way down to your fingertips

[Have them repeat five times]

Now gently move your attention to your feet. See the sun shining brightly and warmly onto your feet

As you breathe in, say, "My feet …"

As you breathe out, say, "… are heavy and warm"

Feel the sun warm your feet and notice the feeling of relaxation that comes with each breath

[Have them repeat five times]

[Move next to the legs, arms and legs, then …]

Now shift your awareness to your abdomen

See the sun pleasantly shining on your abdomen

As you breathe in, say, "My abdomen …"

As you breathe out, say, "… is pleasantly warm"

[Have them repeat five times]

Now focus on your breathing

Feel the air flow as you breathe in … and out

Say these words as you breathe in: "My breathing …"

As you breathe out: "… is free and easy"

As you breathe, imagine something that, to you, is free, like the wind

[Repeat five times]

(Optional section below. Repeat each individually five times)

Now feel the wind as it gently moves across your face, cooling you with every breath in

As you breathe in say, "My face …"

As you breathe out say, "… is pleasantly cool"

Now shift your attention to your heartbeat
As you breathe in say, "My heartbeat . . ."
As you breathe out say, ". . . is calm and regular"
Imagine something that, to you, is calm and regular, like a metronome or the ticking of a clock
(End optional section)
Now gently bring into your awareness the natural state of relaxation you have achieved in yourself
Recognize how this level of relaxation makes you feel and remember that it is OK to feel good, it is OK to feel relaxed
Now gently shift your awareness back to the room and return your breathing to normal

Appendix 6.4 Sample Mindfulness Activity Discussion Questions

1. How did your mind feel? Did you notice any thoughts during the activity?
2. What were the thoughts that you noticed during the activity?
3. What were the emotions that you noticed during the activity?
4. Do you notice a difference in how you connect with your thoughts and emotions when you are mindful of them instead of automatically reacting to them?
5. Did you notice any judgmental thoughts during the activity?
6. What is something new that you noticed during the activity?
7. How did your body feel before, during, and/or after the activity?
8. Did your emotions change during the activity?
9. Did you enjoy the activity? What are some reasons why you did or did not enjoy it?
   If students answer using judgmental language, help them separate emotions and preferences from fact. Example: Student: "It was awesome!" Teacher: "What was awesome about it?" Student: "It made me feel calm, and I like that more than feeling angry."
10. Can you practice mindfulness at home?

Sample Questions to Ask Later in the Academic Year

11. What is something you wish you did mindfully day-to-day?
12. What makes mindfulness helpful for you to practice?
13. How does mindfulness change how you view the world?
14. How does being mindful change how you interact with others?
15. How does being mindful change how you think about yourself?
16. How has adopting a mindful perspective changed how you think about yourself?
17. Describe your relationship with your emotions. How do you react to them?

18. How has your perspective toward stress and difficult situations changed with mindfulness?
19. How do you manage things now versus at the beginning of the school year? What are some examples of this?
20. How do you use your mindfulness skills in school? Has this been helpful for you?

References

Allen, J., Robbins, S. B., Casillas, A., & Oh, I. S. (2008). Third-year college retention and transfer: Effects of academic performance, motivation, and social connectedness. *Research in Higher Education, 49*(7), 647–664. https://doi.org/10.1007/s11162-008-9098-3.

Baer, R. A. (2003). Mindfulness training as a clinical intervention: A conceptual and empirical review. *Clinical Psychology: Science and Practice, 10*(2), 125–143. https://doi.org/10.1093/clipsy/bpg015.

Baer, R. A., Smith, G. T., Lykins, E., Button, D., Krietemeyer, J., Sauer, S., Walsh, E., Duggan, D., & Williams, J. M. G. (2008). Construct validity of the five facet mindfulness questionnaire in meditating and nonmeditating samples. *Assessment, 15*(3), 329–342. https://doi.org/10.1177/1073191107313003.

Beck, A. T. (1991). *Cognitive therapy and the emotional disorders.* New York: International Universities Press.

Brown, K. W., & Ryan, R. M. (2003). The benefits of being present: Mindfulness and its role in psychological Well-being. *Journal of Personality and Social Psychology, 84*(4), 822–848. https://doi.org/10.1037/0022-3514.84.4.822.

Cahn, B. R., & Polich, J. (2006). Meditation states and traits: EEG, ERP, and neuroimaging studies. *Psychological Bulletin, 132*(2), 180–211. https://doi.org/10.1037/0033-2909.132.2.180.

Chan, R. C. K., Shum, D., Toulopoulou, T., & Chen, E. Y. H. (2008). Assessment of executive functions: Review of instruments and identification of critical issues. *Archives of Clinical Neuropsychology, 23*(2), 201–216. https://doi.org/10.1016/j.acn.2007.08.010.

Cristea, I. A., Gentili, C., Cotet, C. D., Palomba, D., Barbui, C., & Cuijpers, P. (2017). Efficacy of psychotherapies for borderline personality disorder: A systematic review and meta-analysis. *JAMA Psychiatry, 74*(4), 319–328. https://doi.org/10.1001/jamapsychiatry.2016.4287.

Davidson, R. J., Kabat-Zinn, J., Schumacher, J., Rosenkranz, M., Muller, D., Santorelli, S. F., Urbanowski, F., Harrington, A., Bonus, K., & Sheridan, J. F. (2003). Alterations in brain and immune function produced by mindfulness meditation. *Psychosomatic Medicine, 65*(4), 564–570. https://doi.org/10.1097/01.psy.0000077505.67574.e3.

DeBerard, M. S., Spielmans, G., & Julka, D. (2004). Predictors of academic achievement and retention among college freshmen: A longitudinal study. *College Student Journal, 38*(1), 66–80.

Durlak, J. A., Weissberg, R. P., Dymnicki, A. B., Taylor, R. D., & Schellinger, K. B. (2011). The impact of enhancing students' social and emotional learning: A meta-analysis of school-based universal interventions. *Child Development, 82*(1), 405–432. https://doi.org/10.1111/j.1467-8624.2010.01564.x.

Farb, N. A. S., Segal, Z. V., Mayberg, H., Bean, J., Mckeon, D., Fatima, Z., & Anderson, A. K. (2007). Attending to the present: Mindfulness meditation reveals distinct neural modes of self-reference. *Social Cognitive and Affective Neuroscience, 2*(4), 313–322. https://doi.org/10.1093/scan/nsm030.

Felver, J. C., Celis-de Hoyos, C. E., Tezanos, K., & Singh, N. N. (2016). A systematic review of mindfulness-based interventions for youth in school settings. *Mindfulness, 7*(1), 34–45. https://doi.org/10.1007/s12671-015-0389-4.

Fronsdal, G. (2006). *Life balance (audio podcast)*. San Francisco, CA: San Francisco Zen Center.

Godfrey, K. M., Gallo, L. C., & Afari, N. (2015). Mindfulness-based interventions for binge eating: A systematic review and meta-analysis. *Journal of Behavioral Medicine, 38*(2), 348–362. https://doi.org/10.1007/s10865-014-9610-5.

Gouda, S., Luong, M. T., Schmidt, S., & Bauer, J. (2016). Students and teachers benefit from mindfulness-based stress reduction in a school-embedded pilot study. *Frontiers in Psychology, 7*(4), 1–18. https://doi.org/10.3389/fpsyg.2016.00590.

Gu, J., Strauss, C., Bond, R., & Cavanagh, K. (2015). How do mindfulness-based cognitive therapy and mindfulness-based stress reduction improve mental health and wellbeing? A systematic review and meta-analysis of mediation studies. *Clinical Psychology Review, 37*, 1–12. https://doi.org/10.1016/j.cpr.2015.01.006.

Gumora, G., & Arsenio, W. F. (2002). Emotionality, emotion regulation, and school performance in middle school children. *Journal of School Psychology, 40*(5), 395–413. https://doi.org/10.1016/S0022-4405(02)00108-5.

Hölzel, B. K., Lazar, S. W., Gard, T., Schuman-Olivier, Z., Vago, D. R., & Ott, U. (2011). How does mindfulness meditation work? Proposing mechanisms of action from a conceptual and neural perspective. *Perspectives on Psychological Science, 6*, 537–559. https://doi.org/10.1177/1745691611419671.

Jennings, P., Lantieri, L., & Roeser, R. (2012). Supporting educational goals through cultivating mindfulness: Approaches for teachers and students. In P. M. Brown, M. W. Corrigan, & A. Higgins-D'Alessandro (Eds.), *Handbook of prosocial education* (pp. 371–397). Lanham, MD: Rowman & Littlefield.

Kabat-Zinn, J. (2011). Some reflections on the origins of MBSR, skillful means, and the trouble with maps. *Contemporary Buddhism, 12*(1), 281–306. https://doi.org/10.1080/14639947.2011.564844.

Kaunhoven, R. J., & Dorjee, D. (2017). How does mindfulness modulate self-regulation in pre-adolescent children? An integrative neurocognitive review. *Neuroscience and Biobehavioral Reviews, 74*, 163–184. https://doi.org/10.1016/j.neubiorev.2017.01.007.

Khoury, B., Lecomte, T., Fortin, G., Masse, M., Therien, P., Bouchard, V., Chapleau, M., Paquin, K., & Hofmann, S. G. (2013). Mindfulness-based therapy: A comprehensive meta-analysis. *Clinical Psychology Review, 33*(6), 763–771. https://doi.org/10.1016/j.cpr.2013.05.005.

Linehan, M. M. (1993). *Cognitive-behavioral treatment of borderline personality disorder*. New York: The Guilford Press. https://doi.org/10.1017/CBO9781107415324.004.

Linehan, M. M. (2015). *DBT skills training manual* (2nd ed.). New York: The Guilford Press.

Lutz, A., Slagter, H. A., Dunne, J. D., & Davidson, R. J. (2008). Attention regulation and monitoring in meditation. *Trends in Cognitive Sciences, 12*(4), 163–169. https://doi.org/10.1016/j.tics.2008.01.005.

McCloskey, L. E. (2015). Mindfulness as an intervention for improving academic success among students with executive functioning disorders. *Procedia - Social and Behavioral Sciences, 174*, 221–226. https://doi.org/10.1016/j.sbspro.2015.01.650.

Mega, C., Ronconi, L., & De Beni, R. (2014). What makes a good student? How emotions, self-regulated learning, and motivation contribute to academic achievement. *Journal of Educational Psychology, 106*(1), 121–131. https://doi.org/10.1037/a0033546.

Meiklejohn, J., Phillips, C., Freedman, M. L., Griffin, M. L., Biegel, G., Roach, A., Frank, J., Burke, C., Pinger, L., Soloway, G., Isberg, R., Sibinga, E., Grossman, L., & Saltzman, A. (2012). Integrating mindfulness training into K-12 education: Fostering the resilience of teachers and students. *Mindfulness, 3*(4), 291–307. https://doi.org/10.1007/s12671-012-0094-5.

Mello, Z. R., & Worrell, F. C. (2004). The relationship of time perspective to age, gender, and academic achievement among academically talented adolescents. *Journal for the Education of the Gifted, 29*(3), 271–289.

Montgomery, C., & Rupp, A. A. (2005). A meta-analysis for exploring the diverse causes and effects of stress in teachers. *Canadian Journal of Education, 28*(3), 458–486. https://doi.org/10.2307/4126479.

Parker, J. D. A., Summerfeldt, L. J., Hogan, M. J., & Majeski, S. A. (2004). Emotional intelligence and academic success: Examining the transition from high school to university. *Personality and Individual Differences, 36*(1), 163–172. https://doi.org/10.1016/S0191-8869(03)00076-X.

Perkins, P., Scherer, S., Palmer, K., & Talley, C. (2015). Do time perspective and year in school influence GPA in African American college students? *American Journal of Educational Studies, 7*(91), 65–72.

Ramel, W., Goldin, P. R., Carmona, P. E., & McQuaid, J. R. (2004). The effects of mindfulness meditation on cognitive processes and affect in patients with past depression. *Cognitive Therapy & Research, 28*(4), 433–455.

Ramirez, G., & Beilock, S. L. (2011). Writing about testing worries boosts exam performance in the classroom. *Science, 331*(6014), 211–213.

Ramsburg, J. T., & Youmans, R. J. (2014). Meditation in the higher-education classroom: Meditation training improves student knowledge retention during lectures. *Mindfulness, 5*(4), 431–441. https://doi.org/10.1007/s12671-013-0199-5.

Rechtschaffen, D. (2016). *The mindful education workbook: Lessons for teaching mindfulness to students*. New York: W. W. Norton & Company.

Sadigh, M. R., & Montero, R. P. (2001). *Autogenic training: A mind-body approach to the treatment of fibromyalgia and chronic pain syndrome*. Binghamton, NY: Hawthorne Medical Press.

Scherer, S. (2012). *Meditation and journaling to reduce anxiety and increase academic performance* (unpublished doctoral thesis. Virginia State University).

Scherer, S., Talley, C. P., & Fife, J. E. (2017). How personal factors influence academic behavior and GPA in African American STEM students. *SAGE Open, 7*(2), 1–14. https://doi.org/10.1177/2158244017704686.

Schultz, J. H., & Luthe, W. (1959). *Autogenic training: A psychophysiologic approach to psychotherapy*. Oxford, UK: Grune & Stratton.

Semple, R. J., & Lee, J. (2014). Mindfulness-based cognitive therapy for children. In R. A. Baer (Ed.), *Mindfulness-based treatment approaches: Clinicians guide to evidence base and applications* (pp. 161–188). London: Academic. https://doi.org/10.1016/B978-0-12-416031-6.00008-6.

Singh, Y., Sharma, R., & Talwar, A. (2012). Immediate and long-term effects of meditation on acute stress reactivity, cognitive functions, and intelligence. *Alternative Therapies in Health and Medicine, 18*(6), 46–53.

Taplin, M. (2011). Silent sitting: A cross-curricular tool to promote resilience. *International Journal of Children's Spirituality, 16*(2), 75–96. https://doi.org/10.1080/1364436X.2011.580730.

Treadway, M. T., & Lazar, S. W. (2009). The neurobiology of mindfulness. In F. Didonna (Ed.), *Clinical handbook of mindfulness* (pp. 45–57). New York: Springer. https://doi.org/10.1007/978-0-387-09593-6_4.

van der Velden, A. M., Kuyken, W., Wattar, U., Crane, C., Pallesen, K. J., Dahlgaard, J., Fjorback, L. O., & Piet, J. (2015). A systematic review of mechanisms of change in mindfulness-based cognitive therapy in the treatment of recurrent major depressive disorder. *Clinical Psychology Review, 37*, 26–39. https://doi.org/10.1016/j.cpr.2015.02.001.

Chapter 7
Silent Sitting in School Counselling: An Educational Practice to Improve Academic Performance and Personal Well-being

Kevin Francis

Abstract Silent sitting is a practice of mindfulness that has been used by many for centuries. To distance the practitioner from the often-implied religious or spiritual connotations associated with meditation and prayer, in recent times, mindfulness has been referred to as silent sitting or stilling the mind. Increasingly in recent years, mindfulness has also become the subject matter of a number of studies, which have consistently shown it to be effective in promoting mental well-being and increasing concentration and cognitive performance, particularly when connected to a values-based approach. Studies have also shown the practice of mindfulness is helpful in alleviating many modern psychological aspects of mental and emotional difficulties, including self-esteem issues, anxiety, depression, stress-related problems, and interpersonal issues.

A myriad of choices of mindfulness practices exist, but the beauty of all mindfulness practices, particularly silent sitting, is that it is quite easy to tailor different styles depending on the needs of any particular clientele. Neurobiological research suggests that mindfulness practices can actually change brain structure and function and is a useful adjunct to mental health and psychotherapy, while promoting improved learning outcomes.

The author is a retired successful secondary teacher and school counsellor with 44 years of teaching practice in science, philosophy, psychology, and religion. This chapter provides an overview of his use of silent sitting (incorporating positive affirmations and cognitive rehearsal), which he has used effectively for the past 36 years in both his teaching and counselling practices.

The first section is a brief introduction and examination of what research has to say about the common elements of silent sitting and mindfulness practices, with some reference to the neurological processes that research has identified as being involved.

The second section is a historical outline of the practices taught and used by the author with secondary school students in Australia.

K. Francis (✉)
Internode, Adelaide, Australia

© Springer Nature Singapore Pte Ltd. 2021   79
S. Parahakaran, S. Scherer (eds.), *A Human Values Pathway for Teachers*,
https://doi.org/10.1007/978-981-16-0200-9_7

The third section reflects on the use of silent sitting over the last 36 years of counselling practice in both state and private schools. The chapter provides a number of successfully used practices for the reader to follow, both personally and with secondary or tertiary students.

Keywords Regular practice · Positive attitude · Self-acceptance

7.1 Introduction

The idea of stilling the mind is not a new one. Many references refer to the need to still the mind, covering centuries of practice in both Eastern and Western contexts. The history of such practices is clearly outlined in The Science of Mindfulness (Siegel 2014). These practices teach us to still the mind and go within, to go beyond the thought-filled mental chattering of our daily lives.

After stressing out about upcoming exams as a university student in 1970, I sought help from a student services psychologist (Dr. James Judd) in the counselling center at the University of New South Wales, who introduced me to the practice of slowing the breath, becoming silent and still to reduce the racing anxiety I was feeling at the time. I am forever grateful for his intervention and teaching me this technique. He started me on my own lifelong journey to further my pursuit of the study of silent sitting to attain mental and indeed physical calm in my personal and professional life. He enabled me to teach and use it with others.

Not long into my counselling career, I came across Herbert Bensen's book *The Relaxation Response* (Bensen 1970) and eagerly waited for his follow-up *Beyond the Relaxation Response* (Bensen 1985), in which he convinced me that these practices were worthwhile to use.

As a secondary school teacher, I would often take the whole 2 weeks of holiday breaks to relax and let go of the term, just in time to go back. By attending two-day workshops on the first weekend of the holidays, at which significant time was taken to still the mind and let go of internal stress, I became aware that I was reaching the state I normally felt at the end of the holiday period. As a result I was truly able to enjoy my breaks with my family. The techniques became part of my daily routine as a result.

This chapter looks at these influences in my life and the increasing research base that has grown over time to confirm the benefits of practicing silent sitting, relaxation, meditation and, in recent terminology, mindfulness. For many years I practiced and taught meditation to adults and adolescents without a true research basis, as when doing so, anecdotally, it just seemed to increasingly help people become more focused in their lives, work, and study and significantly reduce their stress levels.

7.2   Research Evidence

In 1996, I was enrolled in a counselling-focused master's degree course at the University of South Australia and, as my final research paper, was interested in how counsellors in particular coped with the stresses of their jobs. I was saddened at the time and fully aware that four of my colleagues, who had started their counselling careers in the late 1970s, at the same time as me, had become so stressed and overwhelmed that they had suicided. A number of other colleagues had left counselling due to the stresses involved. My unpublished master's research paper sought to find out what, if any, successful techniques were being used by counsellors in state government and Catholic schools at that time to cope with the stresses involved (Francis 1996). It was obviously an issue of concern; nearly 100 surveys were sent, and the response rate was 83%. My own limited research showed that those who practiced some form of mindfulness and/or meditation were happier in their work and had less mental health issues, such as anxiety. This led to many requests for me to run workshops on silent sitting and mindfulness for other counsellors, teachers, and students on a regular basis, which were well attended and appreciated. I revisited much of the work of Herbert Bensen (1970, 1985) at this time to justify the research base of my practices.

In 2011, after years of practicing and teaching silent sitting, in my role as a secondary school counsellor, I was very grateful to be introduced to Dr. Ramesh Manocha, a senior lecturer from Sydney University, through his Generation Next workshops. Generation Next was a national initiative created and convened by him that dealt with youth mental health. At one of these workshops, he outlined his PhD research into meditation, which ultimately led to his publishing his book *Silence Your Mind* (Manocha 2013). This finally ticked all the boxes for me for what I had been doing for the previous 20-odd years.

In Chap. 5 (Mental Silence), Manocha wrote the following:

Mental silence is a phenomenon that has been described in various ways and contexts across histories and cultures.

We are not our thoughts, nor are we the mind that generates them but, in fact, something much more profound that is entirely discoverable in the state of mental silence. Mental silence becomes a window through which we can develop a clearer understanding of ourselves and the world. (p. 61)

In Chap. 9 (Beyond the Mind-body Connection), Manocha summarized many of the outcomes of his research. His analysis showed the following:

There was a robust relationship between the frequency of mental silence experience and health scores, especially mental health. In other words, the more often the meditators experienced mental silence, the higher their levels of health. In the case of mental health, the survey found that even those meditators who experienced mental silence for just a few minutes once or twice a week experienced better mental health than the general population. (p. 162)

This was confirmation of my master's studies (Francis 1996) and ratification for what I was observing in my own counselling and teaching practice.

More recently, Riopel (2019) presents a review of recent neuroscience research on how mindfulness affects the brain. Her summary cites evidence of effects including help in reducing stress, anxiety, and depression and alleviation of chronic pain. Riopel also reports the usefulness of mindfulness practices in helping people to change thoughts that are unproductive, to stabilize and control attention and to recognize and hence regulate what is going on in the mind during mood swings. Other research she reviews has explored helping people to stop smoking and overcome food cravings and identifying what makes people resilient when facing stressful experiences. The role of mindfulness in improving social relationships is also emerging, along with hopeful findings about positive impacts on children with ADHD.

Riopel's (2019) accounts of studies of the brain reveal positive regulatory effects on the amygdala and hippocampus, the regions of the brain that deal with emotions and memory respectively. She cites evidence of decreases in activity in the amygdala, which means the fight-or-flight responses, the reaction to threats, also reactions to perceived stress thus improve. As well, she reports beneficial effects on the prefrontal cortex, the part of the brain associated with both impulse control and maturity.

In summary, the studies reviewed by Riopel (2019) suggested that:

1. Mindfulness positively impacts human functioning.
2. Mindfulness can help improve the quality of attention.
3. Mindfulness, even though it is an internal quality, can impact interpersonal behavior.
4. Mindfulness can provide greater empathy and compassion.

7.3   The Secondary School Experience

Anecdotally, the modern teenager lives in an increasingly demanding and stress-generating world. Apart from school performance, family issues, personal health concerns and part-time jobs, the challenges of social media and other online activities have done little to allow or encourage downtime. Social media has also increased mental health issues as a result of online bullying and unhealthy social competition and expectation, leading to much higher levels of anxiety and depression and reduced levels of resilience from the constant presence of high levels of stress. The increased rates of youth self-harm and suicide are testament to this. All of this clearly suggests that the need for mental stillness has never been greater.

Initially, my training sessions of stilling the mind using silent sitting, coupled with positive affirmations, were mainly delivered to students in Years 8 to 10 in the Excel Programme, a program for gifted students across three schools: a South Australian state high school, a Catholic secondary college (at which I was a staff member), and an independent private school. This program involved gifted students who chose to participate to further enhance their academic excellence.

The technique used was a simple one. Gentle, non-frantic music (I used Steve Halpern (1994a, 1994b) anti-frantic music) played as the participants arrived. When each student arrived in the quiet, low-lit setting, I greeted them individually, then asked them to share one highlight of their day. When all had arrived, the whole group was welcomed. I do not recall anyone ever being late.

The session then started, and I asked the participants to close their eyes lightly to minimize any peripheral visual distraction and become aware of their own breathing patterns, while acknowledging the sounds in the environment around them. This then led into slowing the breath down in an unstrained way by simply repeating the following phrases at an ever-decreasing speed: "I am aware that I am breathing in; (brief pause) I am aware that I am breathing out." If any other thoughts came up, the participants were asked to simply observe them as if from an outsider's vantage point.

In this calm state, I led the participants to silently repeat a positive phrase about themselves and their study inside their own minds:

> I am capable. I can succeed. I will succeed. Today and every day, I will learn the things I need to be successful, knowing I am able to practice and recall them at will. I am capable. I can succeed. I will succeed.

I then instructed them to visualize themselves as being successful, to hold onto that vision for about 15 s, then to go back to the breathing patterns of earlier. They were then gently invited to come back to the present, return their breathing to its normal rate and slowly and gently open their eyes.

Each session was followed by some gentle, conscious stretching before leaving. These sessions ran once a week for eight consecutive weeks at a time. When I followed up with previous participants, a significant proportion reported that they had continued with the practices throughout their secondary schooling and beyond. I was always delighted to meet them later, after they had left school, at shopping centers or even in foreign airports, when they would approach me, introduce themselves and tell me how much silent sitting had helped them. Many delightedly informed me that they were still using those very same techniques.

As a direct result of the perceived success of these workshops, the teacher who was coordinator of the Excel Programme invited me to run similar sessions with her regular classes. She had heard that I was doing these practices in my own senior school classes, not only in philosophy classes, but indeed in my senior chemistry classes, with positive feedback from students and parents alike. In 2004, when I started teaching psychology to Year 11 and 12 students, I again incorporated this methodology as it fitted well into the positive psychology philosophy upon which I based my teaching. The very nature of conducting silent sitting at the start of classes had the added benefit in that I too gained significant clarity of thought and calmness in my teaching and counselling practices, a bonus often commented on by other teachers and students alike. This use of silent sitting led to guest sessions at student leadership camps and retreats, both for students and staff. The feedback was positive and opened a whole new area of my counselling interactions also. This resulted in the compilation of several CD recordings of guided visualizations which included

Steve Halpern's music (Halpern 1994a, 1994b) with his permission, to be used in classes without the need of my actual presence.

The practice of silent sitting expanded to include visualization practices, particularly those involving imagining a successful outcome of goals for whatever task was causing anxiety or concern, then forming a mental picture of the steps needed to arrive at the desired outcome. When I stopped making recordings, many staff members followed up the reference to Dr. Ramesha Manocha's book (Manocha 2013), as well as his free website (www.beyondthemind.com), which provides an easy-to-follow guided meditation.

7.4   Silent Sitting as an Adjunct to Counselling

On a therapeutic level, the techniques of silent sitting were also incorporated very early on into my school counselling practices, both for incidental clients and for regular customers, particularly those on the autism spectrum. Over the years, the college had an ever-increasing number of students with diagnosed Asperger's syndrome, who were regular visitors to the Well Being Centre with varying degrees of anxiety levels.

One particular example comes to mind. A Year 11 student who had been clinically diagnosed with a high level of Asperger's came rushing into my office before school had even started one morning in a highly agitated and incoherent state. I invited him into my office and gently conveyed to him that I could not understand what he was saying in his current state of agitation. I suggested that we both sit down and count our breathing down, in the same way we had in his previous visits. He had been practicing this technique with me over a period of several months on his regular catch-up visits when times were less stressed.

The change was nothing short of spectacular. I had taught him to take his own pulse previously, so while he was slowing his breathing down, I invited him to let go of all the racing thoughts within his head and watch his pulse rate. Over a period of only a few minutes, his pulse reduced by a third, his breathing became regular and he lost his initial agitation. In that stillness, I asked him to calmly visualize the issue that was upsetting him and, when he was ready, to share it with me. He was able not only to articulate the cause of his upset but to come up with two strategies that he could choose to deal with the issue more effectively. We then had a relaxing cup of tea, after which he left.

The following morning, he was waiting outside the Well Being Centre with a smile on his face to tell me that not only had he resolved the situation but that his mother was very proud of him and would be phoning me later in the day to thank me for helping him. One particularly gratifying comment was that it was the first time she had recalled her son showing empathy and compassion, qualities not normally expressed by people diagnosed with his level of Asperger's.

The same techniques were also very effective in dealing with general anxiety issues and anger management. Visitors to the Well Being Centre would enter a large, inviting and comfortable waiting room. The waiting room provided cool, filtered water and positive affirmation posters on the walls, as well as a regular rotation of a large collection of quotations and affirmations collected over my 39 years as a secondary school counsellor.

A Year 9 boy, whose high levels of anxiety exacerbated his stuttering in a high-pitched voice, also benefited significantly from the regular practice of silent sitting. I would simply hold up my hand to him to stop him talking, then calmly ask him to sit, close his eyes and slow his breathing down, focusing on making his abdomen rise and fall with each breath. When the pattern of breathing had slowed, we would sit in silence for 2–5 min. I would then ask him to open his eyes, maintain the calm feeling and articulate his issue for that day in a slow deep voice. The change was always dramatic, again with the side benefit of him displaying more empathy towards those giving him a hard time, making a mental resolution not to react emotionally to the situations in which he would find himself. He maintained these practices for the remaining 2 years of his secondary education, even becoming a popular school leader in his final year at school while undertaking his Year 12 studies, which required regular public speaking.

As another calming strategy, in conjunction with silent sitting, a number of commercially available line-patterned coloring books and an array of good-quality colored glitter gel pens and colored pencils were also made freely available to visitors. While waiting for their appointments, students (and indeed staff members) were invited to select a picture or pattern that appealed to them from one of several books and work silently on coloring them in any way they wished, with soft music in the background. All who used the Well Being Centre understood that if they wrote their names or identifying codes of some sort on the pictures, no one else would complete an unfinished picture in the book. This rule was followed meticulously by all who visited the center, and the completed pictures could either be displayed in the center or taken home by the person who completed them. About half were happy to have their pictures displayed on the walls or to leave them in the books for others to see. This concept of being mindful whilst coloring in has become popular in recent times.

Some pictures were taken from magazines such as Better Homes and Gardens Colour for Spring (2015). Each pattern in this publication also had an inspirational quote attached. One such quote was: "Blessed are they who see beautiful things in humble places where other people see nothing."

This small amount of time spent to quiet the mind and gather thoughts meant that those clients using silent sitting before counselling sessions were able to better express their thoughts and feelings. On many occasions, they were even able to identify their own underlying issues and come up with self-generated strategies to deal with their situations with clarity and some sense of control. They were often able to articulate their perceived shortcomings and the errors of judgment they had made in misinterpreting incidents that had upset them. Indeed, during a number of appointments, just by silent sitting and doing the coloring in, they were able to resolve their angst sufficiently without any real counselling intervention to be able to return calmly to the classroom out of which that they had previously stormed. They would also, without prompting, apologize to the teacher concerned and, on some occasions, even discuss appropriate reparation.

The use of the coloring exercise, coupled with silent sitting, was particularly effective with dealing with students with ADHD. On first reflection, it might seem odd to use a focus on breath for someone whose very condition is about the inability to focus on any task for any length of time. I called the technique I developed the PAUSE method when explaining it to the students involved and their teachers. I often used acronyms in my work, which I printed out on small cards and laminated for the students so they could carry them in their pockets.

PAUSE was a simple technique I worked out in conjunction with my first ADHD student, then printed on a small business-style card. I subsequently used it with many other students over the years, with a personal message on the back pertinent to the particular student who was using it.

Put down any stuff you are using.

Assume a grounded position (feet firmly on the floor, shoulder width apart).

Use your slow breathing count (four in, two hold, four out).

Still your body, then your mind.

Engage back into the task again when you when feel ready.

On the other side of the first card was written: "All people learn in their own special ways."

This technique could be followed in the classroom itself or the student could use a prearranged signal negotiated and agreed to by all the student's teachers. For example, the student could quietly and without any further interaction than a nod from the teacher leave the classroom and walk to the Well Being Centre. They would check in with any of the three staff members who were there and use the waiting area (with the coloring in materials) or go through the procedures in one of the counselling rooms.

After about 10 weeks or so using this method with the initial student, he was able to stay in the classroom and just touch his pocket in which he carried his card to reassure himself and calm his mind to the point where he could refocus on the classroom task without having to leave the room to visit the Well Being Centre. I left the responsibility to the homeroom teacher to let any new staff know of the needs of this student. Without me specifically naming the students involved, this methodology was eventually explained at a yearly professional development day for all staff, including ancillary staff. Many staff saw me after those meetings to ask if they could have such a card also to remind them when they felt they were losing it.

One of the fundamental essentials in resolution through counselling intervention is to be able to define the situation and explore possible alternative choices that might avoid repetition of problems or reactions to circumstances in the future. When used appropriately, this was a major positive outcome of engaging in these techniques.

I used a similar approach for students with ADHD whose lives easily spiraled out of control. One example involved a student whose fight-or-flight response was interfering with his ability to control his angry outbursts and resultant lack of self-esteem and resilience. Silent sitting was again a significant aspect used by this student to modify his attitude. This time it was coupled with a numbered scale that helped him to focus on the moment at hand and accept that such feelings were not only normal but common to most people. The numbers were as follows:

1. I am feeling good about myself, so I think I will do OK.
2. I am starting to feel I am having problems staying on task. I need to still myself and practice my breathing and silence to go back to 1.
3. I need to take a break. I need help to calm down, to go to a quieter place.
4. It is all too much. I need to get out of here right now.
5. I have totally lost it. If I do not get out of here, I will hit someone.

If I saw him in the yard, after sharing greetings, I would simply ask him what number he thought he was at. I encouraged his teachers to do the same, and if he was higher than a two, he was offered the chance to go to the Well Being Centre if he wished. He would most often take up this offer.

On the other side of the card with the numbered scale was a positive affirmation. This would either be the slogan "Help Ever, Hurt Never" or an acronym of the student's name with positive personal qualities for each letter, which we would decide together. Let us use the name Darren as an example.

Determined.
Artistic.
Responsible.
Reliable.
Energetic.
Noticeable.

Obviously, my college was blessed with the Well Being Centre for times such as these, a necessary place of retreat where this student could come as he most often needed some structured guidance to do the silent sitting procedure. In our early interactions, he and I spent some time talking through what actually happened in his brain when he felt and behaved like this, before we first set up the five-point card system. He appreciated this, as he genuinely felt someone was prepared to listen and understand his feelings and behavior and that it had a scientific basis (he was into anything involved with science). It took the better part of a year for him to comfortably own his erratic thoughts and behavior, and his disruptions in class, though never completely disappearing, became less in number and more manageable.

Having used this for a significant number of students over at least 20 years previously, I was surprised and delighted to eventually discover that this technique was used by Buron and Curtis (2013), who wrote about their version of this type of intervention and published a book called *The Incredible 5-Point Scale*. I think the addition of focused exercises and silent sitting enhanced its effectiveness.

Small groups of students could also use the Well Being Centre to resolve their own friendship or other relationship issues by following the silent sitting protocols. While counsellors were available if needed, students often managed to do this on their own.

The basic rules of the Well Being Centre revolved around the seven principles found in *Teach Only Love* (Jampolsky 1983), a book about attitudinal healing. The seven principles are worth listing here:

1. Health is inner peace.
2. The essence of our being is love.
3. Giving is receiving.
4. All minds are joined.
5. Now is the only time there is.
6. Decisions are made by learning to listen to the preference for peace within us.
7. Forgiveness is the way to true health and happiness.

Teach Only Love (Jampolsky 1983) is a book I thoroughly recommend for all teachers. Each of the above seven points can be used individually as a very powerful affirmation phrase during silent sitting.

In my experience, as described above, the practice of taking a few moments at the start of, during and at the end of each day to still the mind by slowing down the breath and practicing silent sitting significantly helps to promote clarity of thought, inner peace and reduced anxiety, enabling one to better face the challenges of everyday living in these current times.

References

Bensen, H. (1970). *The relaxation response*. New York: Berkley Books.

Bensen, H. (1985). *Beyond the relaxation response*. New York: Berkley Books.

Better Homes and Gardens Colour for Spring. (2015). *Better Homes and Gardens Colour for Spring*. Eveliegh, Australia: Pacific Magazines Pty Ltd.

Buron, K., & Curtis, M. (2013). *The incredible 5-point scale*. Kansas: APC Publishing.

Francis, K. (1996). *Effective coping strategies* (unpublished master's thesis, University of South Australia).

Halpern, S. (1994a). *Inner peace* (CD). Sound Rx.

Halpern, S. (1994b). Gifts of the angels (CD). *Inner peace music*.

Jampolsky, G. (1983). *Teach only love*. New York: Bantam Books.

Manocha, R. (2013). *Silence your mind*. Sydney, Australia: Hatchett Press.

Riopel, L. (2019). Mindfulness and the brain: What does research and neuroscience say? *PositivePsychology.com*. Retrieved from, https://positivepsycholgy.com

Siegel, R. (2014). *The science of mindfulness: A research-based path to well-being*. Chantilly, VA: The Great Courses.

Chapter 8
Humanizing Education through Moral Education

Vishalache Balakrishnan

Abstract In the current digital world, every aspect of education has some elements of technology. Teaching and learning have become very complex and often individualistic, especially with the use of technology. In many schools and higher learning institutions, we are missing out on the integration of all types of people, the joy of studying and the purpose of life. It has become a very mechanical world. In some cultures, even preschool children are forced to spend hours studying for a supposedly early head start. By the time they are in secondary school, they have burned out, some even to the extent of taking their own lives because they cannot keep up with parental and societal pressure to excel in their studies. To ensure that the digital education era does not eliminate the human side of education, it is important to employ strategies to ensure this humanizing. One way that this can become a reality is through moral education. Moral education is a subject that is taught in Malaysian schools as a core subject for all non-Muslim students. It aims to develop students as individuals who have integrity and noble values, high moral standards based on universal values founded on moral principles that contribute to the unity, prosperity, and well-being of the individual, the country, and the global society. Through certain pedagogies in moral education, such as visualization and silent learning, students can be encouraged to engage in deep self-reflection, which can place them in a better position to make decisions based on the moral choices available in moral dilemmas that they face at interpersonal and intrapersonal levels.

Keywords Humanizing education · Visualization · Silent learning · Moral choices

V. Balakrishnan (✉)
Faculty of Education, University of Malaya, Kuala Lumpur, Malaysia
e-mail: visha@um.edu.my

© Springer Nature Singapore Pte Ltd. 2021
S. Parahakaran, S. Scherer (eds.), *A Human Values Pathway for Teachers*,
https://doi.org/10.1007/978-981-16-0200-9_8

8.1   Introduction

At the simplest level, education is perceived as the process of giving and receiving knowledge, skills, and values (Balakrishnan 2011). The conventional notion of receiving knowledge at a school or university for a certain duration and then being considered a learned person is no longer the norm. Education is lifelong, and no matter how high the qualifications one has acquired, learning takes place during every second of one's life.

Education at the societal level is the process of acquiring the knowledge, skills, and values that members of a particular society are expected to have. Sometimes, these components are indoctrinated into young children, and they tend to believe in them throughout their lives. A sound education develops critical thought processes along with learning accepted facts. It encourages intellectual curiosity, and this leads to lifelong learning. One subject that leads to exploring life to its fullest is moral education.

8.2   Moral Education

Moral education is becoming increasingly important in the current digital era, particularly for educators who want to ensure the humanness of education. What are seen as universal values are also part of moral education. Now, with current issues like pandemic outbreaks, and the global connectivity represented by, for example, Industrial Revolution 4.0 (IR 4.0), and Smart Society 5.0, there is an even greater need to humanize moral education and ensure that universal values are not just paid lip service but put into action.

Morality, on its own, is a complex term. Puka (1976) argued that without teachers knowing what morality is, it cannot be taught, and it especially should not be taught through "brainwashing." According to the Collins English Dictionary, morality "is the belief that some behavior is right and acceptable and that other behavior is wrong." However, with such a simplistic meaning, morality is still within a gray area because right and wrong, good, and evil, have come to be based subjectively on local norms and cultures.

As the world becomes borderless with the magical touch of the Internet, matters of right and wrong become even more of a gray area. For example, what was wrong in Eastern cultures may be seen as a norm in Western cultures. Thus, do East and West really exist in the current digital era? The answer is both yes and no. Yes, because cultural heritages like societal norms and values are maintained from generation to generation. No, because every individual with digital knowledge is able to reach out for answers and reasons when facing moral dilemmas in their daily lives.

So how can moral education be part of this controversial saga? From a local perspective, this can be education provided for individuals to learn about values, skills, and facts needed to make meaningful decisions that do not jeopardize their rights as individuals. At the same time, decisions made and actions taken should not bring harm to others in society, including the environment, the flora, and fauna.

As simple as it can be, the nature of globalization has brought about many changes. For example, every nation is becoming more and more multicultural. This makes it even more important to ensure that the different domains of moral education (moral reasoning, moral emotions, moral actions, moral motivation, etc.) are taught with clarity and provide the fundamentals for students to fall back on when they are faced with daily moral dilemmas in their day-to-day living.

8.3   Research Findings

A longitudinal research study conducted from 2007 to 2010 in Malaysia concluded that morality is very subjective, based on demography, individual maturity, and influences of different societies on one's moral decisions (Balakrishnan 2011). This is illustrated by the following two cases taken from the study, in which the students' moral dilemmas were closely related to common Asian values, such as the strict role of the father as disciplinarian in the family and the high value parents place on education.

8.3.1   Case Study 1

This research was conducted in an all-girls school. The six students were 15–16 years of age and came from different ethnic and religious backgrounds. When asked to first visualize and then write about one real-life moral dilemma that was really disturbing them, all six girls wrote about dilemmas that involved themselves as individuals (e.g., not being able to control their emotions when meeting with students of the opposite sex); dilemmas that they had with their parents, mostly with their mothers (e.g., mothers over-concerned about their boy-girl relationships); and dilemmas that they had with their friends (e.g., best friends and buddy groups who enjoyed gossiping about other girls).

8.3.2   Case Study 2

In the second research group, which was made up of 16-year-old Form 4 boys, the moral dilemmas were also around the circle of self: self and parents and siblings, self and friends, and self and nature. The boys were more concerned about dilemmas such as a lack of personal freedom with fathers controlling all of their movements in school and at home, even to the extent of how they styled their hair or spoke with their siblings. They also wrote about their parents' concerns with who their friends were and what they planned to do after their secondary school education. The boys in this case study visualized their entire lives as having no freedom or choices about how to lead their own lives.

These cases from 2007 showed that young adolescents in the two different focus groups were more concerned about moral dilemmas concerning their personal lives and their relationships with others. Even though they had studied a set of values in their moral education classes from Year 1 to Form 5 (7 years old to 17 years old), when they faced moral dilemmas in their daily lives, their experiences and surroundings guided their decision-making rather than what was learned in the moral education classroom (such as self, family, school, society, environment, human rights, patriotism and national pride, and international safety). Only one participant mentioned his worry about nations not prioritizing environmental sustainability and the increasing haze pollution in neighboring countries.

In other words, the moral issues and values about which the students were the most concerned were not those covered in the moral education curriculum (Balakrishnan 2011) but rather were relational and context dependent. They prioritized autonomy, self- and mutual respect, trust, freedom, and tolerance as the main conflicting themes in their real-life moral dilemmas.

The analysis also showed that the participants' moral choices were influenced by their parents, culture, religion, need for utilitarianism, collaboration, and friendship within a strong care-based approach. However, most of the time, participants argued that the visions of their teachers and parents were always the priority and their own visualizations of learning and their own real-life daily moral dilemmas were ignored. This raises the need to look more closely at the notion of students' visualization.

8.3.3 Visualization

What is visualization? In everyday language, it is the representation of an object, situation or set of information as a chart or other image. It can also be the formation of a mental image of something. It can be used as a technique for creating images, diagrams or even narratives.

Visualization, in the context of thinking, can be divided into four categories:

1. Consideration, which includes the creation of new images by their repetition and existing elements. This is the basis for a visual analogy.
2. Learning physical skills, which first creates a visual perception that defines the nature of physical movement arising in the performance of a specific movement (for example, tuning the radio, dissecting dead bodies).
3. Understanding verbal description, in which visualization is generated based on propositional statements (for example, the structure of crystalline solids formed on the basis of verbal descriptions).

4. Creativity, which can be either a reassessment of the meaning of an existing image or a change of the frame of reference (Gilbert 2005).

While many subjects, such as computer studies, cognition and thinking, and cartography, use visualization as their main teaching pedagogy, moral education, and other character- and value-based subjects can also use it as an effective teaching and learning pedagogy. Together with silent learning, students can be taught the process of visualization as a part of aspiring to higher-order thinking skills. They can explore their own emotions and make appropriate moral judgments when faced with simple or complex moral dilemmas; that is, the decision process becomes intrapersonal, not interpersonal.

In the two case studies discussed earlier, research participants from both the all-girls and all-boys schools kept repeating things like, "I can imagine that if my mother saw my mobile phone and the content, she would surely flare up." Thus, this virtual perception was fearful and negative when the students saw the consequences of not being able to share their own ideals and emotions with their parents, whom some of them considered "old-fashioned" or "not open minded." However, toward the end of using the pedagogy of discussing real-life moral dilemmas (Re-LiMDD), the students had learned to visualize the situation from their parents' viewpoints, that their parents would feel fear if their children mixed with the wrong group of friends or did not have self-discipline.

Visualization, if applied wisely in the moral education classroom, can enable students to see the positive and negative sides of their moral dilemmas. This continuous and systemic effort can enable them to face gray areas in daily life with more confidence and sense, rationally deciding how to judge a moral dilemma and make wise decisions based on their affirmative visualizations. One simple visualization method that I have found to be particularly useful is the silent way.

8.3.4 Silent Learning the Silent Way

There is a simple story told by Gautama Buddha, who wanted his helper to fetch a pitcher of water from the river near where they were resting. The helper went and came back with an empty pitcher, giving the reason that the water was cloudy, as a bullock cart had just passed through. The wise Buddha sent his helper several times, but the response was the same, and he returned repeatedly with the empty pitcher.

After many attempts, the helper, who was wondering why the Buddha had made him walk to the river so many times to collect cloudy water, came back with clear water in his pitcher. When Buddha took and drank the water, he thanked the helper and told the rest of the group that it was a simple lesson to all. The lesson was that, when one's mind is cloudy with too many thoughts, one needs to wait for it to be silent, just as the helper had to wait for the river water to be clear again. Only then can one think rationally and make decisions wisely.

The silent way is a term used for silent teaching, which originated in the early 1970s and was the brainchild of Gattegno (1963). The basic principles of the approach are as follows:

1. Teachers should concentrate on how students learn, not on how to teach.
2. Imitation and drill are not the primary means by which students learn.
3. Learning consists of trial and error, deliberate experimentation, suspending judgment, and revising conclusions.
4. In learning, learners draw on everything that they already know, especially their native language.
5. The teacher must not interfere with the learning process.

Over the years, Gattegno's (1963) ideas have been tested, adapted, and amended to suit different teaching and learning settings. He used color-coded silent way tools and materials for foreign students to learn foreign languages, which helped students to identify and produce the sounds of the new language.

Similarly, in the moral education class, a teacher can provide a real-life moral dilemma and then observe students when they try to resolve the dilemma based on their own personal experiences. The teacher's silence provides an opportunity for students to reflect on their own experiences and then resolve the dilemma put forward.

Relating back to Case Study 1, one particular student had the dilemma of having sweaty hands whenever she met students of the opposite sex. This situation had led her to many embarrassing moments that she had cried over, even to the extent that she had felt like ending her own life. After several cycles of Re-LiMDD, the student herself started to reflect and tried the silent learning approach. In her reflective journal, she wrote the following:

> I have been quite silly all this while. Knowing that I get sweaty palms whenever I meet boys, I should have learnt to calm myself down. I understand that I am unique and different from others. I do not have to shake hands and make a fool out of myself. I should just say hello and nod my head or do something different. This would have built my confidence and not made me nervous. What a fool I have been all this while (Girl participant, Case Study 1).

When the above research participant started in the first phase of the research, she kept repeating, "I can imagine . . ." When further probed, she said she could see how the boys were laughing behind her back and how her own girlfriends were teasing her. But as she became more reflective, which was part of the Re-LiMDD phase of silent learning and silent self-reflection, she began to understand herself better and to see the entire picture of who she was and what she was trying to resolve. Being silent made her understand herself and the world around her. And being in that equilibrium also helped her to resolve the dilemma of her sweaty palms.

Philips (1994) described a framework devised by Jensen (1973) that identifies five different functions of silence, each function having both a positive and a negative aspect:

1. Linkage: Silence can act as a bond or as a device to separate people.
2. Affecting: Silence can represent respect, kindness, and acceptance and can bring about a time for reflection and a healing period after a confrontation. On the other hand, it can be seen as embodying scorn, hostility, coldness, defiance or even hate.
3. Revelation: Silence can lead to understanding and self-awareness. It can also be used to conceal opinions and feelings.
4. Judgment: Silence can lead to an assumption of assent and agreement with what has been said. It can also be interpreted as disagreement and resentment.
5. Activating: Silence can communicate an attitude of thoughtfulness and consideration or an absence of thought or opinion.

In Case Study 2, six real-life moral dilemmas were discussed using the Re-LiMDD. The boys in this case group reacted differently during the different phases of the Re-LiMDD. When the dilemma of their lack of freedom from their parents was discussed, the students showed linkage (agreed that they do had no freedom to do what they wanted during their free time), affecting (patted the friend who was sharing the "torture" of two pairs of "hawk eyes" that he was undergoing every day), revelation (wrote in their own personal journals of how they appreciated the freedom their parents gave them compared to their friend who shared his moral dilemma), judgment (nodded their heads to show agreement and support for their friend), and activating (shook hands and hugged the friend who shared, without saying a single word).

Thus, the role of silent learning can lead to deep self-reflection and enable one to discover one's own strength in resolving daily moral dilemmas. In moral education, merging visualization and silent learning has much potential to encourage maximum learning to take place as the subject focuses on the holistic development of individuals, such as cultivating the reasoning mind, creating a positive motivating emotion, and concluding with appropriate moral actions.

Many times, moral education teachers wanted to help to solve students' moral dilemmas for them, playing the savior role. However, the students in the research project described above clarified that they wanted autonomy to think through, judge and come up with their own decisions. They said they would not shame their teachers or parents by making immoral decisions but, as one particular student said, "Values are caught and not taught." She made the comment that, in this light, if her parents were taking drugs, she might take after them.

Thus, teachers must withhold their thoughts and offer the silent way for students to think through their own moral dilemmas. In a similar spirit, Jim Scrivener, in his book *Classroom Management Techniques*, recommended that teachers withhold their responses from time to time: "acknowledge student contributions but don't feel the need to say something after each one" (Scrivener 2012, p. 187). Scrivener continued that "often, the space and silence (i.e. the absence of the teacher saying something) is what students need to organize their own thoughts and find something to say" (2012, p. 187).

Kramsch (2009) suggested:

> We may want to leave time in class for students to write in silence, to have a silent, private contact with the shape of a poem and its silent sounds, to listen in silence to the cadences of a student or to our own voice reading aloud, to follow silently the rhythm of a conversation played on tape, the episodic structure of a story well told. We may want to even foster silence as a way of letting the students reflect on what they are right now experiencing. (pp. 209–210).

What both Scrivener (2012) and Kramsch (2009) have suggested is a need for moral education teachers to create the space for students to reflect and decide. Doing so enables their students to make wise moral choices in their daily moral dilemma resolution. To understand further what this involves, the next section examines the concept of moral choices in more depth.

8.3.5   Moral Choices

Why are moral choices necessary? Choices are necessary because, to develop as an individual to one's full potential, one must have more than one course of action available, as well as both the authority and the competence to choose which course of action to follow (Boostrom 1998). Moral education has the capability to allow this natural process to happen. As mentioned earlier, the students' choices can be influenced by several factors, as shown in Fig. 8.1.

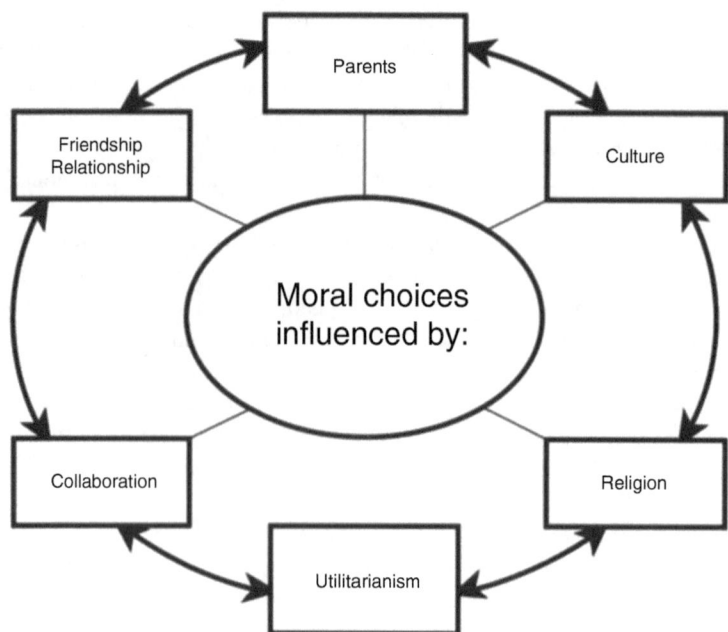

Fig. 8.1 Factors influencing moral choices of secondary school students (Balakrishnan 2011)

The notion of self-decision-making in a pluralist society is particularly important within the Eastern cultural context. Even though students are provided with skills and pedagogies like visualization, silent learning, etc., their final decisions are still based on factors mentioned in Fig. 8.1. Students interact among themselves as a group and also consult their parents if they have warm, positive relationships with their parents and family members. Thorne (1993) once states that adolescents' and children's interactions are not preparation for life; they are life itself.

8.4 Discussion

Good, effective educators choose from a rich set of pedagogies to clearly present ideas and information to their students. However, students need the skills and knowledge for visualization in learning (Balakrishnan 2011). This can include small, practical techniques, such as collaborative learning and learning by learning. Collaborative learning has always been part of moral education with students learning to cooperate on specific tasks in and outside the classroom. Doing a project on service learning or community service is a concrete example of collaborative learning outside the classroom.

Learning by learning is when students are given opportunities to engage in the silent way and visualization to reflect on their own learning and then prepare the materials they can use to communicate and interact with others. This includes the creation of visualizations that are effective in resolving a moral dilemma. After using effective approaches to visualization and silent learning techniques, hopefully, students are able to reach the reflective stage, which is essential in humanizing education. At this stage, students are fully aware that they have clear ideas of what they are facing and how they are going to resolve any moral dilemmas that they encounter. These ideas contribute towards the unity, prosperity, and well-being of self, society, and country, as well as global society.

Through implementing pedagogies in moral education such as visualization and the silent way, students are more likely to be able to engage in self-reflection and deep learning. They are in better positions to make decisions about moral dilemmas at interpersonal and intrapersonal levels based on the moral choices available to them.

8.5 Conclusion

Visualization of desired outcomes is an age-old technique. It involves envisioning oneself achieving a goal. When students visualize, they need space for some silent moments. Visualization and silent learning come hand-in-hand. Students must be trained from a young age to have an internal awareness of their known cognition, emotions, and actions. When students have the space to become complete humans, then no digital era can ever take away their pride, their dignity or their self-worth.

The crucial question here is, "Are we—educators, parents and society on the whole—providing such a platform for our students?"

With the current technology era, students must be encouraged to apply visualization and silent learning in their daily lives. They need to be equipped with specific skills for reflective resolutions, which can enable them to face life based on what is learned. This is an alternative for humanizing education for the twenty-first century.

References

Balakrishnan, V. (2011). *Real-life moral dilemmas in moral education.* Kuala Lumpur: University of Malaya Press.

Boostrom, R. (1998). The student as moral agent. *Journal of Moral Education, 27*(2), 179–190.

Gattegno, C. (1963). *Teaching foreign languages in schools: The silent way.* New York: Educational Solutions.

Gilbert, P. (2005). Compassion and cruelty: A biopsychosocial approach. In P. Gilbert (Ed.), *Compassion: Conceptualisations, research and use in psychotherapy* (pp. 9–74). Abingdon, UK: Routledge.

Jensen, V. (1973). Communicative functions of silence. *ETC: A Review of General Semantics, 30* (3), 249–257.

Kramsch, C. (2009). *The multilingual subject.* Oxford, UK: Oxford University Press.

Philips, D. (1994). The functions of silence within the context of teacher training. *ELT Journal, 48* (3), 266–271.

Puka, B. (1976). Moral education and its cure. In J. R. Meyer (Ed.), *Reflections on values education* (pp. 47–87). Waterloo, ON: Wilfrid Laurier University Press.

Scrivener, J. (2012). *Classroom management techniques.* Cambridge, UK: Cambridge University Press.

Thorne, B. (1993). *Gender play: Girls and boys in school.* New Brunswick, NJ: Rutgers University Press.

Chapter 9
Silent Sitting and Visualization Techniques and the Environment: A Mindful Tool for Developing Awareness

Suma Parahakaran

Abstract Due to the rapid expansion of urbanization in many parts of the world, especially in developing countries, many students are losing their connectedness with the environment at a time when this interconnectedness is crucial. This chapter provides some examples of silent sitting and visualization as an integral part of classroom teaching to create a sense of connection between students and the environment. These ideas have been drawn primarily from successful water education programs in Asia, including selected parts of India and China, and in Africa. Cornell's Flow Learning concept has been adapted as a framework for these techniques. Some examples are provided with lessons learned from the implementation of silent sitting and visualization using elements from the environment. The chapter also refers to a model developed by Jumsai to explain why silent sitting can be helpful in bringing about environmental awareness.

Keywords Visualization · Flow learning · Mindfulness · Environmental education · Sustainable development

9.1 Introduction

Many environmental issues have emerged due to human impact and environmental degradation (Goudie 1993; Haughton and Hunter 1994; Khan 1995). Human actions related to natural disasters in the form of gas emissions, pollution of water and food, and excessive use of energy and water are creating environmental problems. The main problem is that humans are dependent on the earth, and we need to be aware of this fact for the protection and sustainability of all beings in the world. The United Nations' 2030 agenda, for example, elaborates on the following Sustainable Development Goals (SDGs):

S. Parahakaran (✉)
American University of Sovereign Nations, Sacaton, AZ, USA

© Springer Nature Singapore Pte Ltd. 2021
S. Parahakaran, S. Scherer (eds.), *A Human Values Pathway for Teachers*,
https://doi.org/10.1007/978-981-16-0200-9_9

- SDG 3: good health and well-being.
- SDG 6: clean water and sanitation.
- SDG 7: affordable and clean energy.
- SDG 11: sustainable cities and communities.
- SDG 12: responsible consumption and production.
- SDG 13: climate action.
- SDG 14: life below water.
- SDG 15: life on land (UN General Assembly 2015).

These different goals have become crucial for the well-being of the environment globally. While scientific understanding of water issues and management help to protect and conserve the environment, love and care for the environment are also essential.

As well, there is a growing understanding that the environment is a major contributor to human well-being (Triguero-Mas et al. 2015). For example, as more and more rural areas are being urbanized, green urban areas have helped to sustain mental health conditions (Alcock et al. 2014). The field of neuroscience has contributed a lot to our understanding of why the implementation of techniques like silence, mindfulness, and visualization are important to help mental and emotional processes for our well-being and for the development of pro-environmental behaviors. Drawing from successful water education programs in Asia, including selected parts of India, China, and Africa, this chapter provides some examples of how silent sitting and visualization techniques, particularly when used with music, can help students to gain deeper awareness and respect nature.

The concept of Flow Learning, proposed by Joseph Cornell (1989), is used here to explain how silent sitting helps in creating human-nature connections (see Sect. 9.3.1). People have a natural quality to view nature as a resource to be used. They lack a depth of sensory perception and awareness of the beauty of nature and of the problems arising as a consequence of human exploitation (Bonnett 2017). This quality can lead to bad decision-making and the inevitable outcomes of those decisions (Bonnett 2017). Humans become separated from the environment because of their thinking processes (Pepper 1999).

Environmental degradation can be reversed through education if one values the world intrinsically. This means positioning the senses as part of a consciousness in which words, ideas, concepts, and thinking are accepted as only a part of us (Bai 2001). The sixteenth item of the Earth Charter (Earth Charter Associates, 2000) on "promoting a culture of tolerance, culture and peace" states that we must "recognize that peace is the wholeness created by right relationships with oneself, other persons, other cultures, other life, Earth, and the larger whole of which all are a part" (Item IV.16f).

To understand more about the role of education in connecting us to the historical wisdom of environmental protection and conservation, it is important to know more about how the reports of the Earth Charter and the United Nations' SDGs address the development of curricula for schools and universities globally.

9.1.1 Reports of the Earth Charter, UN Sustainable Development Goals and the Environment

As mentioned above, the processes of development and urbanization are leading to mounting ecological state and environmental issues. Scientists warn us that the rate of environmental degradation and the consequences of human actions are intricately related. Reports on environmental issues and sustainability affirm again and again the need for a stronger ethical framework founded on shared values using a spiritual dimension and contemplative practices (Barney et al. 2000; Clugston 1997; Clugston et al. 2002; World Commission on the Social Dimension of Globalization 2004). Without the essential sensitivity and deeper understanding of the energies that bind the universe, humans may not be able to move from the present destructive path to one of the unities.

Referring to the educational goal SDG 4 of the UN General Assembly (2015) to "promote inclusive and equitable quality education and promote lifelong learning opportunities for all," Clugston et al. (2002) explain that if the Earth Charter is to achieve its goal of promoting and implementing access for all to quality education, it has to be done in a values context that engages human capacities and motivation.

> Solutions related to pro-environmental behaviors are related to psychological adaptations. Other factors that also impact behavior changes are attributed to moral, ethical, and altruistic imperatives (Koger et al. 2011). Literature describing the earlier views of how humans protected the environment and conserved the rivers, water sources, and trees are deeply embedded in various ethnic and indigenous groups of the world (Parahakaran 2013). The SSEHV practice of Ceiling on Desires (see Sect. 2.1.4) is therefore integral to environmental protection: "Any use of the elements over and above legitimate bounds is a sacrilege. So too, each element must be used under some limitations, not as and how you like" (Sathya Sai Baba, 1978, p.55).

9.1.2 The Need for Humans to Develop a deeper Contemplative Nature

Many environmentalists have realized that pro-environmental behaviors have to be integrated into education. It has been argued that human values allow us to broaden our understanding of the unifying aspects of the environment (Parahakaran 2020) and hence to do more to conserve it.

The present school curricula aim mostly at providing scientific knowledge about nature and its processes but overlook the affective dimensions such as appreciation, awe, and deep reflection. Clugston et al. (2002) refer to the need to use effective contemplative practices to awaken ourselves to engage passionately with real-world needs. Specifically, Clugston et al. (2002, p. 68) described the need to do the following:

- Engage deeply and effectively in contemplative practices that awaken us to our great work, our vocations, where our deepest passions meet the real needs of the world.
- Experience our interconnectedness and interdependence with the whole living world, embracing diverse cultures of people and animals, agriculture and wilderness, the cycles of life and the seasons, as well as the unfolding cosmos.
- Feel, and act from, compassionate concern for others, doing no harm, reaching out to assist all beings.

Clugston et al. (2002) added that the inculcation of these values requires us to live and to accommodate the lives of others with respect and love and to make decisions that are open to collective participation that uplifts everyone.

Silent sitting practices or guided visualization techniques encourage students to awaken to the aesthetic sense of nature, to explore the similarities of the values inherent in nature and its interconnectedness with all living things. This kind of awareness is related to a sense of awakening within when in contact with nature (King 2010). Due to the emerging recognition of the need to promote this kind of awareness, the next section focuses on literature that talks more about what needs to be done.

9.2 Silence, Mindfulness, Contemplative Practices and their Potential to Reconnect Humans to Nature

Twenty-five quantitative studies examining 2990 participants were analyzed for mindfulness interventions connected to nature, and these interventions had positive psychological, interpersonal, and physiological aspects (Djernis et al. 2019). In addition, another review of 12 studies with 2435 individuals revealed that mindfulness can also help in creating connections with nature (Schutte and Malouff 2018). Contemplative practices, when turned toward the nature of the environment, can help students to be deeply aware of the joy within them when they experience nature with some degree of calmness and concentration (Cornell 1989).

A study by Reid-Howells (2014) explored people's experiences of the opportunities of silence to enable students to absorb complex concepts and expand their space for reflection, thus creating aha moments. Fivush (2009) explored silence and reflected that "creating shared silence" may promote a sense of pulling together, of sharing great emotions, and thus may facilitate identification and affiliation with others (p. 92). Silence enables humans to connect to the energy fields, such as the sun and beauty of creation, while they experience the interconnectedness of everything in nature (Jasmuheen 2011). The following quotation from Van Gordon et al. (2018) illustrates how this can happen:

> Perhaps the best way of appreciating how the principle of interconnectedness relates to our lives as human beings is through our connection with nature. When we breathe in, we breathe in the out-breath of plants, shrubs, and trees. When we breathe out, we breathe out

the in-breath of flowers, animals, and birds. When we drink water, we drink the clouds, rivers, and oceans. When we eat a meal, we eat plants, vegetables, and fruits that have grown out of the earth. (p. 1655)

This awareness is not just about perceiving a feeling or emotion but extends in connection to nature as it includes care and love (Richards 2001). Richards (2001) elaborated on the need to be conscious of the beauty within nature, such as a view of the "sunset streaking the sky with brilliant colours and cloudscapes" (p. 75). We have opportunities to learn more about nature and develop a larger awareness of ourselves and our interconnection with the nature around us. Richards (2001) emphasized the need to "un-condition our conditioned senses and let them fall on a fluid gestalt, giving space for sensing the different rhythms and tones, and gestures by the environment surrounding us" (p. 75).

9.2.1   A Model for Contemplative Awareness through Silent Sitting and Visualization

Jumsai (2003) proposed a theory to explain why the technique of silent sitting has an important potential impact on the learner's mind and hence helps to create the kind of awareness described in the previous section. Figure 9.1 illustrates this theory (see also Sect. 2.1.5 for a brief overview of silent sitting and visualization).

According to Jumsai (1997), the conscious mind of the learner is continuously interacting with the five senses of sight, hearing, taste, touch, and smell. For the conscious mind to focus, learners must attend to what is happening as they receive stimuli from the environment. The conscious mind is able to listen to music and the words of a song or guided visualization. When the learner goes inward as they calm down, they are able to declutter their thoughts and enter into a state of calmness.

Jumsai (1997) proposed that the unconscious mind involves both the subconscious and the superconscious mind. Memory is stored in the subconscious mind like data in a computer. When learners retrieve any information, they interpret it from the

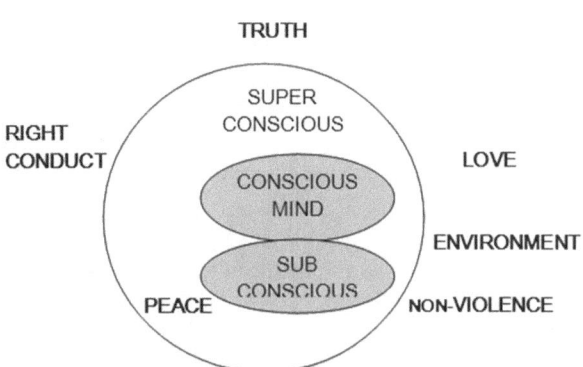

Fig. 9.1 Mind of the learner and use of silent sitting or visualization (Jumsai 1997)

subconscious mind, which is part of their experience. The subconscious mind can be reprogrammed by seeing, learning or reinforcing information.

Jumsai (1997) described the superconscious mind as the space from where learners gain their insights or intuitions. The superconscious mind deals with the Sohar and Marshall tertiary psychological processes (spiritual quotient, or SQ), while the conscious mind is derived from Freud's secondary psychological process (intelligence quotient, or IQ) and the subconscious mind from Freud's primary psychological processes (emotional quotient, or EQ) (Jumsai 2003; United Nations Human Settlements Programme [UN-Habitat] 2001). The superconscious mind, which is rarely discussed within the education system, is related to the spiritual quotient. It is concerned with a "tertiary brain process for synchronous neural oscillations" (Selman et al. 2005, pp. 24–25), which helps to integrate all the data across the brain and supports the transformation of human reasoning and emotional processes (Selman et al. 2005).

9.2.2   SSEHV Program and the United Nations Human Settlements Programme (UN-Habitat) Agenda for Water Education: An Educational Agenda

The SSEHV program, which has been implemented in many parts of the world, responds to the need for shared-values-based learning that raises awareness in children and develops interconnection with nature. The UN-Habitat stated that human values are the missing link and the core component for developing a new water ethic (UN-Habitat 2001; UN-Habitat 2006; UN-Habitat & Southeast Asian Ministers of Education Organization [SEAMEO] 2007; UN-Habitat & The African Institute of Sathya Sai Education 2005).

The UN-Habitat incorporated the Jumsai model (human values-based integrated instructional model) (UN-Habitat 2006). The activities are developmentally appropriate and do not engage young children with complex and abstract concepts. The techniques used are simple and engaging as they can be used both indoors and outdoors. Combining induced teaching techniques with elicitation of values inherent in nature creates motivation in students. For example, a lesson about nature in the SSEHV program integrates the values inherent in the sun into a science lesson. The author recollects memories of classroom experiences with students in the science classes where SSEHV programs were conducted. Students responded positively to such sessions with statements on the inherent values of the sun, such as "Sun shines every day without fail. The sun gives light and heat without expecting anything in return." The lessons become teaching moments to elaborate on the beauty, greatness, and wonder of nature and the need to protect nature.

9.3   UN-Habitat Human Values and Water Education

This section describes a large-scale project implemented successfully in many parts of Asia, as an illustration of how human values can be used to enhance environmental awareness. The Human Value Based Water and Sanitation Hygiene Education (HVWSHE) project has been evaluated as reported by the UN-Habitat (Parahakaran 2013; RCE-Kunming n.d.; UN-Habitat 2011).

The aim of this project was to raise students' awareness about the importance of caring for water sources appropriately and distributing water wisely, unselfishly and without wastage through discussing the human values inherent in water and its life giving nature. This was important to ensure that the participants would learn to value life and realize their interconnectedness to the environment (Jumsai and Parahakaran 2006; Parahakaran 2013).

A study by Parahakaran (2013) explored the use of silent sitting in schools for environmental education with 22 teachers from Indonesia, Thailand, and the Lao People's Democratic Republic (Lao PDR) using explicit expressions about the interconnectedness of all things. The teaching pedagogies (silent sitting and visualizations, group activities, storytelling, music, and quotations) were all utilized and helped the participants to increase their reflective capacity, concentration, and self-awareness practices at all levels. In addition, the pedagogies created awareness in both teachers and students of the values inherent in water, increased their respect for water, and enhanced interpersonal relationships and interconnectedness with the environment.

While these pedagogies were interdependent, silent sitting was one of the most-used pedagogical tools in the HVWSHE project (Parahakaran 2013). It was valuable as a means of stimulating intuition and wisdom and increasing participants' appreciation for elements such as water. It stimulated critical thinking, sharing, caring, peace, and tolerance, hence fostering development of human values required for a good water ethics. Silent visualization techniques of induced imagery, often used along with music, helped students to retrieve direct experiences with nature from their memories. A teacher trainer from Thailand stated that music, apart from silent sitting, helped to motivate her students. When she introduced the values of water, she would use the sounds of water.

Cornell's (1989) concept of Flow Learning was the key framework for the silent sitting and visualization techniques used in the HVWSHE projects. The following section describes this concept in detail and illustrates how it was applied to this project.

9.3.1   Flow Learning

The book *Sharing the Joy of Nature* by Joseph Cornell (1989), a nature consultant in the Grand Canyon, provides us with a lens for visualizing how individuals connect with nature. Cornell chose a popular spot for his study and watched 150 visitors to the Grand Canyon as they observed the view. Only three people gazed at the Grand Canyon for more than 30 s. He realized that not many people had the skill to absorb the beauty and magnificence of nature.

Cornell (1989) collected a range of outdoor activities and used a method called Flow Learning to address this deficit. The stages he identified are awaken enthusiasm, focus attention, experience directly, and share inspiration. These stages, according to Cornell, are significant in connecting students back to nature. For example, to awaken is to motivate an intense flow of awareness; to focus is to help students to bring their attention to a calm focus. As our focus increases, we are more aware of what the senses have awakened in us: the senses of sight, touch, smell, taste, and hearing. Focused attention helps us arrive at a state of calmness and to experience directly without restlessness in our minds. This stage is the direct experience of a deeper awareness. When we are still and our minds are uncluttered, we are able to experience a deep sense of joy, calm, and happiness. We have an increased awareness of our natural state and the connection with the elements in the natural world (Cornell 1989).

The first stage of Flow Learning, therefore, awakens enthusiasm so students can experience alertness and engage in the activity. The second stage helps to cultivate receptivity so students can start paying deeper attention to the subject of experience and leads to receiving and responding by engaging with full attention. The third stage leads students to be fully absorbed and go inwards. The last stage of the activity involves an interactive session in which the teacher facilitates discussion, and creates group bonding and a sharing of personal reflections (Barlow 2010).

9.3.2   Adapting Cornell's (1989) Flow Learning to Visualization Techniques for Connecting to the Environment

In this section, the four stages of Cornell's (1989) Flow Learning are illustrated in relation to their adaption for the HVWSHE projects. Music was often used in conjunction with this model, particularly at the Awaken Enthusiasm and Focus Attention stages. Teachers interviewed during the HVWSHE project indicated that music was not only effective but also helped students to remember the values in the context of the music, and it touched their hearts subconsciously (Parahakaran 2013).

Stage 1: Awaken Enthusiasm.
Cornell (1989) suggested that the purpose of this stage is to awaken learners' enthusiasm. At this stage, the visualization technique can be used with music accompanied by either song lyrics or positive words about nature to attract students' attention.

Teachers can lead students to focus on the sound and let their awareness be with the sounds in the environment. The sound of water and the natural sound of birds chirping usually attract children's attention.

Stage 2: Focus Attention.
According to Cornell (1989), at this stage, learning depends on focusing and bringing scattered thoughts to stillness. The initial enthusiasm now draws students to become more attentive.

At this stage, students slowly draw their attention to music and move into a phase of silence so that they can pay attention to the music and the words.

Stage 3: Experience Directly.
At this stage, students' attention is focused with calmness. This stage allows them to be more aware and sensitive to the different expressions of nature when they are outdoors engaged in a specifically planned activity. This helps students to be engaged through direct experience (Cornell 1989).

When students listen to music and sounds from, or words about, nature (for example, sounds of water), they have direct experience. When they engage with the feeling of being one with the sound of water and experience the flow of water, there is a feeling of deep connection in that calmness and stillness.

The following is an example of a visualization that can be introduced at this stage:

Breathe in slowly and breathe out slowly.

Imagine you are near a flowing river.

The sun is shining, and its rays touch the waters.

Every drop flows, mingling and rushing with the other,

Sounds of burbling and gurgling bathing the grass,

Giving life to all, insects and birds.

You watch the river flow gracefully

Down and down; what a beautiful sight!

You are thankful for this gift from nature ...

Slowly open your eyes when you are ready.

Stage 4: Share Inspiration.
The fourth stage of Cornell's (1989) Flow Learning involves students by sharing inspiration. At this stage they are motivated and inspired by their direct experience with the activity. Teachers can facilitate discussions to involve students and allow them to share reflections.

In the HVWSHE project, this sharing would generally take the form of a debriefing session.

Teachers can ask questions such as the following:

1. How did you feel?
2. What interested you?
3. Did you feel different after you listened to the music?
4. How did you feel about the water?
5. What values are inherent in the water?
6. Do you think we share the same values?
7. Is it important to thank creation? Why?

Teachers use debriefing as a tool by asking students what happened, how they felt about the whole experience and why. They do not question or judge, and they allow as many responses as possible. Students who are exposed to nature and capable of being sensitive to the different rhythms of nature may be able to express their responses better. This exercise after the visualization techniques can help students to interconnect their ideas and learn from each other. Debriefing also enhances student awareness and insights of which they may be unaware.

9.4   Other Examples of Visualizations with Elements from Nature

9.4.1   Using Mountains as an Element from Nature

In the first stage (awaken enthusiasm), the teacher asks students to sit up straight and close their eyes. Students are instructed to breathe slowly while the music plays in the background. They are asked to focus on their breath. In the silent visualization exercise of the mountain, students are able to identify values of mountains such as silence, magnificence, their ability to withstand strong winds and heat and their strength and might and to identify these values inherent in themselves.

Generally, the teacher starts by saying, "Breathe in slowly and breathe out slowly." This exercise can be continued for a minute or two if students are restless.

The second and third stages (focus attention and direct experience) engage students to focus on the lyrics or script about the mountain:

Imagine you are standing in front of a beautiful mountain.

Feel its strength and might,

Holding trees and plants,

Stones and rocks and waterfalls.

You enjoy the sight of this mighty mountain,

Bathed in beautiful rays of sunlight

Coloring the mountains orange and yellow.

Feel the strength of the mountain

Withstanding the strong winds and heat,

Silent and magnificent.

Smell the fragrance of flowers.

Feel the freshness of the air.

And the cool breeze touch your skin.

You thank creation for this experience. . .

Slowly open your eyes when you are ready.

The teacher then debriefs and invites students to share their responses for a few minutes.

9.4.2 Using Trees as an Element from Nature

An example of trees used as a focus point for visualization opens up a number of values inherent in trees during the discussion or debriefing session.

The teacher induces a calm state of relaxation before extending the imagery to students.

Breathe in slowly and breathe out slowly.

Imagine a beautiful tree in your garden

With pink flowers and their sweet fragrance.

The tree stands tall with leaves that are high,

Looking up to the sky and reaching to touch the sun's rays,

With warm light flowing through the branches.

You feel the beauty of the tree with its roots

Deep in the ground, unseen,

Standing strong, giving shade and coolness to all.

You feel thankful to creation for this wonderful experience. . .

Slowly open your eyes when you are ready.

The teacher then debriefs and invites students to share their responses for a few minutes.

9.5 Conclusion

This chapter has used the example of the HVWSHE project to illustrate how education in human values, when integrated into environmental education, can elevate students' interconnections with the environment. The discussion has focused particularly on the important role of silent sitting and visualization as a tool to enhance the connection between human values and environmental awareness.

The chapter has also illustrated how Cornell's (1989) Flow Learning can be used as a guide for implementing visualization techniques or guided imagery with music. These visualization exercises can prompt students to open up with spontaneous responses and expressions about their understanding of nature or the environment. As Sobel (1996) emphasized, it is important that students enjoy nature and feel at one with it as a precursor to protecting and saving it. When they love the smell of the raw earth and grass, the natural sounds and the wonderful sights, they become beholden to nature and step up to becoming stewards of the planet.

References

Bai, H. (2001). Beyond educated mind: Towards a pedagogy of mindfulness. In B. Hockings, J. Haskell, & W. Linds (Eds.), *Unfolding bodymind: Exploring possibilities through education* (pp. 86–99). Brandon, VT: The Foundation for Educational Renewal.

Barlow, J. (2010). Bringing children back to nature. *Green Teacher, 88,* 23–26.

Barney, G. O., Blewett, J., & Barney, R. K. (2000). *Threshold 2000: Critical issues and spiritual values for a global age.* Grand Rapids, MI: CoNexus Press.

Bonnett, M. (2017). Environmental consciousness, sustainability, and the character of philosophy of education. *Studies in Philosophy and Education, 36,* 333–347. https://doi.org/10.1007/s11217-016-9556-x.

Clugston, R. (1997). The earth charter in its context. Satya. Retrieved from http://www.satyamag.com/jun97/earth_charter.html

Clugston, R., Calder, W., & Corcoran, P. B. (2002). Teaching sustainability with the earth charter. In W. L. Filho (Ed.), *Teaching sustainability at universities: Toward curriculum greening.* Bern: Peter Lang.

Cornell, J. (1989). *Sharing the joy of nature: Nature activities for all ages.* Nevada City, CA: Dawn Publications.

Djernis, D., Lerstrup, I., Poulsen, D., Stigsdotter, U., Dahlgaard, J., & O'Toole, M. (2019). A systematic review and meta-analysis of nature-based mindfulness: Effects of moving mindfulness training into an outdoor natural setting. *International Journal of Environmental Research and Public Health, 16*(17), 3202. https://doi.org/10.3390/ijerph16173202.

Earth Charter Associates. (2000). *The Earth Charter.* Retrieved from, https://earthcharter.org

Fivush, R. (2009). Speaking silence: The social construction of silence in autobiographical and cultural narratives. *Memory, 18,* 88–98. https://doi.org/10.1080/09658210903029404.

Goudie, A. (1993). *The human impact on the natural environment* (4th ed.). Oxford: Blackwell.

Haughton, G., & Hunter, C. (1994). Urban development and the environment. In *Sustainable cities: Regional development and public policy* (pp. 9–29). London: Jessica Kingsley.

Jasmuheen. (2011). *Biofields and bliss trilogy.* Queensland, Australia: Self-Empowerment Academy.

Jumsai, A. (1997). *Integration of human values and human excellence.* Thailand: The Institute of Sathya Sai Education.

Jumsai, A. (2003). *A development of the human values integrated instructional model based on intuitive learning concept.* Bangkok: Chulalongkorn University.

Jumsai, N. A., & Parahakaran, S. (2006). HVWSHE: Experiences in Thailand and Human Values (conference presentation). In *In Proceedings of Regional Workshop on Developing Teaching and Learning Materials for Integrating HVWSHE in Southeast Asian Schools.* Manila, Philippines: SEAMEO Innotech.

King, U. (2010). Earthing spiritual literacy: How to link spiritual development and education to a new earth consciousness? *Journal of Beliefs & Values, 31*(3), 245–260. https://doi.org/10.1080/13617672.2010.520998.

Koger, S. M., Leslie, K. E., & Hayes, E. D. (2011). Climate change: Psychological solutions and strategies for change. *Ecopsychology, 3,* 227–235.

Parahakaran, S. (2013). *Human values-based water, sanitation and hygiene education: A study of teachers' beliefs and perceptions in some SEA countries* (doctoral dissertation, University of Sydney).

Parahakaran, S. (2020, July 23–24, in press). Spiritual human values and bioethics integrated knowledge management tools for sustainable development (conference presentation). *2nd world conference on Children & Youth 2020, Malaysia.*

Pepper, D. (1999). The roots of technocentrism. In M. J. Smith (Ed.), *Thinking through the environment* (pp. 22–31). New York: Routledge.

RCE-Kunming. (n.d.). Human values-based water, sanitation and hygiene education in Kunming City (HVBWSHE). *Global RCE Network.* Retrieved from, https://www.rcenetwork.org/portal/sites/default/files/HVBWSHE-RCE-Kunming.pdf

Reid-Howells, B. (2014). *Experiences of silence: An exploration of peoples' experiences of intentional silence* (honors thesis, College of Sustainability, Dalhousie University).

Richards, R. (2001). A new aesthetic for environmental awareness: Chaos theory, the beauty of nature, and our broader humanistic identity. *Journal of Humanistic Psychology, 41*(2), 59–95. https://doi.org/10.1177/0022167801412006.

Sai Baba, S. (1978). Nature is the best teacher. In *Sathyam Sivam Sundaram* (vol. 4, p. 55). Sri Sathya Sai Books and Publications Trust (SSSBPT).

Schutte, N. S., & Malouff, J. M. (2018). Mindfulness and connectedness to nature: A meta-analytic investigation. *Personality and Individual Differences, 127,* 10–14. https://doi.org/10.1016/j.paid.2018.01.034.

Selman, V., Selman, R. C., Selman, J., & Selman, E. (2005). Spiritual-intelligence/–quotient. *College Teaching Methods & Styles Journal, 1*(3), 23–30.

Sobel, D. (1996). *Beyond ecophobia: Reclaiming the heart in nature education.* Great Barrington, MA: The Orion Society and the Myrin Institute.

Triguero-Mas, M., Dadvand, P., Cirach, M., Martínez, D., Medina, A., Mompart, A., Basagaña, X., Gražulevičienė, R., & Nieuwenhuijsen, M. J. (2015). Natural outdoor environments and mental and physical health: Relationships and mechanisms. *Environment International, 77,* 35–41.

UN General Assembly. (2015). Transforming our world: The 2030 agenda for sustainable development. *Refworld.* Retrieved from, https://www.refworld.org/docid/57b6e3e44.html

UN-Habitat. (2006). *Facilitators & trainers guidebook.* Nairobi, Kenya: UN-Habitat.

UN-Habitat. (2011, September 13–17). Water, sanitation & hygiene (WASH) (Conference presentation). *Sustaining the blue planet: Global water education conference,* Bozeman, MT: UN-Habitat.

UN-Habitat & Southeast Asian Ministers of Education Organization (SEAMEO). (2007). In P. Pannen, K. Ng, J. Ikhsan, & D. Mustafa (Eds.), *SEAMEO resource package: Human values-based water, sanitation and hygiene education (HVWSHE).* Indonesia: SEAMEO Regional Open Learning Center (SEAMOLEC) and United Nations Centre for Human Settlements (Habitat).

UN-Habitat & The African Institute of Sathya Sai Education. (2005). Water for African cities programme phase II. *UN-Habitat.* Retrieved from, http://www.unhabitat.org/water-for-african-cities-programme-phase-ii

United Nations Human Settlements Programme (UN-Habitat). (2001). Recommendations of Expert Group Meeting (EGM) on Water Education in African Cities, Johannesburg, 30 April to 2 May 2001. In *Human values in water education: Creating a new water-use ethic in African cities* (pp. 38–39). Nairobi, Kenya: UN-Habitat, United Nations Centre for Human Settlements.

Van Gordon, W., Shonin, E., & Richardson, M. (2018). Mindfulness and nature. *Mindfulness, 9,* 1655–1658. https://doi.org/10.1007/s12671-018-0883-6.

World Commission on the Social Dimension of Globalization. (2004). *A fair globalisation: Creating opportunities for all.* Geneva: International Labour Office.

Chapter 10
A Reflective Practice Model for Introducing Teachers to Silent Sitting and Visualization Strategies

Margaret Taplin

Abstract This chapter suggests a process for facilitating teachers to become adept at and willing to use silent sitting and visualization in their practices. It is intended primarily for teacher educators and others responsible for professional development who may wish to introduce this strategy. Brookfield's critical lenses of reflective practice are used as a framework for this model. The model creates opportunities for participants to see the benefits for themselves and their students, take ownership of its implementation, and develop their skills and knowledge to use it through ongoing collegial discussions in a community of practice. The model draws on approaches that have been used around the world to introduce teachers to silent sitting and visualization as part of the Sathya Sai Education in Human Values (SSEHV) model.

Keywords Silent sitting · Visualization · Professional development · Reflective practice

10.1 Introduction

Two aspects required for teachers to adopt innovations successfully are capability, which goes hand-in-hand with security and confidence, and willingness, in the form of motivation and commitment (Benveniste and McEwan 2000). Teachers may be unwilling, even i f hey have the capability to adopt innovations, for several reasons. One major obstacle can be a lack of faith in the pedagogy (Benveniste and McEwan 2000). It is also difficult for teachers to become committed to implementing a new idea in their classrooms if they do not have a sense of "ownership" of it (Benveniste and McEwan 2000) or do not recognize the importance of its contribution (Richards 1996). Often this can arise from asking them to implement something they have never experienced for themselves (Klein and Riordan 2011).

M. Taplin (✉)
Institute of Sathya Sai Education, Kowloon, Hong Kong
e-mail: mtaplin@hotkey.net.au

© Springer Nature Singapore Pte Ltd. 2021
S. Parahakaran, S. Scherer (eds.), *A Human Values Pathway for Teachers*,
https://doi.org/10.1007/978-981-16-0200-9_10

Another potential obstacle arises if the demands imposed by the innovation are too great on top of teachers' already over-packed schedules (Benveniste and McEwan 2000). With competing teaching, pastoral and administrative tasks, little time is available in the school day to introduce something extra, particularly if it threatens to take away from the time needed for other activities (Pyle and Esslinger 2014), so the innovation is often given low priority (Richards 1996). Another potential inhibitor can be parental opposition to something that they perceive to be "beyond the basics" (Richards 1996).

On the other hand, certain critical elements can make teacher professional development both meaningful and worthwhile (Dyer 2013). These include giving teachers choices to determine their own priorities (Dyer 2013), flexibility to modify the innovation to suit their contexts (Dyer 2013; Tondeur et al. 2016), and incremental steps to develop the practice (Dyer 2013; Klein and Riordan 2011). It is also important for the innovation to become an integral part of the teacher's routine (Dyer 2013). In planning and implementing a new initiative, teachers' voices must be both heard and acknowledged (Zide and Mokhele 2019). Learning through inquiry is important (Tondeur et al. 2016); teachers need to be "seen as active participants in learning, rather than empty vessels to be filled by the 'expert' trainer" (Thompson and Pascal 2012, p. 314). They need opportunities to experience firsthand the kinds of innovations to be implemented (Tondeur et al. 2016) and to take ownership through making meaning of these personal experiences (Klein and Riordan 2011).

Another component of successful, sustainable adoption of teaching innovation is a sharing of workplace projects that allows for professional learning in practice and opportunities for collegial discussion about ideas and initiatives (Klein and Riordan 2011; Makopoulou and Armour 2014; Tondeur et al. 2016). However, while the "practical wisdom" to be obtained from this kind of sharing is a key ingredient, it should be supplemented with theory and research findings (Makopoulou and Armour 2014).

A professional development program that can meet all of these needs and encourage teachers to engage fully with the initiative requires a combination of a professional knowledge base, a value base, and practice (Thompson and Pascal 2012). Reflection on learning from one's own experience is a powerful ingredient in establishing mindful and well-informed practices (Mathew et al. 2017; Thompson and Pascal 2012; Tondeur et al. 2016). In the words of Mathew et al. (2017):

> A person who reflects throughout his or her practice is not just looking back on past actions and events, but is taking a conscious look at emotions, experiences, actions, and responses, and using that information to add to his or her existing knowledge base and reach a higher level of understanding (p. 127).

A model that has stood the test of time, has been cited multiple times as influential (for example, by Benade 2015; Jacobs 2016; Thompson and Pascal 2012), and addresses all of the components referred to above as important to successful, sustainable professional development is Brookfield's four lenses for critically reflective practice (Brookfield 1995, 1998, 2017). This is an inquiry-based process that guides teachers to discover and research rather than being told in a lecture how to

Table 10.1 Brookfield's (1995, 1998, 2017) four lenses for critically reflective practice

Level	Characteristics
Critically Reflective Lens 1: Our Autobiography as a Learner of Practice	• Recognizing our personal experiences in the stories others tell. • Analyzing ourselves as learners • Explaining the parts of the learning we feel strongly committed to.
Critically Reflective Lens 2: Our Learners' Eyes	• What are our learners seeing and hearing? • What is happening to them?
Critically Reflective Lens 3: Our Colleagues' Experiences	• Talking to colleagues about what we do. • Sharing experiences of dealing with the challenges and successes. • Hearing ideas that may not have occurred to us. • Helps us to know what our assumptions are and to change our power structure.
Critically Reflective Lens 4: Theoretical Literature	• Teachers who research, present or publish scholarly literature display an advanced vocabulary for teaching practice, which can become a "psychological and political survival necessity, through which teachers come to understand the link between their private [teaching] struggles and broader political processes" (Brookfield 1995, pp. 37–8). • Engagement with scholarly literature supports understanding.

adopt the innovation. As teachers get better at reflection, it can effect changes in their beliefs and practices and give them a feeling of ownership because they are not just given information secondhand. Rather, discussion of their reflections with colleagues helps to develop a sense of community as common understandings emerge (Brookfield 1998). The summary in Table 10.1 lists the four lenses, with a brief descriptor of each.

Brookfield's model has been adopted as the framework for the silent sitting and visualization professional development program described in this chapter because of its capacity to develop both capability and willingness simultaneously. When introducing SSEHV, we want teachers to realize that the tools are intended to help them personally as well as their students. Silent sitting is a short, tangible activity that they can do relatively easily and in a short time without cutting too much into lesson time, so we introduce it as one of the earliest strategies.

In introducing silent sitting to teachers through this professional development program, Brookfield's lenses are not used in a linear way—in fact, they are more cyclic in nature. Hence in this description of a teacher professional development program, some lenses are revisited more than once. In the following program outline, each step is listed with the lens to which it relates.

10.2   A Framework for a Professional Development Program

10.2.1   Objectives

On completion of this module, participants will be able to do the following:

- Describe various purposes for silent sitting.
- Explain to children why silent sitting is beneficial, in the context of the five human values categories of truth, right conduct, peace, love, and non-violence (see Chap. 1 for more information).
- Design and implement silent sitting regularly in their classes for different purposes.
- Document the benefits of regular silent sitting for their pupils and themselves.

10.2.2   Preliminary Preparation

10.2.2.1   Critically Reflective Lens 4: Theoretical Literature

Teachers read *Silent Sitting: A Resource Manual* (Taplin 2010). This booklet gives an overview of the rationale for silent sitting and visualization in the context of the SSEHV framework, a theoretical explanation of its purpose and why it works, some examples of how it can be used for different purposes and some comments from teachers who have used it. This preliminary reading aims at setting the context and giving teachers some background information before the first group session. A free digital copy of this book can be obtained from the Institute of Sathya Sai Education Australia website.

10.2.3   Group Session 1

10.2.3.1   Critically Reflective Lens 1: Our Autobiography as a Learner of Practice

Teachers are given the experience of participating in a short silent sitting and visualization activity, led by a course facilitator, at the beginning of each session (i.e., at the beginning of the day, after lunch). At this stage, there is no discussion or reflection; they are simply asked to experience it.

10.2.3.2   Critically Reflective Lens 4: Theoretical Literature

After the teachers have experienced the silent sitting at least once, but preferably several times, a brief lecture is presented on the purpose of silent sitting and visualization and its impacts on different levels of the mind (see Chap. 1 for an overview of the kind of information introduced here). This is based on and supplementary to the preliminary reading.

10.2.3.3   Critically Reflective Lens 3: Our Colleagues' Experiences

In this activity, the new teachers have the opportunity to share in the experiences of teachers who have adopted silent sitting and visualization as a regular technique in their teaching. The new teachers are invited to watch and discuss videos of these teachers applying the strategy in their classrooms. After watching the videos, they engage in small-group discussion. Prompt questions can include the following:

- Does it appear that these children have learned to focus and concentrate well during silent sitting?
- What should we do if some do not participate?
- What can you observe about the teachers' behaviors and mannerisms?

Teachers are encouraged to raise questions at this stage, and the facilitator then conducts a theory-based question-and-answer session.

The next step in colleagues' sharing of experiences in this early phase of introducing the innovation is for teachers to work in small groups to take turns leading their group mates in different types of silent sitting:

1. For relaxation and settling down.
2. For introducing a lesson topic.
3. For thinking about a behavior, moral, or value that the children need to work on.
4. For solving a problem or reflecting on what has been learned.

If the professional development is being done in a school setting, this can be extended over some time, with teachers leading their colleagues at the beginning of staff meetings or at the start of the school day.

10.2.4   In-Class Follow-Up to Session 1

10.2.4.1   Critically Reflective Lens 1: Our Autobiography as a Learner of Practice

Teachers are asked to submit monthly written reflections on their experiences and challenges. They may be asked to complete a silent sitting diary (see Appendix).

10.2.4.2 Critically Reflective Lens 2: Our Learners' Eyes

The teachers are asked to conduct a common mini action research project in their classes. A minimum of three sessions per week, each of a short duration, has been suggested because we want teachers to feel that the innovation is manageable and is not going to burden them or sacrifice time meant for other activities. Three sessions weekly is sufficient practice for them to detect changes over time.

- Do silent sitting in at least three lessons per week (for 2–5 min). (Teachers can be encouraged to work in teams and share each other's scripts to reduce the workload.)
- Select six students. Every month, interview the students, and bring your interview results to Session 2. In order to ensure some consistency in what teachers need to look for, some interview questions are structured for them to ask their students:

  - Do you like doing silent sitting? Why/why not?
  - What are your favorite kinds of silent sitting?
  - Does silent sitting help you in your schoolwork in any way? How?
  - Does silent sitting help you in your daily life in any way? How?
  - Has your use of silent sitting had any effect on anyone else (for example, your friends or family)?

10.2.5 Group Session 2

10.2.5.1 Critically Reflective Lens 1: Our Autobiography as a Learner of Practice

Teachers are asked to share from their reflective diaries and their personal experiences of how silent sitting has impacted upon them personally. Some may focus on the effects of using it regularly with their students, such as creating a more peaceful classroom environment, while others may have been doing it regularly as their own practice, either individually or with colleagues (see Chap. 11), and can share these experiences.

10.2.5.2 Critically Reflective Lens 3: Our Colleagues' Experiences

This second group session is held at least 2 months after Session 1 to allow time for the teachers to explore implementing the silent sitting strategies in the most appropriate ways for their specific contexts. Even more importantly, teachers have time to reflect on these experiences and become aware of the benefits for themselves and their students. This awareness becomes a major motivator for them to continue and to find out more.

- Teachers share examples of silent sitting they have been using and share the findings from their monthly interviews with six pupils.
- In small groups, teachers discuss their experiences, the benefits, the challenges, and their questions about silent sitting.
- A question-and-answer session is conducted with the course facilitators about issues raised in the discussion.
- In small groups, the teachers form plans for making any necessary modifications to their silent sitting plan for the coming months.
- In some cases, teachers can be invited to bring their own video clips of silent sitting and visualization practices in their classes and to share the scripts they have developed. They can watch and analyze each other's videos in small groups (for example, discussing the purposes of the activities and the children's engagement).

10.2.5.3 Critically Reflective Lens 4: Theoretical Literature

Depending on the teachers' needs and interests raised in the group discussions, a lecture is given to present further theoretical information about silent sitting and visualization.

Teachers are also given time to encourage them to move to deeper levels of implementation and particularly to focus on embedded values messages (see Chap. 4 for an explanation and some examples). One way to do this is to share examples of silent sitting and visualization scripts that teachers can use in their own lives (see the Appendix to Chap. 11 for some examples).

10.2.6 Follow-Up to Session 2

10.2.6.1 Critically Reflective Lens 1: Our Autobiography as a Learner of Practice

Teachers write and submit monthly journals about the impact on their students and themselves. The focus can include children's behavior and concentration, quality and effectiveness of the learning that occurs, changes in academic achievement over time, and the teacher's feelings about teaching.

10.2.6.2 Critically Reflective Lens 2: Our Learners' Eyes

Teachers continue to use silent sitting in at least three lessons per week and continue to interview the same six students every month until the end of the project.

10.2.6.3 Critically Reflective Lens 3: Our Colleagues' Experiences

Teachers introduce silent sitting into staff meetings, invite other teachers to take turns to lead it, and discuss the effects from time to time in staff meetings.

10.2.7 Program Evaluation

While the program evaluation is ongoing, based on teachers' written reflections, their reports on interviews with their students, and the decisions and questions raised in small-group discussions, a post-course evaluation can provide additional opportunity for the teachers to reflect on themselves as learners of the practice and to listen to colleagues' voices.

10.2.7.1 Critically Reflective Lens 1: Our Autobiography as a Learner of Practice and Critically Reflective Lens 3: Our Colleagues' Experiences

Focus group interviews can be conducted to evaluate the program and provide additional opportunity for the teachers to reflect on their own journeys and to listen again to their colleagues' experiences.

Interview questions can be semi-structured to enable facilitators to collect needed information and to allow flexibility for the teachers to add new information of their own. The important thing is that they are encouraged to reflect on the outcomes not only for their students but also for themselves. The following are examples of interview questions:

1. Please share a story about how silent sitting has changed your professional or personal life.
2. Share a story about how using silent sitting changed any of your students. Did that have any impact on you? If so, please share.
3. From your experience, which types of silent sitting and visualization have been the most helpful for your students? For you?
4. Give your ideas about why the strategies described in Question 3 have been helpful.
5. Share your future plans for using silent sitting and visualization in your teaching and in your life in general.

10.3   Discussion

This chapter has briefly described a professional development program designed to develop teachers' willingness and capability to incorporate silent sitting into their practices. The program was designed in line with Brookfield's (1995, 1998, 2017) critical lenses of reflective practice and to mirror principles described by others as critical to bringing about effective implementation of an innovation. For example, a loosely designed brief to do silent sitting three times per week gives the teachers flexibility to decide when and how to incorporate it in the most suitable ways for their own contexts (Dyer 2013; Tondeur et al. 2016). This brief specifies a minimum of three times per week for 2–5 min, which is long enough to have some impact over time but not considered to be too much of an added burden or to take too much away from the lesson time—this being one of the main obstacles to teachers adopting innovations (Pyle and Esslinger 2014). At the same time, the program allows teachers flexibility to use the strategy more frequently or for longer periods as they start to experience its benefits, along with freedom to determine their own priorities, flexibility to modify the innovation to suit their contexts, and opportunities to develop the practice in incremental steps (Dyer 2013; Tondeur et al. 2016). This approach is anticipated to enable the silent sitting and visualization intervention to become a part of the teacher's routine over time.

The opportunities built in for teachers to reflect on their own experiences and the impact of silent sitting on their students and themselves is an important component of allowing them to develop a sense of its purpose and benefits (Mathew et al. 2017; Thompson and Pascal 2012; Tondeur et al. 2016). Collegial discussion is another feature of this professional development model (Klein and Riordan 2011; Makopoulou and Armour 2014; Tondeur et al. 2016). Frequent sharing of their stories and experiences with each other creates opportunities for teachers' voices to be both heard and acknowledged (Zide and Mokhele 2019) and opportunities to engage them as active participants in the intervention (Thompson and Pascal 2012). Discussion gives them ownership (Benveniste and McEwan 2000), since their decisions about its use are coming from them and each other rather than being told what to do and how to do it (Thompson and Pascal 2012). Another aspect of collegial sharing is the opportunity to observe and discuss videos of expert teachers implementing the innovation in their own classes and, later, for the participating teachers to share videos of their own experiences.

Engaging in a mini action research activity in their own classrooms between seminars creates a chance to listen to their students' voices and look at what is happening through their eyes, which can also help to build a sense of the purpose behind the intervention. It also gives the teachers a common experience to discuss with colleagues.

The opportunities for practice, reflection, and discussion are supplemented by theory presented at strategic stages of the program when teachers are most likely to be receptive. At the beginning, they are given some background reading and a short lecture to set the context and introduce the concepts and benefits of silent sitting. At

Table 10.2 Silent sitting diary

Day/ Date	How many times did you do silent sitting today?	How did you feel during and just after the silent sitting?	Did silent sitting have any lasting effects on you during the day? If "yes" please write a few words to describe the change.	Has there been any unexpected change in your behavior or another family member's behavior? If "yes" please write a few words to describe the change.

subsequent face-to-face meetings, they are given further input through lectures to answer the questions they have raised themselves; and after they have reached a certain level of willingness and competence, they are given further theoretical input to challenge them to move to deeper levels, such as linking values and lesson topic content.

10.4 Conclusion

The model described here is based on principles of reflective practice and aimed at leading teachers incrementally to accept, believe in, and implement silent sitting and visualization as a component of their regular practice. Hopefully, this model will be useful for teacher educators and others interested in preparing teachers, at both primary and secondary school levels, to develop faith in the pedagogy (Benveniste and McEwan 2000) and hence adopt the initiative. A longitudinal study would be valuable to investigate the teachers' growth through using this model (Table 10.2).

Silent Sitting Diary

Do silent sitting for about 5 min at least once every day for the next 2 weeks. Once a day is enough, although the results will be better if you do it twice a day.

Please fill in the diary every day. Most questions can be answered simply (e.g., yes or no), but sometimes it would be a good idea to write a few words to remind you of what happened. Please note that this diary is only for your benefit. You do not have to hand it in and be "marked" on it.

References

Benade, L. (2015). Teachers' critical reflective practice in the context of twenty-first century learning. *Open Review of Educational Research, 2*(1), 42–54.

Benveniste, L., & McEwan, M. (2000). Constraints to implementing educational innovations: The case of multigrade schools. *International Review of Education, 46*, 1–2.

Brookfield, S. (1995). *Becoming a critically reflective teacher*. San Francisco: Jossey-Bass.

Brookfield, S. (1998). Critically reflective practice. *The Journal of Continuing Education in the Health Professions, 18*, 197–205.

Brookfield, S. (2017). *Becoming a critically reflective teacher* (2nd ed.). San Francisco: Jossey-Bass.

Dyer, E. (2013, November 6–8). *Pushing the envelope: How can digital resources increase collaboration and standards success for teachers?* [Conference presentation]. Evanston, IL: Teaching Channel's Research and Design Conference, North Western University.

Jacobs, S. (2016). Reflective learning, reflective practice. *Nursing, 46*(5), 62–64.

Klein, E., & Riordan, M. (2011). Wearing the "student hat": Experiential professional development in expeditionary learning schools. *Journal of Experiential Education, 34*(1), 35–54.

Makopoulou, K., & Armour, K. (2014). Possibilities and challenges in teachers' collegial learning. *Educational Review, 66*(1), 75–95.

Mathew, P., Mathew, P., & Peechattu, P. (2017). Reflective practices: A means to teacher development. *Asia Pacific Journal of Contemporary Education and Communication Technology, 1*, 126–131.

Pyle, B., & Esslinger, K. (2014). Utilizing technology in physical education: Addressing the obstacles of integration. *Delta Kappa Gamma Bulletin, 80*(2), 35–39.

Richards, C. (1996). Innovation in primary education. *European Education, 28*, 20–26.

Taplin, M. (2010). *Silent sitting: A resource manual*. Hong Kong: Institute of Sathya Sai Education.

Thompson, N., & Pascal, J. (2012). Developing critically reflective practice. *Reflective Practice: International and Multidisciplinary Perspectives, 13*(2), 311–325.

Tondeur, J., Forkosh-Baruch, A., Prestridge, S., Albion, P., & Edirisinghe, S. (2016). Responding to challenges in teacher professional development for ICT integration in education. *Educational Technology and Society, 19*(3), 110–120.

Zide, L., & Mokhele, M. (2019). Role of clusters in improving teachers' classroom practices: Distinctions and challenges. *Journal of Social Sciences and Humanities, 16*(9), 209–223.

Chapter 11
Teachers' Perceptions of Silent Sitting as a Buffer to Their Problems

Margaret Taplin and Li Lingli

Abstract The study reported in this paper was not intended as a research project to address problems with teachers' morale or their sense of well-being. However, in the course of the teachers' reflections during a professional development program to introduce the Sathya Sai Education in Human Values (SSEHV) model to a group of primary school teachers in mainland China, it emerged that many of the teachers were applying the strategies in their own lives and reporting positive effects on their professional and even personal problems. A brief survey indicated changes, over a two-year period, in their perceptions of the seriousness of problems, including student behavior, excessive workload, exhaustion, feeling angry, doubting their sense of mission, and personal health. Focus group interviews conducted with a small convenience sample suggested that the teachers attributed this improvement to the silent sitting strategies they had adopted. Two possible explanations emerged: that the use of the strategies changed children's behaviors, which in turn changed the teachers' coping, and that the strategies empowered the teachers to look at their problems differently.

Keywords SSEHV · Teachers' problems · Silent sitting · Inner peace · Love

Visiting scholar at time of research.

M. Taplin (✉)
Institute of Sathya Sai Education, Kowloon, Hong Kong

Centre for Research and Development in Values Education, South China Normal University, Guangzhou, China
e-mail: mtaplin@hotkey.net.au

L. Lingli
Centre for Research and Development in Values Education, South China Normal University, Guangzhou, China

© Springer Nature Singapore Pte Ltd. 2021
S. Parahakaran, S. Scherer (eds.), *A Human Values Pathway for Teachers*,
https://doi.org/10.1007/978-981-16-0200-9_11

11.1 Introduction

Worldwide, for the past two decades at least, an abundance of research has been conducted about issues relating to teacher well-being, teacher stress, and teacher burnout. For example, Arens and Morin (2016) identified emotional exhaustion, and Maslach et al. (2001) a combination of depersonalized attitudes toward their students and surroundings and a reduced sense of personal accomplishment. Reports have indicated that issues like budget cuts and declining public support are leading to teachers becoming increasingly discouraged (Mackenzie 2007). Stress and lack of responsiveness and enthusiasm by students can drain their enjoyment of their work (Harmsen et al. 2019; Helou et al. 2016) and cause them to doubt whether teaching was the right choice for them (Helou et al. 2016).

On the other hand, a sense of well-being and control of their problems can lead to positive outcomes for teachers. For example, Schnaider-Levi et al. (2017) developed a framework for such outcomes, based on theories of psychological well-being. The framework included a large number of factors, such as the following:

- Higher levels of self-acceptance.
- Self-awareness and more peaceful inner selves.
- Acknowledging their abilities as well as accepting their weaknesses.
- Positive reciprocal relationships with others, expressed through empathy and affection.
- Better interactions with their surroundings due to less emotional involvement and more flexible attitudes.
- Improved ability to set boundaries and maintain their personal standards and values irrespective of pressure from external surroundings.
- A feeling of mastery of the external surroundings.
- A sense of purpose in life defined by personal values and goals as a source of meaning and fulfillment.
- A sense of realizing their potential and openness to new experiences.

This gap identified between the negative consequences of teachers suffering from stress or burnout and the positive outcomes for those with a high sense of well-being highlights the need to explore ways to support teachers to address the problems that cause the stress and burnout in the first place. Some previous literature has paid attention to the main sources of these problems, their potential consequences, and the support needed to overcome them.

11.1.1 What Are the Main Sources and Consequences of Teachers' Problems?

The causes of teacher stress or burnout are many and complex and have been the subject of numerous studies from multiple theoretical perspectives. Generally these studies have suggested an interplay of multiple stressors that can be both personal and interpersonal (Richards et al. 2018). Different aspects of teacher stress or burnout can be affected by different issues (Skaalvik and Skaalvik 2017). As a source of teachers' problems, excessive workload is high on the list (Fernet et al. 2012; Grayson and Alvarez 2007; Skaalvik and Skaalvik 2010; van Droogenbroek et al. 2014). Time pressure is another problem that can have a significant effect on emotional exhaustion (Skaalvik and Skaalvik 2017).

Additionally, concerns about student welfare and behavior can increase teachers' stress (Geving 2007; Harmsen et al. 2019; Mackenzie 2007; Skaalvik and Skaalvik 2010). Foremost among these concerns are disruptive students (Grayson and Alvarez 2007), low academic achievement (Geving 2007; Helou et al. 2016), and the associated need for teachers to "prove" their competence (van Droogenbroek et al. 2014). Another concern is the students' disengagement (Covell et al. 2009). According to McCormick and Barnett (2010), these student behavior issues can cause problems for teachers in two ways: one is to create feelings of failure; and the other is that the corresponding range of negative emotions can lead to their treating students impersonally, which can give rise to further negative emotions and reduced management of the student behavior. Perceptions of being unable to manage the behavior, in turn, can lead to further symptoms of burnout (Helou et al. 2016).

Other problems contributing to teacher stress are related to school conflict (Harmsen et al. 2019); interpersonal conflicts (Fernet et al. 2012; Helou et al. 2016); and the quality of the social interactions within the school community (Pieterinen et al. 2013). These problems can come from a variety of sources: student-peer and parent/community relations (Grayson and Alvarez 2007), conflicts with or lack of support from colleagues (Fernet et al. 2012; Pieterinen et al. 2013; Skaalvik and Skaalvik 2010; van Droogenbroek et al. 2014), and perceived lack of support from school leadership (Skaalvik and Skaalvik 2010). These depersonalized relationships can be a cause of emotional stress (Grayson and Alvarez 2007) and can be compounded by discipline problems, low student motivation, and value dissonance (Skaalvik and Skaalvik 2017).

The consequences are also many and, if left unaddressed, can be dire for teachers and for their students (Martin et al. 2012; Pei and Zhang 2007). Increasing demands on their time and resources mean that teachers do not have enough time or opportunity to take actions to look after their morale and job satisfaction (Helou et al. 2016). Emotional exhaustion can lead to diminished feelings of personal accomplishment (Grayson and Alvarez 2007; Maslach et al. 2001). The negative impacts can be even greater on their health than on their work outcomes (Pei and Zhang 2007). Low teacher morale can lead to teachers losing heart, developing cynical attitudes, or taking increased sick leave—with the practical consequence of increased costs incurred in covering their absenteeism (Grayson and Alvarez 2007).

11.1.2   What Strategies Can Address These Problems?

The reality is that most of these problems are persistent in schools. It is important, therefore, to understand why some teachers cope better than others. Some investigations have revealed that the teachers most likely to suffer are those who are influenced by external events rather than by internal beliefs that the problems can be overcome (Farber 2000). Evidence has been found of a possible relationship between teachers' self-efficacy and their ability to cope with problems (Skaalvik and Skaalvik 2010).

It is not always possible to remove the causes of stress, but it is possible to change the way teachers react to them. One strategy that can help to reduce the impact of their problems is to foster work environments in which they can feel free to disclose their stress (Grayson and Alvarez 2007). Whole-school initiatives to tackle problems such as student misbehavior can help them to cope better (Grayson and Alvarez 2007; McCormick and Barnett 2010).

It is also important for teachers to feel that they belong to professional communities that promote trust and well-being (Pieterinen et al. 2013). Additionally, they can feel supported by strong staff relationships, collegial support and collaborative relationships between themselves and their students' parents (Grayson and Alvarez 2007; Juhasz 1990; Pas et al. 2012). When a healthy school environment exists and their morale is high, teachers can feel good about themselves and their jobs (Beltman et al. 2011). For example, Covell et al. (2009) reported that a school climate of students and staff showing respect for the rights of others had significant impacts on the teachers because of changes in the students' behaviors. Such positive changes, for example, in students' respect for property and the rights of others, were seen to reduce teachers' emotional exhaustion and to predict their empathy and a sense of accomplishment from teaching.

Opportunities and encouragement to reflect on and rethink their practices, and indeed to reflect generally on the focus and direction of their professional lives, can lead teachers to develop a deeper level of appreciation for the work they are doing (Fernet et al. 2012). According to Richards et al. (2018), such opportunities for reflection can enable teachers to recognize that obstacles can be catalysts for change and growth and can lead to the understanding that they can and do make a difference in their pupils' lives. Some potentially successful reflective strategies are positive psychology and guided visualization (Schnaider-Levi et al. 2017).

11.1.3   The Specific Context of China

The discussion so far has examined the impact of student behavior on teachers in a global context. As the investigation described in this paper was conducted in China, it is necessary to consider the specific problems with which teachers are typically faced in this country.

Two papers published in English and several in Chinese have reported causes of occupational stress for teachers in China. In fact, in a nation-wide survey, almost 80% of middle school teachers reported feeling burned out during their daily work (SINA 2005, cited in Ju et al. 2015). The exam dictates the curriculum, and there is a strong expectation from education authorities, parents, and children for teachers to prepare their students adequately and achieve high scores (Feng 2007a; Li et al. 2011; Pei and Zhang 2007; Peng 2012; Romanowski 2006). Romanowski (2006) reported further that large classes taught using traditional methods cause teachers to spend a lot of time disciplining students rather than teaching. This means that, with so much time being used to correct behavior, teachers are unable to give individual attention to students who are struggling.

As in the global context, in China other issues can impact a teacher's ability to cope with problems: frequent changes in educational policy (Peng 2012), teaching reforms (Cao and Lu 2006; Li et al. 2011), unsupportive leadership (Cao and Lu 2006), workload (Feng 2007b; Li et al. 2011), pressure from management (Feng 2007b), miserable work conditions (Cao and Lu 2006), low income (Li et al. 2011), collegial relationships (Cao and Lu 2006; Zhu et al. 2009), and students' academic and behavioral problems (Jin et al. 2008; Li et al. 2011; Zhu et al. 2009). Needless to say, teachers' health and well-being can suffer because of these problems, with evidence of anxiety, tiredness, and negativity (Li 2007) and a tendency to view their teaching not as a vocation[1] but only as a way of making a living (Lin 2007). Somewhat alarmingly, there have also been reports of bad behavior by teachers, such as rudeness (Li 2007), lack of professional morality (Zhu et al. 2009), and controlling or even abusive behavior with students (Jin et al. 2008).

A summary of the key issues described in the literature (Fig. 11.1) has led to the development of a framework to inform the development of an instrument to measure teachers' perceptions of their problems for the purpose of this investigation. The factors influencing teachers' problems can be categorized as personal, interpersonal, or contextual. Those marked with asterisks in Fig. 11.1 are consistent with the problems described specifically by the participants in the professional development program on which the current investigation was based. Those in italics were mentioned specifically in the literature relating to China.

11.1.4 The Context of the Study

The study reported here was not designed initially to address these teacher problems directly. Rather, it was an initiative to introduce the Sathya Sai Education in Human Values (SSEHV) philosophy, with its emphasis on children's character development, into a school system.

---

[1] According to the Cambridge English Dictionary, a vocation is "a type of work that you feel you are suited to doing and to which you should give all your time and energy."

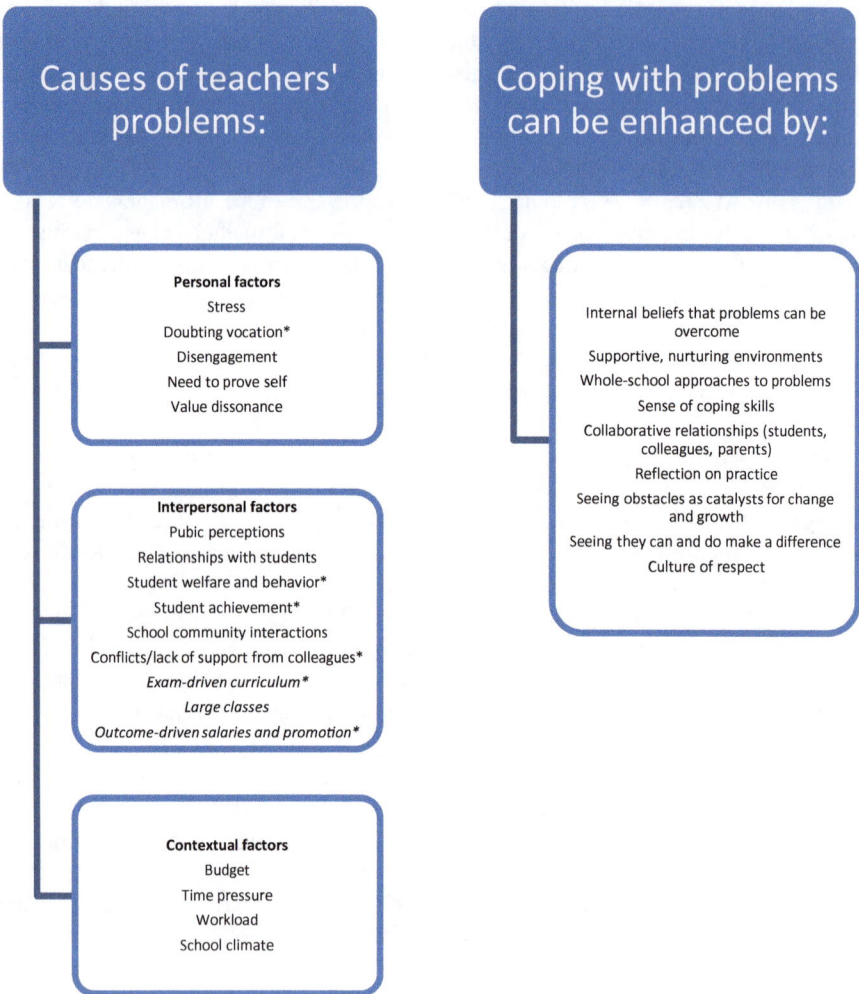

Fig. 11.1 Framework of factors causing teachers' problems and contributing to their coping ability

The intervention was a two-year project in which clusters of teachers were selected from 10 primary schools in each of three school districts in mainland China. The teachers engaged in a series of classroom-based activities to integrate SSEHV, as described in Chaps. 1 and 2, into their curricula. The teachers who participated in this project were selected by their district education bureaus because they were recognized as experienced and innovative teachers. As emphasized above, this study was not intended to be an alternative to the intervention models for teacher stress or burnout, as described earlier in this chapter. Rather, the focus was to explore these issues that arose as one consequence of the teachers' participation in the project.

During the project, the teachers were asked collectively to consider the five human values and their corresponding values messages (see Chap. 1) and to identify those important to their school and community cultures. They were shown strategies for introducing these values indirectly and directly. The indirect strategies included teacher modeling of the values, particularly the value of love, in their interactions with their students and the creation of a values-rich environment in which the children were immersed in the values messages in and out of the classroom. The direct strategies focused on embedding important values messages in topics across the curriculum and encouraging children to reflect on these messages in their own lives.

The teachers participated in three-day seminars held every three months, during which they were introduced to the philosophies and strategies of SSEHV, including suggestions for integrating these strategies into their subject teaching. Between seminars they were asked to explore how they could best implement the strategies in their classroom teaching and extracurricular activities. As well, they were visited in their schools twice by the project team and given feedback for improving their classroom practices. As a professional development program, the teachers were guided on how to use the strategies in their teaching but were also given the autonomy to introduce them as they felt necessary and feasible. This understanding was in line with research that has suggested teachers adopt innovations at different paces and with different levels of understanding (Bitan-Friedlander et al. 2004; Cheung 2010). Their experiences became the focus of written reflections and discussions during the face-to-face seminars.

Successful implementation of this program depended on the teachers' perceptions of the importance of the values and whether they were prepared to adopt them in their own lives, their classrooms, and all aspects of the school culture. Among other strategies introduced to the teachers in this project, silent sitting and guided visualization (see Chap. 1 for details) played a significant role, both as a tool to use with children and as a means for the teachers to practice the values in their own daily lives.

The specific tools that were introduced to the teachers included the following:

- Silent sitting and guided visualization, a technique of self-inquiry whereby teachers invite children to sit and listen to music, to silence, or to teacher-led visualizations (Taplin 2010) that enables the children to tap into their inner depths to reflect on aspects of their own values beliefs and solve their own problems more effectively. Refer to the Appendix for examples.
- Opportunities and challenges to practice and reflect on the values in daily life and reflect on their experiences through questioning and discussion.
- Teacher role-modeling of the values, especially being loving toward the children even when they are not behaving in a way that is likeable (Taplin 2008).

The teachers were asked to practice these strategies between workshops. They submitted regular written reflections on their experiences with these tasks. For example, when they were introduced to the strategy of silent sitting, they were asked to use it in at least three lessons per week for one month and to interview selected students about their perceptions of the experience. Emphasis was placed on the importance of teachers modeling the human values in their own lives, but they were not asked specifically to do so.

In a previous round of this project in a different province of China, the teachers' reflections over time had revealed that they actually were starting to use some of the strategies not only with their pupils but also for themselves. Many of them stated toward the end of the project that the strategies aided them in managing some of the personal and professional issues they faced. While some teachers, typically in the early stages of an intervention, perceived the implementation of the strategies as a burden (consistent with Castro-Villarreal et al. 2014; Zhai et al. 2011), others said that the use of these strategies seemed to make their lives easier. This was important to us because we wanted the teachers to see the intervention as a helpful tool and not as an extra burden. Consequently, we became interested in this surfacing trend and set up a small-scale investigation to find out more about it in the next round of the project.

11.2 Method

The purpose of this investigation was to explore whether and how the SSEHV intervention affected the participating teachers' perceptions of their professional and personal problems. Our intention was not to "prove" the effectiveness of the strategies. An experimental control group study was not appropriate at this stage for a number of reasons. For example, we were only able to access the teachers who were a part of our project; as well, the teachers were exploring and developing the new initiative at their own pace; thus it was not appropriate to address fidelity issues (Gersten et al. 2000). Rather, we were interested in what the teachers were doing and how they perceived their strategy use to address their problems. A simple survey was conducted at the beginning of the two-year project and again at the end, followed by interviews and analyses of reflective writing.

11.2.1 Survey

The survey was not intended to be a rigorous instrument but rather a means of exploring further the patterns that had been hinted at in the previous round of the project. We compiled a list of the professional and personal problems that the teachers had mentioned in their reflective writing and face-to-face discussions throughout the previous round (see Fig. 11.2 for a list of the problems addressed). While this list did not cover all of the issues raised in the literature as relating to teacher well-being, stress, and burnout, there was a reasonable amount of overlap, as can be seen by comparing Fig. 11.2 with Fig. 11.1 presented earlier in this chapter. The respondents were asked to rate their perceptions of the given problems on a five-

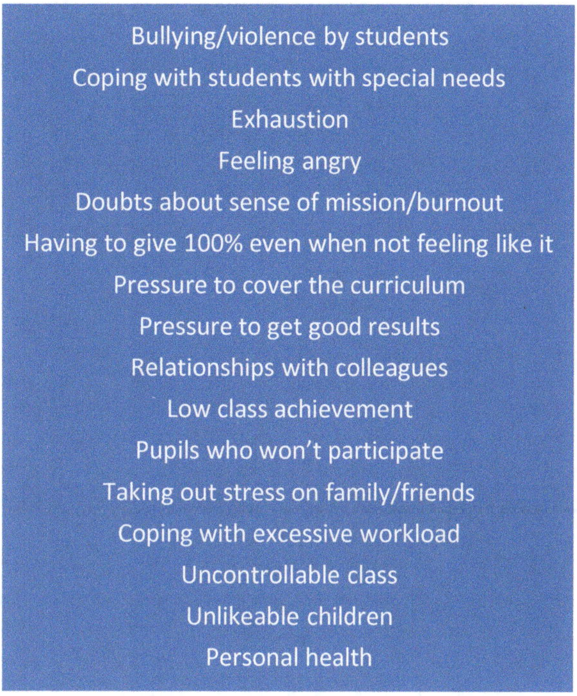

Fig. 11.2 Teacher problems addressed in this investigation

Bullying/violence by students

Coping with students with special needs

Exhaustion

Feeling angry

Doubts about sense of mission/burnout

Having to give 100% even when not feeling like it

Pressure to cover the curriculum

Pressure to get good results

Relationships with colleagues

Low class achievement

Pupils who won't participate

Taking out stress on family/friends

Coping with excessive workload

Uncontrollable class

Unlikeable children

Personal health

point Likert scale, where 1 represented "not at all serious for me" and 5 represented "extremely serious for me." The survey was compiled in English, translated into Chinese, and then back-translated by separate translators (Brislin 1970).

11.2.2 Interviews

In order to probe more deeply into the teachers' beliefs about how and why the SSEHV strategies may have contributed to a decrease in their problems, data were collected from a series of individual and focus group interviews with a convenience sample of teachers who had been engaged in the project for the full two-year duration. The interviews were conducted three months after the project completion and collection of the second round of survey data. Semi-structured questions were used to guide the reflections.

The interview questions were designed to elicit the teachers' opinions about how and why the initiative helped to address the problems that were identified in the survey as serious/extremely serious for a large percentage of the teachers (see Sect. 11.3). Specifically, they were shown a list of these problems and asked to describe the strategies that they had used to address them. They were asked to share their experiences of how the SSEHV strategies had helped them to reduce the seriousness of the problems and to describe their views about which of the strategies had been the most helpful. They were also asked to suggest why these strategies might have helped them to cope better with their problems.

The interviews were conducted in Mandarin Chinese by the second author, who translated the first author's probing questions and the responses simultaneously during the interviews. The interviews revealed a great deal of support for silent sitting as the tool that had the most impact on the teachers; hence the focus here is mainly on the ways in which they described their use of this tool and its impacts.

11.2.3   Sample

Convenience sampling was used for both the survey and qualitative data collection (O'Leary 2010). A sample of 91 primary school teachers who were present at the opening seminar of the SSEHV project completed the survey. They were all primary school teachers, with 35 teaching Grades 3 and 4, 28 teaching Grade 2, 14 teaching Grade 1, and 14 teaching Grade 6. In China, primary school teachers teach specialized subjects: 35 taught mathematics, 42 taught Chinese language, and 14 taught English as a foreign language. Most (84) were female. The teachers were selected by their education bureau as leading teachers in their respective schools, which meant they were mature in terms of age and experience. The largest group (77) was in the age range of 31–40 years and had 16–20 years of teaching experience. Of these, 72 completed the same questionnaire 2 years later. The questionnaires were administered during the first and last group meetings of the project to all teachers who were willing to respond, and responses were anonymous.

The interviews were conducted in small focus groups with 25 teachers who were easily accessible after the post-intervention surveys had been analyzed. The demographics of these groups reflected the gender, age, and years-of-experience characteristics of those who completed the survey.

11.3   Results

11.3.1   Survey

Descriptive statistics were used to summarize the patterns arising from the survey. A Cronbach's Alpha coefficient of 0.98 suggested a good level of reliability. Even though the pre-intervention mean ratings were relatively low, the highest being 3.45 for coping with excessive workload, there were six items that around 25% or more of the teachers rated as serious/extremely serious, as shown in Table 11.1. These items were coping with excessive workloads, exhaustion, personal health, pressure to get good results, feeling angry, and low class achievement.

Table 11.1 Independent samples *t*-test to compare mean ratings before and after the intervention

	Pre-intervention			Post-intervention			*t*-test		% rating items serious/extremely serious	
	N	M#	SD	N	M#	SD	*t*	*p*	Pre-intervention	Post-intervention
Coping with excessive workload	91	3.45	1.20	70	2.61	0.97	−4.91	0.00*	52.7%	21.4%
Exhaustion	91	3.25	0.95	72	2.53	0.92	−4.91	0.00*	42.9%	12.5%
Personal health	91	2.90	1.26	70	2.40	1.06	−2.69	0.01*	28.6%	17.1%
Pressure to get good results	90	2.91	1.10	70	2.49	1.00	−2.52	0.01*	27.8%	12.9%
Feeling angry	91	2.92	0.98	72	2.03	0.86	−6.22	0.00*	26.4%	5.6%
Low class achievement	91	2.75	1.03	70	2.09	0.90	−4.35	0.00*	24.2%	8.6%
Doubts about sense of mission/burnout	92	2.41	1.06	71	1.80	0.89	−3.99	0.00*	15.2%	4.2%
Having to give 100% even when I don't feel like it	90	2.50	1.04	69	2.13	0.89	−2.41	0.02**	15.6%	7.2%
Pupils who won't participate	90	2.37	1.11	71	1.94	0.91	−2.66	0.01*	16.7%	7.0%
Bullying/violence by students	92	2.28	1.03	72	1.58	0.73	−5.09	0.00*	13.0%	1.4%

1 = not at all serious, 5 = extremely serious
*significant, $p < 0.01$, ** significant, $p < 0.05$

Interestingly, in the end-of-course survey, the means for all of these items had decreased significantly (mostly $p < 0.01$) according to an independent samples t-test, as had the numbers of teachers rating them as serious/extremely serious. Quite large differences occurred in the percentages of teachers rating serious/extremely serious for exhaustion (42.9% in the pre-intervention survey and 12.5% in the post-intervention survey), coping with excessive workload (52.7% and 21.4%), feeling angry (26.4% and 5.6%), and low class achievement (24.2% and 8.6%). Although doubts about sense of mission was only rated highly by around 15% of the teachers, it has been included in Table 11.1 because it also had a significantly lower mean rating, and the percentage of teachers rating it highly had reduced to 4.2% by the end of the project. Similarly, three other items (having to give 100% even if I don't feel like it, pupils who won't participate, and bullying/violence by students) had significantly decreased means and slight decreases in the ratings as serious/extremely serious, even though the low pre-intervention rating suggests that the teachers were not overly concerned with these issues in the first place. We were particularly interested in the larger decreases, and these gave us further incentive to conduct interviews to find out more about what the teachers had been doing to bring about these apparent changes.

11.3.2   Interviews

The interviews were semi-structured and designed to gather more information about the issues identified from the survey as being of particular interest. This means that the analysis was deductive as the categories of interest had been pre-determined (Crabtree and Miller 1999). The initial coding was done by the first author and validated by the second. It was evident by the end of the interviews that saturation had been reached, with no new categories being introduced (Glaser and Strauss 1967).

The following sections describe the teachers' comments about how their use of SSEHV strategies had helped in relation to the problems listed. As there was considerable overlap between their comments on exhaustion and coping with excessive workload, these two have been grouped together.

11.3.2.1   Exhaustion and Coping with Excessive Workload

Not surprisingly, exhaustion and excessive workload were not only rated the highest for seriousness in the survey but were also the issues described most often by the teachers in the interviews and written reflections. When asked how the SSEHV strategies had helped them to cope with the exhaustion associated with teaching, 14 of the respondents said they used silent sitting and/or deep breathing to achieve peace of mind:

> Every day, early in the morning, I close my eyes and breathe deeply three times and fully concentrate on the day's work... Then the day's work goes smoothly—everything is under control, and I feel full of joy.

One of the effects of silent sitting was to help the teachers to change how they viewed the situations that were making them exhausted:

> I am the principal and also teach classes—a very heavy workload—I often feel exhausted. Teachers call me when they have problems they cannot deal with. I was starting to dislike the job of being a teacher... I had doubts about my career and responsibility. When I feel exhausted I use silent sitting—deep breathing—to calm down.

In one focus group, there was an indication of some linkage between exhaustion and anger (see next section). The teachers mentioned how silent sitting had helped them to overcome exhaustion, explaining that if they could calm themselves down after getting angry, they would then find that they were also less exhausted.

It was not only their own personal use of silent sitting that seemed to be helpful. One group explained how using it with their students helped indirectly to cope with their own exhaustion. They commented that dealing constantly with problem behavior can be exhausting. After silent sitting was used for 5–10 min daily, along with values-based discipline strategies, the children's behavior improved, consequently the teachers felt more relaxed and less tired. This, in turn, helped them to be able to cope better with heavy workload pressure.

Another way in which the teachers had found silent sitting helpful in overcoming their exhaustion was by changing how they viewed their students. One of the important aspects of SSEHV is the value of love—this means that we ask teachers to try to develop self-love and a sense of love for their students. To facilitate this, as mentioned above, we talk about strategies for loving children even in their most "unlikeable" moments. Two teachers commented that they were able to utilize guided visualization to address their exhaustion by learning to change how they looked at their students. Their comments reveal that their focus on positive visualization enabled them to actually experience the desired feeling of love, which helped them to find meaning in their teaching and feel happier:

> Later I imagine my students sitting in the classroom, and I focus on each student's face, imagining each of them as a beautiful flower or something else beautiful. Then I have a sense of love from my heart. I feel full of strength and energy all over.

11.3.2.2 Feeling Angry

Six of the teachers commented specifically on how they had used strategies consciously to overcome their anger. Previously, they had often lost their tempers easily in class, often in relation to children's poor academic performances, and responded in anger. Silent sitting was mentioned by three of them as a tool to deal with anger issues. One chose to do it alone, while another described how doing it with her class had an impact on her own sense of peace:

The children in my Grades 1 and 2 classes like to do silent sitting at the beginning of the lesson—this can settle them and also can give me the strength to calm down and be peaceful, so I will not be influenced by the children's behavior.

This does not necessarily mean that they no longer became angry but rather that they felt they were equipped with the skills to manage it better:

Maybe when something happens I will be angry, but I will calm down and not lose my temper.

11.3.2.3 Burnout and Doubts About Sense of Mission as a Teacher

Three of the teachers reflected specifically on the impacts of SSEHV on their self-doubts about their sense of mission as teachers and another discussed this in the context of exhaustion (see previous section). The following example describes the complex issues that can lead to this feeling of burnout:

In this country [China], the government pays a lot of attention to academic scores. Another thing is that there are many, many problems in students. I have been teaching for 15 years and have the feeling it has become harder and harder to teach children. One-child families, left-behind children [children who live in the school because their parents have moved away for work], single-parent families—more and more—so children's characters are very strange—this makes the communication between teachers and students harder. Nowadays, there are more and more bad messages about teachers in the media, and this influences our social status and authority in the eyes of parents. A teacher's income is not high, but expenses are high. I spend about eight hours at school working so have less time for my family. So I felt very unhappy about these problems and had no ways to deal with it.

Another of these teachers found new impetus through utilizing silent sitting to reflect on the meaning of the human values and the consequent transformation in her own feelings:

Though I had thought myself to be a teacher, only pursuing the academic score was really superficial. I have learned the "human" side of the work, to "take the love as the starting point," even if the student's outcomes are not so good. I try as much as possible not to look at the superficial things but to discover the students' true intrinsic selves. I feel my teacher's sense of mission more strongly, love the students more deeply, am more harmonious in my relationships with the students, and more creative in my methods of work.

11.3.2.4 Pressure to Get Good Results (i.e., Achieve High Academic Scores)

It has been mentioned earlier in this chapter that teachers in China are under intense pressure to ensure their classes achieve high academic scores. This pressure comes from school leaders, parents, and the children themselves. Ten respondents commented on how SSEHV helped them to cope better with this pressure; although it was still there, the teachers believed they had changed how they responded to it:

Now that I know about SSEHV, I don't care about my return on teaching. It's more important for me to love my students.

Three teachers did, however, feel that the problem actually had been alleviated by the introduction of silent sitting. They felt that, by helping to improve the children's focus and concentration, it often led to the desired outcome of academic success:

Silent sitting can make students concentrate more on their study. It really does work.

11.3.2.5 Personal Health

On the issue of personal health, the effect of the silent sitting in promoting greater peace of mind was again mentioned by the teachers in the interviews:

Before, it took too much time to deal with problems—now I feel I am more tolerant—emotionally better, more communicative with children, positive changes in the children have made me happier, and this has had positive effects on my health.

11.3.2.6 Bullying/Violence by Students

Eight of the teachers spoke specifically about how silent sitting and guided visualization had helped to improve how they dealt with student behavior problems, particularly bullying and violence. Two teachers mentioned that they had started to feel less affected by violent behavior in the classroom because they reacted more calmly than they would have done in the past. Furthermore, five said that the regular use of silent sitting with the children had actually reduced instances of behavioral problems and also that they had defused potentially violent or disruptive students effectively by using this technique. They found that students were able to calm down and reflect on their behavior rather than erupting in inappropriate ways.

11.3.3 Why Do the Strategies Work?

In order to understand in more depth how and why the silent sitting strategies were beneficial to the teachers, we asked them to speculate about why these might have worked. Their responses have been classified into two potential explanations. The first was that the teachers' practices changed the children in their classes, which reduced some of the problems that had existed previously. The second was that some changes happened in the teachers so that they were no longer affected by problems as much as they had been in the past. In the following section, evidence is presented to support each of these explanations.

11.3.3.1   Explanation 1: The Teachers' Practices Changed the Children

Many of the teachers' comments suggested that their implementation of silent sitting strategies resulted in positive changes in the children's behaviors, which in turn had positive effects on the teachers' coping strategies. One teacher explained this process clearly:

> Since participating in the values education, the children in the class and I have grown together, letting me realize the value of the human values. Their forgiveness, loyalty, sympathy, love, selflessness, peace, patience and so on have given my own life a focus and have caused me to have warmth, forgiveness and love.

One suggestion was that the children responded positively to the changes that occurred in their teachers:

> First, I think that we have to improve ourselves… if we persist to form a good habit, our thinking and behavior will be improved… if our hearts are kind, our children will be positive and, in this condition, we can all feel happy.

Some teachers gave more specific indications of how the changes actually affected them, such as in this written reflection:

> More children are willing to communicate with me. I feel that they begin to trust me. This feeling is very good. Teachers can be closer to the children's hearts, to see what they need. Student management is much easier than before.

11.3.3.2   Explanation 2: The Teachers Changed, so They Were Not as Affected by Challenges

Another group of teachers' comments suggested that, due to implementing the silent sitting and guided visualization strategies in their own lives, they were no longer affected as much by challenges as they were previously:

> I have no problems these days because I have changed my mood, so life is easy for me.

Others described the impact of love on how they viewed their situations:

> Love benefits the most. Love all the colleagues and the children, and they can feel it. Before, when it was very chaotic around me, I would feel very bad—many students would tell tales—I disliked this kind of thing. Then Love entered—love them when they are unlovable. When we can really love them, the children will love us too. So my inner-world benefit is that it makes me become a happy teacher.

Another perspective change the teachers mentioned was tolerance:

> I can look at things from another perspective when I communicate with children or parents. I am more tolerant.

Again, silent sitting was viewed as a tool to support looking at problems differently:

First, we do reflection and silent sitting, and then we feel love, then we feel happy. If we feel
happy, then we can deal with the exhaustion and other problems—even if the problems don't
go away, we can deal with them better.

11.4   Discussion

This chapter has reported an investigation of a group of Chinese primary school
teachers' perceptions of how the strategies for an education in human values
(SSEHV) program, particularly silent sitting and guided visualization, helped them
to address some of the common professional and personal problems they had
experienced prior to the intervention. While it cannot be claimed that the SSEHV
intervention was solely responsible for bringing about positive changes, the interview data do suggest that the teachers' adoption of the strategies and their attempts to
practice them in their own lives had some impact on how they viewed and coped
with some of their professional and personal problems.

A limitation of the study was that we only examined a small number of teaching
problems. As well, due to the long-term nature of the professional development
program, there was some attrition, and the sample size was small. Furthermore, the
study was limited in that it relied on teachers' self-report measures (Geving 2007).
As this was a part of a professional development program in which the participating
teachers were developing at different paces, it was not appropriate to attempt to
establish fidelity (Gersten et al. 2000). Similarly, it was not appropriate to conduct a
controlled study; hence, it cannot be claimed that the SSEHV intervention alone
contributed to the changes reported by the teachers over the two-year period.

The teaching-related problems addressed in this study did not have particularly
high mean ratings for seriousness before the intervention, but statistically significant
decreases were found in the pre- and post-intervention means for nine items. These
were teachers' perceptions of their coping with excessive workloads, exhaustion,
their personal health, pressure to get good results, feeling angry, low class achievement, having doubts about their sense of mission as teachers, seriousness of bully-
ing/violent students, pupils' lack of participation, and having to give 100% even
when they did not feel like it. Around 25% to 50% of teachers rated the first five of
these as serious/extremely serious, and the decreases in mean ratings and percentages of respondents rating the problems as serious/extremely serious were mostly
small.

The problems on which the changes occurred were consistent with those
described in the literature as being among the most major challenges for teachers.
These include workload pressures (Beltman et al. 2011), anxiety about students'
performances on public examinations (Feng 2007a) and personal health (Pei and
Zhang 2007). The teachers also perceived positive changes in their students' behavior to have helped them to cope better, consistent with the suggestion of Beltman
et al. (2011) that behavioral issues influence teachers' sense of well-being. The
problems the teachers reported were not discrete, and it seemed that addressing one

sometimes contributed to changes in another. For example, by becoming less angry, they also found they were less exhausted and subsequently able to cope better with other problems, such as heavy workloads. These changes helped them to rediscover the meaning in their teaching.

Of the SSEHV tools the teachers used, silent sitting and guided visualization was the most accessible and popular. The teachers used it to achieve peace of mind and feelings of love, which may have resulted in a shift in how they viewed their problems, especially if they were feeling overwhelmed, angry, or out of control. Schnaider-Levi et al. (2017) also reported similar effects of this type of activity. According to the teacher interviews, the most useful values to practice in their daily lives were peace and love. The teachers found the values of understanding and tolerance particularly useful for loving children in their most challenging moments. Some teachers admitted that sometimes they had to pretend to be loving at first but found it became easier to practice the values and the strategies genuinely as time went on.

The strategies and the values are difficult to separate. For example, we cannot claim that silent sitting or guided visualization alone helped with anger or exhaustion. Rather, it is likely to be the combination of this and other strategies, such as consciously becoming more loving. Practicing any one of the human values alone is unlikely to have resulted in the shift reported by the teachers but rather the strategies and values could have interacted to bring about changes that had positive effects on the original problems. Nevertheless, it is clear from the data that silent sitting and guided visualization was the strategy the teachers used the most and found to be the most helpful.

From the interview data, two possible explanations emerged about why the SSEHV strategies might have helped the teachers to address their problems and enhance their well-being. The first of these was that their practices to implement the human values education initiative resulted in changes in the children's behaviors, which in turn had positive effects on the teachers' coping strategies. Certainly this makes sense in the light of the viewpoint of Grayson and Alvarez (2007), that teachers' well-being is affected most by how their students view them and how they respect and care for each other, and that of Covell et al. (2009), that teachers have a stronger sense of achievement and accomplishment as students become more respectful. As Richards et al. (2018) proposed, it is the confirmation that they do make a difference in their students' lives that can help them to cope better. Interestingly, some of the teachers reported that, as children's concentration and behavior improved, often the desired outcome of higher academic achievement followed, hence helping to alleviate that problem too.

The second explanation was that, in implementing the strategies in their own lives, the teachers became better able to handle the problems that arose. Grayson and Alvarez (2007) explained this as an inverse relationship between teacher satisfaction levels and negative emotional reactions. This is in accordance with Beltman et al. (2011), who advocated that teachers can best help themselves by taking active responsibility for their own well-being. Furthermore, Gu and Day (2007) suggested that positive emotions fuel psychological resilience. Some factors here are consistent with the framework for teacher well-being developed by Schnaider-Levi et al. (2017). These include the teachers' perceptions of increased peace, positive relationships with peers and students, their ability to maintain personal values, more flexible attitudes, and a sense of purpose in life defined by their own personal values and goals.

Additionally, the teachers' reports of the benefits of the silent sitting and visualization strategies align with Farber (2000) and Skaalvik and Skaalvik (2010), who suggested that teachers who feel they have control over their problems are more likely to cope with them effectively. It also fits with the suggestion of Schnaider-Levi et al. (2017) that mindfulness practices can contribute, among other things, to a sense of environmental mastery that can make teachers feel less emotionally involved, more flexible in their attitudes, and thus better equipped to handle interpersonal dynamics. Similarly, several researchers have found that this type of reflection provides a framework for teachers to rethink their practices (Fernet et al. 2012).

Another possibility for the second explanation is that the SSEHV project strategies and values influenced how the participating teachers construed success and their goals for teaching (Butler 2007). For example, they became less caught up in the belief that success as a teacher is only measured by their students' academic scores and hence were less worried about whether the scores would be low.

11.4.1 Questions for Further Investigation

The results of this study have suggested that aspects of the SSEHV intervention had positive impacts on the participating teachers' perceptions of the seriousness of some common professional and personal problems. However, the results also give rise to additional questions regarding the efficacy of SSEHV. For example, further research can look at the impacts of the SSEHV initiatives on other problems to see if there are any patterns in the types of issues with which the strategies can be the most effective.

The interview data hinted that the SSEHV strategies enhanced relationships between colleagues, even though this was not rated highly in the survey as a serious problem. Nevertheless, there is empirical support regarding the importance of teachers having opportunities to share common goals, values, and problem-solving strategies as a school community (Grayson and Alvarez 2007; Pieterinen et al. 2013; Skaalvik and Skaalvik 2010). It is worth investigating further exactly how SSEHV strategies contribute to positive collegial relationships.

The teacher interviews suggest that the practice of the human values and coping strategies may have resulted in a greater sense of internal control. Some earlier studies have suggested that a sense of self-efficacy can be brought about by teachers feeling confident and competent and if they receive credit for and draw sustenance from their accomplishments (Beltman et al. 2011; Skaalvik and Skaalvik 2010). A deeper investigation of the impacts of practicing SSEHV on internal control and self-efficacy may be beneficial (Ju et al. 2015).

This study was conducted in one specific context, mainland China, and only focused on primary school teachers. There is a need to explore whether the findings can be replicated in other contexts and cultures and at other levels of education.

Another potential question for further investigation is whether there is any link between gender and the effects of silent sitting and visualization or other SSEHV strategies on teachers. The sample in this study consisted predominantly of female teachers. Future studies could investigate whether there were any gender differences in the strategies they used and their impacts.

11.5   Conclusion

In China, teacher stress is high because of intense pressures—hence this study has contributed some useful data to suggest that the SSEHV intervention described here was helpful for teachers. This was most likely due not to one specific SSEHV strategy but rather to a combination, although the use of silent sitting and visualization was a common factor mentioned by most of the teachers interviewed. The findings suggest that the application of the values and strategies helped the teachers to perceive themselves to be coping better with their pressures and problems and even to increase—or, in some cases, get back—their sense of purpose, meaning, and vocation (Gu and Day 2007). These strategies seem to have given them a framework for developing or rekindling, or at least reflecting on, the kinds of personal factors advocated by Beltman et al. (2011) as critical to teacher well-being, such as altruism, moral purpose, a sense of vocation, emotional stability, patience, a sense of competence and pride, and the ability to let go, to look at challenging situations differently, and to know their students.

This chapter has some implications for addressing the types of professional and personal problems that can impact negatively on teachers and their students. Through integrating SSEHV into their programs and into their personal lives, teachers can potentially help themselves to make their own lives easier.

Funding   These data were collected as part of an ongoing project funded by the Institute of Sathya Sai Education of Hong Kong. The first author is a volunteer consultant for this organization.

Sample Visualizations for Teachers' Own Use or to Use with Children

Problem Solving (from Taplin 2010)

First, read the problem. Then put it aside. Close your eyes and just listen to the inner silence of your mind for a few moments. Focus your concentration on the back of your closed eyelids at the point where your eyebrows meet. Don't try to think about anything—just allow your mind to be still and empty, and concentrate on the blankness behind your eyes. When you feel that your mind is completely still, think for a moment about the problem you need to solve. You can either repeat the whole question in your mind, or you can simply say, "I need to find the solution to the problem I am about to tackle." Once you have asked this question, return your attention to focusing on the silent, blank emptiness of your mind behind your closed eyelids for a few more minutes. Then visualize your subconscious mind working like a computer. First, it sorts the knowledge you already have that can be used to solve the problem. Then, it sorts out what else you need to know. Next, it puts this knowledge together in a logical way. Finally, it sends the output into your conscious mind so you can work on the problem. Take three slow, deep breaths; then open your eyes and start to work on the problem (p. 37).

Removing Worries or Fears (from Taplin 2010)

Visualize a golden wheel with a black hole in the middle. Breathe all your worries and fears into the black middle, and breathe in the golden spokes to replace it (p. 40).

Resolving Anger (Alderman 1996, p. 155, cited by Taplin 2010)

Think of a time when you felt angry with someone....Feel the anger....Look carefully at what made you angry....Is it because you wanted something and did not get it?....Is it because there was some injustice involved?....Imagine yourself telling the person gently that you felt angry and why....Or if you think it would be better, just walk away from the situation. Imagine yourself drinking a cool glass of water and the heat of anger leaving you....You feel calmer.... You were able to resolve the situation without shouting, insulting or hitting the person. So congratulate yourself on your self-control....You begin to feel more peaceful and happy (p. 40).

Resolving Violence in Thought, Word or Deed (Alderman 1996, p. 205., cited by Taplin 2010)

Think of a time that you regret because you were violent in thought, word or deed. . . See yourself doing that action. . . See the consequences of your action for the other people. . . And for yourself. . . Silently say sorry to everyone involved, including yourself, for all the hurt you caused. . . Feel yourself surrounded with love and forgiveness. . . Imagine yourself acting differently in this situation, so that no one, including yourself, is hurt. . . Think of a time when you did something to reduce conflict... or stop something hurtful happening... or imagine something you would like to have done... See yourself doing it... Feel the pleasure of achievement... Imagine goodness spreading out from your action like ripples in a pond. (p. 40)

Opening the Heart Connection (from Taplin 2010)

As usual, take some deep, slow breaths and feel yourself relaxing. Imagine you are looking at your own heart. What does it look like? What color/colors is it? How big is it? Is it plump and happy looking, or is a part of it shriveled up or wrinkled? What kinds of feelings come up in it when you think about your friends? Your classmates and schoolmates? Your family and relatives? People who you don't know?

Now, think about using your heart for its main purpose, which is to pump out Love, first into your own body and then into other peoples'. Imagine your heart filling up with loving thoughts and feelings, until it is plump, brightly colored and full. Watch as it starts to overflow so that the feelings and thoughts of Love start to flow over into your own veins and arteries until it is flowing freely through your whole body. After that, allow it to flow from your heart towards the other people in the room. Try to keep the habit of doing this all through the day. (p. 45)

Courage in the Face of a Challenge (from Taplin 2010)

With your eyes closed, imagine a tiny ant at the foot of a large rock that looks like a towering mountain. The ant needs to find a way to cross to the other side of this mountain, but it seems to be too big and the task seems to be hopeless. It takes in a big, long, deep breath full of courage and as it breathes out, it lets go of all the doubts and anxieties that are the obstacles getting in its way. Imagine the ant, filled with courage, taking the first step forward. Watch the ant as it continues its journey up the mountain. Sometimes the path is rough or slippery and it stumbles or falls, but when this happens it picks itself up and finds a better path. It doesn't give up. Every time it has a setback or seems to have failed, it gets up again. If the path it is on looks hopeless, it thinks about what went wrong and changes the plan. With every mistake or setback it gets a little bit braver and a little bit stronger. Step by step, meter by meter, the ant goes forward until at last it reaches its goal (p. 45).

Making a Difference with Difficult Students (or Colleagues) (from Taplin 2010)

Close your eyes, and take 3 slow, deep breaths. On each outward breath feel yourself relaxing more and more. Take your attention to the classroom/s you will be working in today. If there is more than one, mentally go to each in turn. Imagine that you are painting the whole classroom with something that symbolizes peace. It might be a peaceful scene from nature, or it might simply be a peaceful color such as pink. Quickly but thoroughly mentally paint each room in the way that you think is best.

Next, take your attention to the pupils. Imagine your pupils sitting in the classroom/s. Focus your attention for a moment on their faces—in a split second, allow yourself to see each one as a separate and beautiful individual. Now take your attention to focus on the feeling of pure unconditional love—that is the feeling of giving without expectation to receive. You might symbolize this by a color, by a flower, or simply by allowing yourself to feel the sensation. Or you might have another method of your own. Allow this symbol to build up, stronger and stronger, and then allow it to burst so that it showers the whole room and every individual in it. See everyone surrounded by this sense of unconditional well-being, and see yourself as being the source of it throughout the whole day.

When you are ready, bring your awareness back to where you are now, open your eyes and go on in confidence that you have created the right energy patterns for a successful day for yourself and all of your pupils (p. 48).

Visualization to Help You to Open Yourself to the Six Desirable Qualities of a Loving Person (Adapted from Lazarus: Unconditional Love) (from Taplin 2008)

Relax your body and mind. Slowly count backwards from ten, and with each count feel yourself relaxing and letting go more and more. Let down your guard and your resistance to knowing the value of love and allow yourself to seek to find the unconditional within yourself. Imagine yourself in a place where you feel completely safe and secure... Imagine that a small bubble of light appears before you, and grows bigger and bigger until it engulfs you. Allow yourself to feel that you have impact—let go of any conditioning you may have that you do not have any impact or that your impact is negative. Tell yourself, "I have impact" and let it be... Now open yourself to the fact that you are worthy—not because of what you have done or who you know but because of the spark within you. Allow yourself to feel and appreciate the worth that has always been there within you... Next open yourself to the compassion and esteem you have earned for yourself—allow the integrity, the honesty, the responsibility and the trust to come forward from within you... Let in the security and the pleasure and the honesty and vulnerability—let it in. Let in the caring and the intimacy and the trust. Feel the security. You will not lose this love. Let it be... Feel the tingle of confidence... the joy and laughter of knowing that confidence, of holding that confidence, to honor your emotions... allow yourself to respect these emotions... Allow yourself to catch a glimpse of yourself as a purely, unconditionally loving being.

Visualization for Getting in Touch with Your True Self (to Be Used on a Daily Basis) (from Taplin 2008)

(Begin with a few slow, deep breaths to encourage relaxation.) Take your concentration deep inside your chest. Hidden there is your true self. This is the part of you that knows no fear and is always courageous. It is the part of you that never knows loneliness because it always knows love. It is the part that knows no attachments to external things because it is always complete within itself. Hold your attention on that deep, inner part of yourself and imagine that a beam of light is shining down through the top of your head onto that spot. Continue to allow the beam to pour onto that spot. Watch as the light touches your inner self and allows it to expand, like a flower opening. As the flower unfolds, your inner self grows and grows, larger and stronger, until it fills your whole body, your mind, and your emotions with an intense feeling of peace and love. This is the time when you can trust yourself the most to make the best decisions and to have your own strength and completeness. Open your eyes slowly in your own time and appreciate the inner strength you have unlocked (p. 126).

References

Arens, A., & Morin, A. (2016). Relations between teachers' emotional exhaustion and students' educational outcomes. *Journal of Educational Psychology, 108*(6), 800–813.

Beltman, S., Mansfield, C., & Price, A. (2011). Thriving not just surviving: A review of research on teacher resilience. *Educational Research Review, 6*, 185–207.

Bitan-Friedlander, N., Dreyfus, A., & Milgrom, Z. (2004). Types of "teachers in training": The reactions of primary school science teachers when confronted with the task of implementing an innovation. *Teaching and Teacher Education, 20*, 607–619.

Brislin, R. (1970). Back-translation for cross-cultural research. *Journal of Cross-Cultural Psychology, 1*(3), 185–216.

Butler, R. (2007). Teachers' achievement goal orientations and associations with teachers' help seeking: Examination of a novel approach to teacher motivation. *Journal of Educational Psychology, 99*(2), 241–252.

Cambridge English Dictionary. https://dictionary.cambridge.org

Cao, T., & Lu, N. (2006). 学校变革进程中的教师压力管理 [Teachers' pressure management in the school reform]. 教育发展研究 [*Research in Educational Development], 6*, 34–38.

Castro-Villarreal, F., Rodriguez, B., & Moore, S. (2014). Teachers' perceptions and attitudes about response to intervention (RTI) in their schools: A qualitative analysis. *Teaching and Teacher Education, 40*, 104–112.

Cheung, M. (2010). The process of innovation adoption and teacher development. *Evaluation & Research in Education, 13*(2), 55–75. https://doi.org/10.1080/09500799908666947.

Covell, K., McNeil, J., & Howe, R. (2009). Reducing teacher burnout by increasing student engagement: A child rights approach. *School Psychology International, 30*(3), 282–290.

Crabtree, B., & Miller, W. (1999). A template approach to text analysis: Developing and using codebooks. In B. Crabtree & W. Miller (Eds.), *Doing qualitative research* (pp. 163–177). Newbury Park, CA: Sage.

Farber, B. (2000). Treatment strategies for different types of teacher burnout. *Psychotherapy in Practice, 56*(5), 675–689.

Feng, B. (2007a). A study of teacher job satisfaction and factors that influence it. *Chinese Education and Society, 40*(5), 47–64.

Feng, D. (2007b). 教师的疲惫与疲惫的教师:问题与对策 [Teachers' tiredness and tired teachers: Problems and solutions]. 教育理论与实践 *[Theory and Practice of Education], 1*, 21–24.

Fernet, C., Guay, F., & Senécal, S. (2012). Predicting intra-individual changes in teacher burnout: The role of perceived school environment and motivational factors. *Teaching and Teacher Education, 28*, 514–525.

Gersten, R., Baker, S., & Lloyd, J. (2000). Designing high-quality research in special education: Group experimental design. *The Journal of Special Education, 34*(1), 2–18.

Geving, A. (2007). Identifying the types of student and teacher behaviours associated with teacher stress. *Teaching and Teacher Education, 23*, 624–640.

Glaser, B., & Strauss, A. (1967). *The discovery of grounded theory: Strategies for qualitative research.* Chicago: Aldine.

Grayson, J., & Alvarez, H. (2007). School climate factors relating to teacher burnout: A mediator model. *Teaching and Teacher Education, 24*, 1349–1363.

Gu, Q., & Day, C. (2007). Teachers' resilience: A necessary condition for effectiveness. *Teaching and Teacher Education, 23*, 1302–1316.

Harmsen, R., Helms-Lorenz, M., Maulana, R., van Keen, K., & van Veldhoven, M. (2019). Measuring general and specific stress causes and stress responses among beginning secondary school teachers in the Netherlands. *International Journal of Research and Method in Education, 42*(1), 91–108.

Helou, M., Nabhani, M., & Bahous, R. (2016). Teachers views on causes leading to their burnout. *School Leadership and Management, 36*, 551–567.

Jin, D., Xing, S., & Yu, G. (2008). 教师心理健康对学生发展的影响 [The influence of teachers' mental health on students' development.]. 教育研究 *[Educational Research], 1*, 56–59, 98.

Ju, C., Lan, C., Li, Y., Feng, W., & You, X. (2015). The mediating role of workplace social support on the relationship between trait emotional intelligence and teacher burnout. *Teaching and Teacher Education, 51*, 58–67.

Juhasz, A. (1990). Teacher self-esteem: A triple-role approach to this forgotten dimension. *Education, 111*(2), 234–241.

Li, Q., Zhang, G., & Zhou, J. (2011). 中小学教师的职业压力源研究 [A study of the sources of occupational stress of primary and secondary school teachers]. 心理发展与教育 *[Psychological Development and Education], 1*, 97–104.

Li, Z. (2007). 教师课堂问题行为及其预防策略 [Teachers' problematic behaviors in class and their countermeasures]. 高教学刊 *[Journal of Higher Education], 11*, 44–48.

Lin, D. (2007). 教师职业幸福感缺失的背后——'生活方式'抑或'谋生手段'的教师职业观探讨 [Behind the absence of teachers' vocational happiness: A discussion of teachers' vocational views about 'lifestyle' and 'a way of making a living']. 教育发展研究 *[Research in Educational Development], 6*, 46–50.

Mackenzie, N. (2007). Teacher morale: More complex than we think? *The Australian Educational Researcher, 34*(1), 89–100.

Martin, N., Sass, D., & Schmitt, T. (2012). Teacher efficacy in student engagement, instructional management, student stressors, and burnout: A theoretical model using in-class variables to predict teachers' intent-to-leave. *Teaching and Teacher Education, 28*, 546–559.

Maslach, C., Schaufeli, W., & Leiter, M. (2001). Job burnout. *Annual Review of Psychology, 52*, 397–422.

McCormick, J., & Barnett, K. (2010). Teachers' attributions for stress and their relationships with burnout. *International Journal of Educational Management, 25*(3), 278–293.

O'Leary, Z. (2010). *The essential guide to doing your research project*. London: SAGE.

Pas, E., Bradshaw, C., & Hershfeldt, P. (2012). Teacher- and school-level predictors of teacher efficacy and burnout: Identifying potential areas for support. *Journal of Psychology, 50*, 129–145.

Pei, W., & Zhang, G. (2007). Survey of occupational stress of secondary and elementary school teachers and the lessons learned. *Chinese Education and Society, 40*(5), 32–39.

Peng, X. (2012). 关于小学教师工作压力的调查分析 [Investigative research on working stress of teachers at elementary school]. 课程·教材·教法 *[Curriculum, Teaching Material and Method], 3*, 106–111.

Pieterinen, J., Pyhalto, K., Soini, T., & Salmela-Aro, K. (2013). Reducing teacher burnout: A socio-contextual approach. *Teaching and Teacher Education, 35*, 62–72.

Richards, K., Hemphill, M., & Templin, T. (2018). Personal and contextual factors related to teachers' experience with stress and burnout. *Teachers and Teaching, 24*(7), 768–787.

Romanowski, M. (2006). A changing nation: Issues facing Chinese teachers. *Kappa Delta Pi, Winter*, 76–81.

Schnaider-Levi, L., Mitnik, I., & Zafrani, K. (2017). Inquiry-based stress reduction meditation technique for teacher burnout: A qualitative study. *Mind, Brain and Education, 11*(2), 75–84.

SINA. (2005). *Occupational stress and mental health survey among Chinese teachers*. SINA. http://edu.sina.com.cn/l/2005-09-09/1653126581.html.

Skaalvik, E., & Skaalvik, S. (2010). Teacher self-efficacy and teacher burnout: A study of relations. *Teaching and Teacher Education, 26*, 1059–1069.

Skaalvik, E., & Skaalvik, S. (2017). Dimensions of teacher burnout: Relations with potential stressors at school. *Social Psychology Education, 20*, 775–790.

Taplin, M. (2008). *Teacher survival: A practical human values approach to professional fulfillment and happiness*. Hong Kong: Institute of Sathya Sai Education.

Taplin, M. (2010). *Silent sitting: A resource manual*. Hong Kong: Institute of Sathya Sai Education.

van Droogenbroek, F., Spruyt, B., & Vanroelen, C. (2014). Burnout among senior teachers: Investigating the role of workload and interpersonal relationships at work. *Teaching and Teacher Education, 43*, 99–109.

Zhai, F., Raver, C., & Li-Grining, C. (2011). Classroom-based interventions and teachers' perceived job stressors and confidence: Evidence from a randomized trial in Head Start stings. *Early Childhood Research Quarterly, 26*(7), 442–452.

Zhu, J., Chen, H., Shen, J., & Zheng, Q. (2009). 教师问题行为的初步探索 [A preliminary study of teachers' behavioral problems]. 心理科学 *[Psychological Science], 32*(2), 507–510.

Chapter 12
Silent Sitting and Meditation: Building Teachers' Acceptance, Implementation, and Self-awareness in a Malaysian School

Suma Parahakaran

Abstract This chapter explores challenges teachers faced while implementing silent sitting in a primary school in Malaysia. The objectives of the study were focused on exploring three areas: teachers' acceptance and implementation of silent sitting in classrooms; the challenges they faced while exploring the implementation of silent sitting and Light Meditation as a new practice; and their perceptions of any changes in their self-awareness as an outcome of the practice.

The relationship between meditation and silent sitting is introduced briefly. Training sessions were conducted over a period of six months with a small sample of teachers in Malaysia, within the context of Sathya Sai Education in Human Values (SSEHV). Teachers' personal stories and their perceptions of the benefits of the practice are explored briefly.

Keywords Teacher self-awareness · Silent sitting · Human values · Challenges · Acceptance

12.1 Introduction

As described in Chap. 2, the practice of silent sitting is one of the key components of Sathya Sai Education in Human Values (SSEHV) programs. This study was conducted in a model Sathya Sai primary school in Malaysia. The school's mission is to facilitate the development of human values in children in line with the philosophy of SSEHV (see Chap. 2).

A whole school approach to SSEHV is practiced in this school, based on the view that this helps to create a positive ethos and a good school climate (in line with Toomey 2006). The Light Meditation (see Sect. 2.1.5.1) is used during the assembly so that all staff and students are involved. This technique brings focused attention, thus fulfilling the mission of the school. Silent sitting is conducted in classrooms for

S. Parahakaran (✉)
American University of Sovereign Nations, Sacaton, AZ, USA

© Springer Nature Singapore Pte Ltd. 2021
S. Parahakaran, S. Scherer (eds.), *A Human Values Pathway for Teachers*,
https://doi.org/10.1007/978-981-16-0200-9_12

one to three minutes depending on the level of restlessness of students in the classrooms. This school has about 30 students in each class, yet it is still possible to conduct silent sitting successfully.

A previous study conducted in 2013 by the authors explored teachers' perceptions of teaching techniques implemented in another model Sathya Sai school in Thailand (Parahakaran 2013). In that study, the teachers perceived positive effects of silent sitting. Interviews with teachers who had implemented this technique and/or experienced the practice said that it "increased their calmness, awareness, and memory capacity, concentration, motivation, and intuitive capacity" (Parahakaran 2013, p. 173). The transformation was seen in students after 12–20 months of practice. The teachers perceived the main impacts on the students to be positive thinking, positive behavioral outcomes, and love and support demonstrated to their teachers. When asked to rate their perceptions of the five teaching pedagogies for the SSEHV program (prayers, silent sitting, group activities, storytelling, and songs), these teachers felt that silent sitting was the second most preferred after storytelling (Parahakaran 2013).

12.1.1 Light Meditation as a Whole School Approach (General Assembly)

The primary school in Malaysia starts each day with visualization methods during morning assembly. The most beneficial type of visualization is the Light Meditation, which incorporates mindful practice, along with positive mental pictures. The Light Meditation is usually accompanied by background music.

A commonly used script for the Light Meditation can be found in Sect. 2.1.5.1, Figure 1.2. Jumsai (2001) explained why it is a powerful tool.

> So, let us talk a little bit about why the Light Meditation is so powerful. The first part of the Light Meditation is to practice concentration. We concentrate on the light. So, the first step to meditation is concentration, and it is contained in the Light Meditation. At the same time that we concentrate on the light, we take the light to various parts of the body (p. 7).

According to Jumsai (2001), the Light Meditation enables practitioners to reprogram their subconscious minds with positive thoughts (e.g., "I will speak only what is good and useful"). Later, when they visualize the light being spread to their friends, families, and communities, they expand their consciousness and include every living being. As well as being a metaphor for purity and wisdom, the image of the light gives a focal point to concentrate on and for their mental well being.

12.1.2 Silent Sitting and Visualization Activities Used in the Classroom

In the classroom in the Malaysian school, silent sitting is used for one to three minutes at the start of each teaching session. Silent sitting exercises allow students to prepare their minds to focus on their lessons. Debriefing about how the students feel at the end of the practice helps to solidify the benefits of the practice (Taplin 2011).

Typically, the teacher instructs students to do the following:

- Sit up straight, close their eyes, and breathe in and out in a relaxed manner.
- Relax their legs, hands, and muscles by breathing slowly for two minutes.
- Breathe in and out slowly, focusing on their own breath until the teacher tells them to stop.
- Open their eyes slowly.

In addition to silent sitting, simple visualization exercises are also used. An example of a visualization exercise is as follows:

Let us all sit in silence. Breathe in slowly and breathe out slowly. Let us relax our bodies and feel the calmness.

We are taking a walk in a beautiful garden.

The grass is green and there is calmness everywhere.

There are white flowers moving in the wind.

We thank nature for this beautiful scene.

We can see white birds flying in the big, blue sky.

We feel peace and see beauty everywhere.

12.2 Introducing Teachers to Silent Sitting and Visualization Techniques

While there is little doubt that silence and reflective contemplation have a significant role in educational settings (Weeks 2018), few studies have explored how teachers use these techniques in their teaching processes in primary schools. As well, research has suggested that teachers have very little opportunity to learn how to use silence in teaching (Zembylas and Michaelides 2004).

A professional development program conducted in the Malaysian school provided an opportunity to find out more about how teachers experienced learning to use silent sitting. It was of particular interest to explore how teachers develop a belief in its importance and the skills to implement it successfully in their teaching, as well as learning about the challenges and obstacles they experience in doing so. The program was also an opportunity to explore the teachers' perceptions of how the silent sitting benefited themselves.

An opportunity was also created in the professional development program for the 12 participating teachers to reflect on their own self-awareness while engaging in the silent sitting activities. When individuals turn their attention toward themselves to witness their own experiences as subjects, they are being self-aware (Carver 2003). Self-awareness theory conceptualizes that individuals are able to focus on themselves and evaluate how they think and feel against internal standards (Duval and Wicklund 1972). The benefits of self-awareness and its link with mindful practices have been mentioned in several studies (Coholic 2011; Heatherton and Baumeister 1991; Richards et al. 2010).

12.3   Context of the Current Study

The training program for silent sitting was conducted with 12 teachers (see Appendices 1 and 2 for details). The professional development program consisted of three workshops.

First Workshop

During the first workshop, the teachers were given a 10-minute presentation on the impact of silent sitting based on existing literature. They were then asked how they felt about using silent sitting. There was an interesting difference in the views of teachers who had been in the school and using the technique for several years and those who were new to it.

The teachers who had been in the school the longest made comments such as the following:

> I practice regularly in my personal life... it has helped me to be more concentrated and focused.

> It is easier to control the class.

> More calm, relaxed.

> I feel more grateful.

> I have a broader perspective of things.

> I use silent sitting to get children to be calmer and to get their attention.

> I find it difficult to concentrate.

> I am more alert about what to do.

On the other hand, the teachers who were relatively new to the school expressed some reservations:

> I cannot sit for long hours.

> I have not practiced for long.

> I do it only in school.

> I do not implement it every day.

> Not every day.

During this session, the trainer felt that it was important to let all teachers share their views freely.

Second Workshop

In the second workshop, the teachers were given sample scripts for silent sitting visualizations (Taplin 2010). They read the passages and chose some that they felt were interesting to them. The teachers engaged well with the contents from the teachers' manual.

Some discussion arose about the challenges that teachers may face in the initial stages of introducing the technique into the classroom. For example, they were concerned that some students would refuse to close their eyes, particularly those who are curious about what is going on around them.

Some strategies were discussed for addressing this situation. For example, students who cannot sit silently can be given a pencil to draw concentric circles from the inside out and from the outside in until the session is over. This exercise calms them down, and they are not separated from their classmates. The practice of watching their own breathing and experiencing silence helps students to calm down and reduce their restlessness.

Third Workshop

The third workshop was held one month after the second and focused on how to use silent sitting in the classroom. Each teacher was invited to demonstrate the use of their version of silent sitting. Seven teachers came forward to demonstrate. The other five remained silent.

An evaluation questionnaire was given to the participants after this workshop (see Appendix 2), addressing three broad areas:

- Were the teachers able to accept, accommodate, and implement the idea of silent sitting in their classrooms?
- What were the challenges the teachers faced while exploring the new practice of silent sitting and Light Meditation?
- Was there any increase in the teachers' perceived self-awareness after implementing silent sitting for six months?

The written statements from the questionnaire were coded and then organized into themes. From these themes, emergent categories were itemized in tables. The process of analysis followed the strategies suggested by Teddlie and Tashakkori (2009). The categories were then analyzed.

During all three workshops, over a five-month period, the trainer followed up personally by calling teachers to find out whether they had any difficulties with practicing silent sitting. This mentorship was considered an important aspect of the teachers' adoption of a new practice.

One month after the third workshop, a follow-up questionnaire was administered to explore how the teachers had implemented silent sitting in their classrooms and the challenges they faced during the initial period of implementation. After three months of implementation, the teachers were requested to write reflections of their experiences relating to their practice of silent sitting and Light Meditation.

12.4   Analysis and Results

12.4.1   Overview of Teachers' Experiences (First, Second, and Third Workshops)

The data presented below summarize the teachers' experiences at the various phases of the training. These findings are summarized in Tables 12.1 and 12.2.

First Workshop

Many of the teachers had difficulty with issues relating to the presentation of the silent sitting scripts, such as reading the text using the right intonation, voice modulation, and breath control. The challenge was to get them to read slowly and give time for students to visualize the imagery or scenes presented in the vignettes.

The teachers shared their views with each other on how to improve. Seven teachers used the material after the first training session, and five of them did not.

When asked to reflect on their use of silent sitting in the classroom, most teachers said they did not have a formal practice and worked toward engaging in a daily practice. Most teachers were quiet and two teachers stated that they had their own methods. Although teachers stated that they were using silent sitting in classes, they could not implement it regularly because of time constraints.

Second Workshop

The teachers had started to become more aware of their thoughts at this stage, as they began to assimilate and implement what they had been learning. Four of the twelve teachers stated that silent sitting helped them to become calmer and to solve problems. One teacher stated that she felt less emotional.

When asked how the silent sitting had affected their emotions, their answers included:

Aware of other issues other than academic challenges.

More broad minded.

Reduced anger and stress.

Table 12.1 Emergent categories and frequency counts of teachers' responses (Emergent themes and respective categories are from Teddlie and Tashakkori 2009)

Themes	Categories	Number of teachers
Increased awareness of their thoughts	Increased self-awareness	8
More connectivity with people around them	Increased self-awareness	1
Self-control	Increased resilience (emotional regulation)	5
Increased awareness of issues other than academic challenges	Increased awareness of the environment around them	1
Struggling to keep the practice consistent	Needed more effort	1
Problem-solving skills	Increased resilience	4

Table 12.2 Emergent themes and their categories in teachers' narratives about the use of silent sitting and visualization. Emergent themes and respective categories are from Teddlie and Tashakkori (2009)

Excerpts of narratives	Themes	Category
First Workshop		
Not enough time to practice silent sitting due to insufficient time to conduct the lesson	Challenged with new information	Pre-contemplative stage
Sometimes silent sitting is used and sometimes not, depending on the syllabus	Accommodating the new information	Contemplative stage
Second Workshop		
• Concentrate better • More focused • More alert about what to do • Did not practice	Awareness of their own thoughts	Assimilation and implementation stage
Third Workshop		
• Problems are solved subconsciously • Better focus on teaching • Work is getting organized, helps for the whole week • Broader perspective of things, feel less sensitive to emotions • Controls anger • When I think of a problem I find a solution	Self-awareness Resilience Problem-solving skills	Assimilating and implementation stage Experiential stage

Easy to control.

Have greater focus, more alert about what to do.

Calmer.

Reduced anger and stress.

Concentrate better and more focused.

The rest of the teachers were still contemplating and had not reached a stage where they thought of implementing silent sitting.

Third Workshop

During the third workshop, the teachers were beginning to respond more favorably to the idea of implementing silent sitting. In this workshop, they were reminded to report their practices, and a few found that silent sitting was benefiting them. These teachers who were positive were classified as being in the assimilation and implementation stage (see Sect. 12.4.2), where they had realized that if they continued the practice it would be beneficial to themselves. These teachers had started to become more self-aware and had access to their own personal feelings, interests, values, and potential. Those who still did not practice were classified as being in the pre-implementation stage.

Still, at this stage, the responses were varied. Some had implemented silent sitting sessions in their classrooms on an average of three to four times a week, while one had not implemented the practice at all. The challenges they described ranged from lack of time, chores to attend to, and the issues of managing their classroom teaching.

The responses indicated that not all teachers were serious about the practice but that those who practiced found it beneficial.

From the responses in their narratives, the teachers had evidently moved past the stage of worrying about their syllabus and the time constraints and were showing more confidence and willingness to implement silent sitting and the Light Meditation.

At this stage, the most common responses were that silent sitting and visualization practices made them more peaceful (mentioned by four teachers), and that the practices helped them to solve problems (also mentioned by four teachers). Only one said she did not want to practice, although another stated the belief that it was more important to focus on teaching.

Table 12.1 provides emergent categories from themes after the three training workshops. As illustrated in Table 12.1, eight of the 12 teachers made comments suggesting they had increased awareness of their own thoughts and behaviors, and one said that her relationships had improved. Five teachers felt that they could control their minds and were more alert. They said they had more self-control and did not get stressed or become angry. Their emotional regulation was better. Another one stated that she had increased awareness of issues around her other than academic challenges. Four of the teachers felt that they could solve problems when they practiced silent sitting.

12.4.2   Themes Emerging from Evaluation Questionnaire

The trans-theoretical theory of change (Prochaska and DiClemente 2005) was adopted to assess the levels of changes in the teachers. According to this theory, behavioral change is a process involving progress through a series of stages. Using this model, the teachers' statements were categorized into pre-contemplative, contemplative, assimilation and implementation, and experiential stages.

Expanding on the categorization of evaluation question responses in Table 12.2, the following observations were made.

Are teachers able to accept and accommodate the idea of silent sitting in classrooms?

The teachers' responses fell into two main categories. Those who were accepting and planning to practice were said to "accommodate new information," and those who were reluctant due to perceived obstacles were said to be "challenged with new information." Those who accommodated the new information were said to be in the contemplative stage, and those who were still not interested in practicing were said to be in the pre-contemplative stage because they were worried about other issues such as the syllabus. Eight of the twelve teachers were in the contemplative stage at the second training session and moved to the experiential stage after six months of practice. This suggests that, with appropriate support and sufficient time to make their own progress, teachers are able to integrate silent sitting and visualization techniques effectively into their classrooms.

What were the challenges teachers faced while exploring the new practice of silent sitting and Light Meditation?

Five of the teachers found reading the vignettes with the right intonation, voice modulation, and breath control difficult at the beginning. Peer guidance helped them to overcome this challenge. For eight of the teachers, in the initial stage of the training, a lack of ideas was a challenge; this was addressed by providing sample materials, which they were able to use successfully. Another challenge in the early stage was that not all students wanted to close their eyes, while some could not concentrate.

However, as time went on, seven out of twelve teachers stated that their children were maintaining silence and sitting in their classrooms. Responses included the following:

Students are calmer.

They loved it and feel it.

Some can follow and some do not.

They like the scenarios I relate to them.

They ask me to do [silent sitting] after class as they [enjoy it].

Year 3 students respond to the sessions.

The teachers' comments on peer sharing were interesting. For example, they were influenced by positive outcomes experienced by their peers. One stated that she saw her peer using music from a radio and decided to adopt the same idea. The idea of peers sharing their experiences and observing their friends implementing silent sitting reinforced the practice and had a positive impact.

By the end of four months, from teachers' statements, a certain level of increased awareness of their thoughts, relationships with people around them, and issues related to other situations apart from academic challenges was evident.

Was there an increase in self-awareness and resilience after a six-month implementation?

The teachers' feedback suggests that they began to use silent sitting and creative visualization mindfulness practices over time to deal with their stress and that this led to increased self-awareness. The practice of silent sitting and Light Meditation helped the teachers to experience moment by moment without engaging in their own emotional aspects of their personal experiences. This appears to have led them to be more aware and even possibly to build resilience. Consistent with the findings of Fang et al. (2010), the teachers said that their stress was reduced as a result of their practice and they did not shout as an instant reaction but instead responded to their students more calmly. This reflected the finding that mindfulness practices can lead to positive changes in participants' psychosocial and physical functioning (Santorelli et al. 2017). More rigorous research has to be done to understand the relationship between self-awareness and resilience and the underlying mechanisms of how emotional regulation is impacted.

12.4.3 Written Reflections and Interviews

From the written reflections three months after the third workshop, eight of the twelve teachers elaborated on their experiences of regulating their emotions and behaviors:

- Teacher 1 stated that she was doing silent sitting with her students every day and she shouted less in class. She talked more to students and found a lot of changes in herself. She no longer lost her cool as often and became less tense.
- Teacher 2 said that she was doing more silent sitting and she felt she could control her anger. Her students were friendlier with her.
- Teacher 3 believed that she was more aware of what she said and did. She said she had become more careful about how she spoke so as not to hurt anybody. She also thought that, after the training, the relationships among teachers had improved.
- Teacher 4 stated that she was practicing the silent sitting every day and she felt that she could handle her students better.
- Teacher 5 stated that she was practicing silent sitting herself and also with the children. She had reduced shouting at students and, instead, tried to explain things to them in a calm manner.
- Teacher 6 was practicing silent sitting herself. She felt her mind was calmer and settled. She used the phrases, "I'm sorry," "please forgive me," "thank you," and "I love you" with students and said that they were better behaved in class.
- Teacher 7 was more cheerful and she could manage her students much better, especially the Year 4 students. She said she was closer to her students and she could engage better with them.
- Teacher 8 stated that silent sitting had become a part of his daily routine and he could talk positively to students. He felt that his students were more disciplined.

When asked to relate the challenges they had faced, one of the teachers shared the following:

For me, I felt it's not easy to practice silent sitting in a day or even in a week. It takes time for me to really go into it seriously. I practiced silent sitting perfectly till this moment. At the beginning I did silent sitting before I went to bed. It worked out well but unfortunately I couldn't sleep after it because my mind was too fresh. Then, I started to do silent sitting in the morning, but not frequently.

Nevertheless, this teacher was able to overcome her personal challenge:

Still I tried my best to do it frequently. Now, I'm doing it frequently whenever I feel my mind is not stable or disturbed. I love to listen to songs and music, so it's easy for me to do silent sitting with music. I have downloaded a music app named "Relax Melodies" which helps me a lot in doing my silent sitting.

She went on to write very positively about her experience:

"Silence is source of great strength – Lao Tzu." It's a true statement. I feel the satisfaction in myself after I do silent sitting. The silence in me makes me happy and relaxed. It helps me to shape my thoughts too. All unnecessary things in my mind fly away. I can control my thinking. I am not too emotional and am more practical. By doing silent sitting, I can share and spread my love to everyone around me without saying a single word. I'm sending my love through light and its [sic] really working! Silent sitting also helps me to see how much I took for granted and how much I have to be grateful for in my life. I feel blessed with what I have around me. I have started to appreciate a simple things [sic] in my life.

When the same teacher was asked about her students' responses to her silent sitting sessions, she shared the following:

All my students are young and it's really hard for me to make them to close their eyes. But still I managed to do the silent sitting with them and they improved a lot compared to the beginning of the session. I use music and tell a story to make them enjoy the silent sitting. Most of them respond well. Doing silent sitting before starting my lesson helps me a lot to keep the class under control. The students are able to focus on the lesson after the silent sitting.

After the second workshop, the teachers discussed their own experiences in their staff room. Aspects of the professional development activity, including peer sharing, encouragement from peers, and their observation of others practicing, were additional motivational factors for the teachers (consistent with van Aalderen et al. 2014):

I sat with a few teachers and we had a small discussion about practising silent sitting. All shared their views and what they experienced. We faced a lot of challenges to do silent sitting but still managed to improve ourselves in practising it. The teachers agreed that they had learnt to be calm and were more positive in making any decision. By doing silent sitting, we improved and had a better relationship with everyone and shared good thoughts. There are changes in the way of thinking and we take things in a good way. Overall, well-being improved in ourselves and we are in control of our emotions.

Overall, it was encouraging to see that the teachers, especially those who were new to the concept of silent sitting, overcame their initial challenges and found that it improved relationships and helped them to remove stress and focus on students' needs (consistent with Dorman 2015). Their comments suggested that their experiences of silent sitting had led to positive outcomes for themselves and their students, more self-awareness, more emotional regulation, improved relationships with others, motivation to continue enjoying the relaxing experience, and the interest to take the experience out of school to their homes and other areas of their lives. Over time, the participants realized that their students responded better when the teachers changed their ways; this is also consistent with Dorman's (2015) findings. Changes were noted as the training was implemented, including teacher-student relationships and teachers' awareness of their own actions.

The teachers' comments about their practices resonate with the statements made by Hölzel et al. (2011) and Deshmukh (2006). Hopefully, with consistent practice, the teachers can cultivate and develop compassion through inquiry (Feldman 2005). According to Feldman (2005), "with mindfulness and investigation, you find in your heart the generosity and understanding that allow you to open rather than close" (pp. 141–142). The development of awareness could be a transformative factor for teachers. As one teacher said, she "can share and spread my love to everyone around me without saying a single word." The reinforcement of the five values in the Light Meditation has helped her to be more aware of the values, particularly the value of love. If the Light Meditation is done regularly as a whole school approach, the reprogramming of the subconscious mind by reaffirming positive and loving statements can become a reality (Jumsai 2001). The practices can enhance new ways of thinking, opening teachers' minds to be inclusive of others (Hölzel et al. 2011).

12.5 Conclusion

This chapter has explored a group of teachers' experiences of introducing silent sitting and visualization practices into their classrooms. It has described the initial challenges they faced and has given some indicators of how the experience affected the teachers' self-awareness of personal changes.

The evaluation of a three-workshop training program over five months suggests that silent sitting and visualization practices in SSEHV may have helped to reduce the teachers' stress, increase their self-awareness, promote greater resilience, improve relationships, and motivate them to view outside experiences differently.

The sample was small, and the data collection process was opportunistic, hence not rigorous. Nevertheless, the teachers' experiences presented in this chapter suggest that one important factor helping them to overcome their initial challenges was the peer support from colleagues sharing their experiences of improved personal well-being, increased self-awareness and inner peace. As the teachers' self-awareness increased, they also noticed a shift in their students' behavior. These experiential moments provided positive feedback to teachers that encouraged them to continue with the intervention.

Appendix 1 Overview of the Professional Development Program

Module: Silent Sitting/Silent Visualization Techniques in Classrooms	
Content:	• Significance of practicing silent sitting in classrooms. • First practicing and then implementing silent sitting in the classroom. • Challenges teachers face when silent sitting is implemented in classrooms with new groups of children. • Daily practice and reflections of teachers practice.
Objective:	Teachers will be able to do the following: • Explain why the practice of silent sitting is important for children. • Explain why teachers have to practice silent sitting themselves before they implement it in classrooms. • Identify and manage the challenges of implementing silent sitting in the classroom. • Reflect and improve on the practice of silent sitting.
Method of training:	• Explain the importance of silent sitting and the outcomes of the practice from evidence-based practices in international Sathya Sai schools.

(continued)

Module: Silent Sitting/Silent Visualization Techniques in Classrooms	
	• Use examples of visualization scripts to enable each teacher to read, practice, and improve during the training sessions. • Teachers' discussion about the use of the material and whether they found the contents easy to use. • Peer feedback on the tone, method, and time taken to use the material for silent sitting with their peers during the training sessions.
Duration:	2 hours of training + 4 hours of presentation by teachers
Evaluation:	• Teachers' understanding of the significance of the use of silent sitting using a feedback form. • Trainers' training evaluation form.

Appendix 2 Evaluation Questionnaire

No.	Question
1	Are you able to use the contents as a guide to conduct silent sitting in your classrooms? Give reasons.
2	Are you able to set the tone, pace, and time yourself to support children in their silent sitting?
3	Do you think children in your classroom are responding to their sessions? Give reasons.
4	Do you need more training sessions to conduct silent sitting sessions in your classrooms? Give reasons.
5	Are you confident to use silent sitting as part of your teaching techniques?
6	Have you shared your experiences with at least two of your peers and listened to their experiences? Please write their reflections. You do not have to name them.

References

Carver, C. S. (2003). Self-awareness. In M. R. Leary & J. P. Tangney (Eds.), *Handbook of self and identity* (pp. 179–196). New York, NY: Guilford Press.

Coholic, D. A. (2011). Exploring the feasibility and benefits of arts-based mindfulness-based practices with young people in need: Aiming to improve aspects of self-awareness and resilience. *Child & Youth Care Forum, 40*, 303–317. https://doi.org/10.1007/s10566-010-9139-x.

Deshmukh, V. D. (2006). Neuroscience of meditation. *The ScientificWorld Journal, 6*, 275–289. https://doi.org/10.1100/tsw.2006.244.

Dorman, E. (2015). Building teachers' social-emotional competence through mindfulness practices. In D. J. Flinders & C. M. Moroye (Eds.), *Curriculum and teaching dialogue: Vol. 17 # 1 & 2* (pp. 103–119). Charlotte, North Carolina: Information Age Publishing.

Duval, T. S., & Wicklund, R. A. (1972). *A theory of objective self-awareness*. New York, NY: Academic Press.

Fang, C. Y., Reibel, D. K., Longacre, M. L., Rosenzweig, S., Campbell, D. E., & Douglas, S. D. (2010). Enhanced psychosocial well-being following participation in a mindfulness-based stress reduction program is associated with increased natural killer cell activity. *Journal of Alternative and Complementary Medicine, 16*, 531–538.

Feldman, C. (2005). *Compassion: Listening to the cries of the world*. Berkeley, CA: Rodmell Press.

Heatherton, T. F., & Baumeister, R. F. (1991). Binge eating as escape from self-awareness. *Psychological Bulletin, 110*, 86–108.

Hölzel, B. K., Lazar, S. W., Gard, T., Schuman-Oliver, Z., Vago, D. R., & Ott, U. (2011). How does mindfulness meditation work? Proposing mechanisms of action from a conceptual and neural perspective. *Perspectives on Psychological Science, 6*(6), 537–559. https://doi.org/10.1177/1745691611419671.

Jumsai, A. (2001, September). *Significance of Light Meditation* [Conference presentation]. Northern California & Nevada Regional Annual Conference, United States. http://region7saicenters.org/saidocuments/Meditation.pdf

Parahakaran, S. (2013). *Human values-based water, sanitation and hygiene education: A study of teachers' beliefs and perceptions in some SEA countries* [Doctoral dissertation, University of Sydney].

Prochaska, J. O., & DiClemente, C. C. (2005). The transtheoretical approach. In J. C. Norcross & M. R. Goldfried (Eds.), *Handbook of psychotherapy integration: Oxford series in clinical psychology* (2nd ed., pp. 147–171). Oxford; New York: Oxford University Press.

Richards, K., Campenni, C., & Muse-Burke, J. (2010). Self-care and well-being in mental health professionals: The mediating effects of self-awareness and mindfulness. *Journal of Mental Health Counseling, 32*, 247–264. https://doi.org/10.17744/mehc.32.3.0n31v88304423806.

Santorelli, S. F., Kabat-Zinn, J., Blacker, M., Meleo-Meyer, F., & Koerbel, L. (2017). *Mindfulness-based stress reduction (MBSR) authorized curriculum guide*. University of Massachusetts Medical School. https://www.umassmed.edu/contentassets/abe554ad1ced45b98c57e455441d3f95/mbsr-curriculum-guide-2017.pdf

Taplin, M. (2010). *Silent sitting: A resource manual*. Hong Kong: Institute of Sathya Sai Education.

Taplin, M. (2011). Silent sitting: A cross-curricular tool to promote resilience. *International Journal of Children's Spirituality, 16*(2), 75–96. https://doi.org/10.1080/1364436X.2011.580730.

Teddlie, C., & Tashakkori, A. (2009). *Foundations of mixed methods research*. Los Angeles, CA: Sage.

Toomey, R. (2006). *Values as the centrepiece of the school's work: A discussion paper on learnings from VEGPSP stage 1*. Curriculum Corporation. http://www.curriculum.edu.au/verve/_resources/Dr_Ron_Toomey_Discussion_Paper_final_2.pdf.

van Aalderen, J. R., Breukers, W. J., Reuzel, R. P., & Speckens, A. E. (2014). The role of the teacher in mindfulness-based approaches: A qualitative study. *Mindfulness, 5*, 170–178. https://doi.org/10.1007/s12671-012-0162-x.

Weeks, D. (2018). *The value of silence in schools: Intentional silence in the school day offers opportunities for deep reflection and learning*. George Lucas Educational Foundation. https://www.edutopia.org/article/value-silence-schools.

Zembylas, M., & Michaelides, P. (2004). The sound of silence in pedagogy. *Educational Theory, 54*(2), 193–210.

Chapter 13
Students' Acceptance of Silent Sitting/ Visualization and Its Effect on Their Affective Dimensions

Suma Parahakaran

Abstract This chapter explores some primary school children's reflections on their experiences of silent sitting, particularly their feelings about participating in it, and its effects on affective aspects of their lives. These responses have been linked to Krathwohl's hierarchy of affective domain taxonomy. The data were collected from a sample of 53 students. Some were from a Malaysian primary school where the SSEHV model is embedded in the whole-school environment and silent sitting/ visualization is a regular component of their daily activity. The others were from informal classes where silent sitting/visualization was used on a weekly basis. The students' reflections are discussed in relation to existing literature related to mindfulness.

Keywords Affective development · Silent sitting · Self-regulation · Emotional regulation

13.1 Introduction

The development of the affective domain is important in education at all levels. This requires educators to shift their positions from just teaching, explaining, and motivating students at a cognitive level.

This chapter explores the use of silent sitting/visualization as a strategy that can help teachers to address affect in the classroom. Krathwohl's (1973) affective domain taxonomy was used as a framework to explore students' affective domains after they had practiced silent sitting. Studies exploring the affective domain and studies from the field of neuroscience have suggested that affective factors such as self-regulation, self-awareness, compassion, and deeper learning are influenced by the practice of mindfulness (Flook et al. 2014; Hölzel et al. 2011; Kaunhoven and Dorjee 2017; Menezes et al. 2012; Shephard and Fasko 1999; Vago and Silbersweig

S. Parahakaran (✉)
American University of Sovereign Nations, Sacaton district, Arizona, USA

© Springer Nature Singapore Pte Ltd. 2021
S. Parahakaran, S. Scherer (eds.), *A Human Values Pathway for Teachers*,
https://doi.org/10.1007/978-981-16-0200-9_13

2012). Other studies have revealed a range of benefits when silence is practiced, such as compassion (Neff 2003; Neff and Dahm 2015), moral decision-making (Shapiro et al. 2012), and increased concentration (Massachusetts General Hospital 2011).

13.1.1 Categorizing Affective Levels in Learning

A significant contribution to work on the affective domain was that of Krathwohl (1973).

Krathwohl defined affect as the emotional area of learning and proposed a five-level hierarchy for its development (Krathwohl et al. 1973):

- Receiving: At this level, the student has an awareness or attitude or willingness to hear, receive, or accept particular stimuli (classroom activities, textbook, music, etc.).
- Responding: At this level, the student has an active attention to the object or stimuli and shows a willingness to discuss or participate.
- Valuing: At this level, the student accepts and moves to a level of commitment.
- Organizing: At this level, the learner develops a value and relates or synthesizes the value.
- Characterizing: This is the highest level under the affective domain, and at this level, the learner has already internalized and behaves consistently with the values associated with the object or stimulus.

13.2 Literature Review

13.2.1 Affective Learning and Teaching Processes

Affective learning involves learners' feelings, attitudes, and opinions (Miller 2005). It is important that children value these concepts and then internalize them. The role of emotions is important, but the affective dimension is interdependent with the cognitive dimension (Storbeck and Clore 2007; Weare 2010).

While no research has been conducted on affective learning and the SSEHV approach to silent sitting, some evidence suggests that affective development can be enhanced by similar practices, as discussed in the next section.

13.2.2 *Effects and Associated Outcomes of Mindfulness, Meditation, and Silent Practice*

Mindfulness practice and silent sitting have similarities in that both practices involve the individual in being silent and aware of the breath. Hence, the studies reviewed here are related to the identifiers of mindfulness, meditation, and silent practice.

Several studies have explored the effects of mindfulness practice on affective factors. For example, Kabat-Zinn (1990) referred to awareness and Goleman and Davidson (2017) to self-regulation as possible effects of the outcome as a result of mindfulness practices. Improved self-regulation occurs in pre-adolescents when mindfulness is practiced (Kaunhoven and Dorjee 2017), and another outcome of mindful practice has been identified as compassion (Neff and Dahm 2015). Various mental functions, such as self-observation, self-judgment, and self-reaction, are all functions of self-regulation (Bandura 1986). Self-regulation, according to Bandura, is a process in human behavior that is capable of having an impact on the external environment by engaging in different ways. People have capabilities by which they can self-reflect, and this prompts them to exercise some control over their own thoughts, feelings, motivations, and actions. When individuals want to self-direct, they adopt specific behaviors that will guide and motivate them and control their actions. These processes are regulated by anticipatory processes within themselves through self-reactive processes. Bandura further asserted that individuals are able to self-direct their thought patterns and actions (Bandura 1991).

Affective processes are usually operationalized as emotions and feelings that are related to actions (Wrightsman and Sanford 1975). One of these feelings is stress. Evidence suggests that when mindful practices are implemented, practitioners experience nonjudgmental awareness, which produces greater well-being and reduces stress-related symptoms (Hölzel et al. 2011). Other studies have also reported reduction of stress as a result of mindfulness practices (Tang et al. 2015).

During mindful meditation, emotional regulation is enhanced. This is one of the reasons for the recent rise in mindful practices in schools and higher education institutions to help students manage difficult emotions (Menezes et al. 2012). According to Menezes et al. emotional regulation is the individual's capacity to perceive and attend to emotional responses to the environment. When individuals are able to regulate their attention and can enter a relaxed state, they are able to refocus their attention and regulate strong emotions (Menezes et al. 2012). Furthermore, the effects of meditation and emotional regulation should be seen as an outcome of the practice (Menezes et al. 2012).

Because of the evidence supporting the importance of affective development and the role of mindfulness-type practices similar to silent sitting in promoting this aspect of the child, a small study was conducted to explore students' feelings about silent sitting and their perceptions of its effects on their affective aspects.

Krathwohl's (1956) hierarchical model as described above was used to categorize the students' comments. The purpose of this investigation was to give readers a glimpse, albeit a limited one, of the impact of the practice.

13.3   Method

An informal study was conducted in a private primary school in Malaysia where the SSEHV model is embedded into the whole-school program and silent sitting/visualization is implemented daily. The school principal invited the schools' students to submit written comments about their experiences. As the students were studying online from home at the time of this data collection due to pandemic lockdown, the invitations were issued via their parents. Responses were received from 28 students who accepted the invitation. These students' teachers conducted daily silent sitting, including daily use of the Light Meditation (see Sect. 2.1.5.1 for details).

In order to capture an older age group, a further 25 students were recruited from an informal SSEHV class that was conducted weekly. The ages of the participants in this group ranged from 10 to 16 years. They had all participated in SSEHV classes and had been practicing silent sitting regularly from seven years of age at least once a week in their classes.

All of the student participants had been using silent sitting practices regularly for three to nine years, at least daily in the primary school and at least weekly in the informal classes. Over this time they would have been exposed to a range of silent sitting approaches including the Light Meditation (see Chap. 2 for an overview), and in some, suitable background music may have been used. The time spent on these activities would have varied from two to eight minutes. The teachers who led these sessions had all been trained in the SSEHV model by the researcher and had experience implementing silent sitting/visualization for two to ten years. Clearly, the outcomes of this investigation are limited by the range of teachers' experience and students' years of exposure. Nevertheless, it is considered valuable to have a glimpse from the students' perspectives.

The students were required to respond to two questions:

- How did you find the practice of silent sitting at the beginning?
- How has silent sitting benefited you?

13.4   Data Analysis and Findings

This section discusses the children's responses to the two simple questions listed above. Fifty-three students responded.

The responses received were coded according to Teddlie and Tashakkori (2009). The first level of analysis consisted of organizing responses according to the interpretation of student responses aligned to the five affective levels of Krathwohl's taxonomy (Krathwohl et al. 1973).

Themes from the findings are summarized in Table 13.1, along with the frequencies. These themes gave some useful insights about the effects of silent sitting practice on students.

Table 13.1 Students' responses by Krathwohl's taxonomy levels

Krathwohl's taxonomy level	Excerpts from students' responses	Number of students responding in this category (N-53)
Receiving	Very calming and relaxing It was boring at the beginning At the beginning, I felt sleepy and could not concentrate I am angry during silent sitting It was difficult in the beginning because there were interruptions from teachers At the beginning, I didn't know what silent sitting was I found silent sitting a bit challenging in the beginning	53 (100%)
Responding	After that I found it was interesting I found the practice at the beginning very calming and relaxing	50 (94%)
Valuing	It keeps me calm and relaxed It helps me to develop my memory and concentration power I feel silent sitting is something precious I feel it gives me satisfaction and helps me to pay attention As the days passed by, I felt it gave me satisfaction. It helped me to pay attention	17 (32%)
Organizing	I get to concentrate well in my study and keep my mind fresh When I am angry during silent sitting, the peace when doing silent sitting will calm me down	14 (26%)
Characterizing	Silent sitting helped me to handle problems calmly and make me feel confident with the choices I have made. I do silent sitting at home and in school Silent sitting really helped me throughout my life and I thank the teachers who guided me to have this ability	10 (19%)

Krathwohl's taxonomy was adapted as the basis for categorizing developments in the children's acceptance of silent sitting/visualization. For the purpose of categorizing the children's reflections, the following interpretations of Krathwohl's categories were used:

- Receiving: At this level, students are aware of the technique and know that the silent sitting technique involves them sitting down for a few minutes. They may or may not be interested in the silent sitting technique.
- Responding: At this level, students value the idea of the silent sitting and respond to the practice.

- Valuing: At this level, students start valuing the idea of silent sitting and are committed to silent sitting.
- Organizing: At this level, students not only value the idea of silent sitting but also commit to practicing it.
- Characterizing: At this level, the students model the technique and it becomes part of their lives. They internalize the practice of silent sitting.

13.4.1   Responses According to Krathwohl's Five Levels

Table 13.1 illustrates the students' responses according to the interpretation of the levels of affective taxonomy (Krathwohl et al. 1973).

13.4.2   Thematic Categorization of Students' Responses

The students' responses were compiled and organized according to the themes described below.

Receiving Stage

Typical student responses at this stage suggested at the receiving stage their feelings about silent sitting were negative. In particular, they found it boring and difficult to concentrate.

Silent sitting was boring for me in the beginning. (13-14 year-old)

It was very difficult for me to concentrate. (13-14 year-old)

It was really difficult because I kept on getting distracted. (13-14 year-old)

Honestly, I felt bored and at the same time, surprised because everybody was closing their eyes. (13-14 year-old)

In the beginning, silent sitting was hard for me because I have to stay silent and also keep my mind calm and not think about anything else. (13-14 year-old)

Responding Stage

At the responding stage, we can see evidence of students starting to recognize the benefits of silent sitting. Typical comments included:

Silent sitting has benefitted me in many aspects of my life. It helps me in my studies and also for my spiritual development. (13-14 year-old)

It helps me reduce the tension from my body and forget about what has happened. (13-14 year-old)

It helps me to remove unnecessary thoughts and makes my mind calm without any interruptions. It has also made me not to get angry too fast and to deal with every situation calmly. (13-14 year-old)

Valuing Stage

Most of the students' responses were related to this stage, suggesting that they accepted the idea of silent sitting, were prepared to make an effort to develop the skill, and started to find it of value to their lives.

> I tried harder and challenged myself not to get distracted. I could sit for more than five minutes. I realised that I am progressing slowly to overcome my weaknesses. (13-14 year-old age group).

> Silent sitting was boring for me in the beginning but as days passed by, I felt it gave me satisfaction and helped me pay attention. Through it, I learned about culture and became more loving and caring. (10-year-old).

> The first time I did silent sitting, I felt very calm and confident. That was on my first day of school. It made me feel energetic. (10-year-old).

> I became calmer and understood myself better. I improved in my awareness, focus and studies. My level of understanding became better. (10-year-old).

Organizing Stage

The following example of a response at the organizing level suggested emotional self-regulation:

> I feel calmer and control emotions better. (10-year old)

> Helped in increasing emotional capacity to deal with stress. (13-14 year old)

> Increased focus on the present moment. (13-14 year old)

> Creates peace in classroom and a better environment. (13-14 year old)

Characterizing Stage

Responses from students of different ages depicted that they had internalized the silent sitting practice and were now viewing it as a part of their lives.

> Silent sitting really helped me throughout my life and I thank the teachers who guided me to have this ability. (10-year-old)

> At the beginning, I could not focus whenever I did silent sitting. I started to do silent sitting when I was eight. I was really young then and didn't really understand the purpose of silent sitting. I couldn't close my eyes for the whole process and didn't feel anything. After I started doing silent sitting properly with knowing the purpose for doing it, it benefitted me a lot like helping me to focus and to be patient. (13-year-old)

> I actually found silent sitting a bit challenging in the beginning especially the sitting posture because I was not used to sitting like that for a long period of time. Now, I have overcome that problem because I listened to my mind not my body. (13-year-old)

> Silent sitting actually benefitted me a lot in a few aspects. It gradually increased my concentration level and now, whatever task or problem, I handle them with full concentration. (14-year-old)

Responses that Suggested Transition between Categories

In some cases, the students' responses did not fall into just one thematic category but showed signs that they were in transition from one to another.

Student 1 *(10-year-old boy)*

At first when I did silent sitting, it was very difficult for me to concentrate but after a few days, I felt relaxed and found it easy to concentrate. Now, I'm happy to do silent sitting. I always do silent sitting with my mom before we go to sleep...thank you, Madam, for teaching us silent sitting.

The following shows how this child described his transition from the Receiving stage to Valuing, Organizing, and even Characterizing:

- Receiving stage: "At first when I did silent sitting, it was very difficult for me to concentrate..."
- Responding stage: "...but after a few days, I felt relaxed..."
- Valuing and Organizing stages "... found it easier to concentrate. Now, I'm happy to do silent sitting."
- Characterizing stage "I always do silent sitting with my mom before we go to sleep."

Student 3 *(13–16-year-old girl)*

This student also indicated her experience at the Receiving Stage, but her next comment suggested the Responding Stage:

- Receiving stage: "In the beginning, I was unable to sit still. I would always move around and by doing that I would also disturb the others around me. I was also unable to concentrate on my homework."
- Responding stage: "...but after practicing silent sitting, I am able to sit still much more than before and I am able to concentrate more when doing my homework."

Student 4 *(13–16-year-old boy)*

This student also indicated a transition from the Responding stage to the Receiving, Valuing, and Organizing stages:

- Responding stage: "I initially found it tedious as I would rather get something else done instead of sitting still for a couple of minutes."
- Receiving, Valuing and Organizing stages: "It also helps realign my thoughts since my mind is all over the place thinking and worrying about various things throughout the entire day. It also calms down my anxiety as I'm focusing on my breathing throughout the process."

Student 3 *(13–16-year-old boy)*

This boy's response indicated his progression across the four stages:

- Receiving stage: "In the beginning, silent sitting was hard for me because I had to stay silent and also keep my mind calm and not think about anything else."
- Responding and Valuing stages: "It helps me to remove unnecessary thoughts."
- Organizing stage: "It makes my mind calm without any interruptions."
- Characterizing stage: "It has also made me not to get angry too fast and to deal with every situation calmly."

13.4.3 Comments on Specific Affective Domains

Three particular affective domains seem to have been addressed more than others in the students' comments. These are comments that could be categorized, respectively, as self-awareness, self-regulation, and values. Examples of the comments relating to each of these are listed below.

Self-awareness

At the beginning, it was difficult for me to concentrate. But now, it helps me clear my mind and it also benefits me in my self-reflection. (13-14 years age-group).

To be honest, it was pretty boring for me at first but after more practice, I started liking it. (13-14 years age-group).

I felt calmer and more refreshed after doing it. It is definitely good for everyone to practice. (13-14 years age-group)

I was unable to concentrate on my homework but after practicing silent sitting, I was able to sit still much more than before and was able to concentrate more when doing my homework. (13-14 years age-group).

Increases my focus on the present moment. Creates peace in the classroom and a better environment. Improves my academic performance. (10-year-old)

I became calmer and understood myself better. I improved in my awareness, focus and studies. My level of understanding became better. (10-year-old)

Silent sitting makes me release my stress and makes me feel relaxed at the same time. It makes me feel calm too. (12-year-old).

Self-regulation

I actually found silent sitting a bit challenging in the beginning, especially the sitting posture because I was not used to sitting like that for a long period of time. Now, I have overcome the problem because I listen to my mind not my body. (13–14-year-old)

I feel calmer and I can control my emotions better. (10-year-old)

It has helped in increasing my emotional capacity to deal with stress. (10-year-old)

I used to shout at my friends when they made mistakes, but now I advise them quietly. (12-year-old)

Silent sitting helps me to focus on what I want. (15–16-year-old)

Values

It has made me become a good example to others and it helps me think positively. (10-year-old)

It has made me loving, caring, patient, truthful and polite. (10-year-old)

13.5   Discussion

This section provides an interpretation of the students' responses aligned with
Krathwohl's five stages. It then offers a comment on some age-related patterns
that were observed and on individual students' development.

13.5.1   Student Responses by Krathwohl's Five Stages

Receiving Stage

The students' comments about the Receiving stage were based on a retrospective
question about their feelings when they first started using silent sitting/visualization
and not at the time of the data collection. Most suggested that they were just aware of
the existence of the practice (77%) rather than seeing it as beneficial, and 78% of the
sample stated that they had found it challenging in one way or another. Student
responses such as the following are a few examples of how they found the practice at
the beginning:

> Silent sitting was boring for me in the beginning.

> It was very difficult for me to concentrate.

> It was really difficult because I kept on getting distracted.

> Honestly, I felt bored and at the same time, surprised because everybody was closing
> their eyes.

> These comments were common across ages 9 to 16.

Responding Stage

Table 13.1 shows that 50 students (94%) made comments consistent with the
Responding stage, which indicates that they had started to comply with the idea of
silent sitting/visualization and welcomed the idea of practicing it. The students
whose comments fitted into this category ranged in age from 13 to 16 and mostly
had been using silent sitting regularly at least once a week since they were seven
years old. Nineteen students (44%) stated that they felt that they could concentrate
better. Thirteen students' responses (30%) indicate that they were aware of positive
effects on aspects of their affective development, such as improving their energy,
clarity, ability to think, problem-solving, confidence, reflective capacity, and values
in their behavior (such as being more patient, loving, caring, truthful, or polite).
Other comments at the Responding stage included the following:

> Silent sitting has benefitted me in many aspects of my life. It helps me in my studies and also
> for my spiritual development.

> It helps me reduce the tension from my body and forget about what has happened.

> It helps me to remove unnecessary thoughts and makes my mind calm without any
> interruptions. It has also made me not to get angry too fast and to deal with every situation
> calmly.

Valuing and Organizing

At the Valuing stage of the hierarchy, 17 students (32%) indicated they had started committing to the practice, and 14 students (26%) were suggesting they had developed an intrinsic commitment to practicing it. It would be interesting to explore further the extent to which students at this stage do silent sitting of their own accord in addition to that which they do at school.

Characterizing

Ten students (19%) gave responses consistent with the highest level of the hierarchy, the Characterizing stage. At this level, the students indicated they could relate to the challenges they faced and how they overcame them. All ten students valued the practice of silent sitting and had internalized it in different ways.

13.5.2 Age-Related Patterns

Some age-related patterns were noted. Most students in the age range from 9 to 12 stated that they felt calm and peaceful and that they could focus better and improved their performances. Those whose ages ranged from 13 to 16 stated quite similar views about the benefits of silent sitting: that it made them calm and peaceful and had self-regulatory effects. They emphasized how silent sitting has helped them to control their anger or raise their tolerance level.

The distinction from student responses between the third and fourth levels of the taxonomy was not very clear. The responses from the 9- and 10-year-olds were notably different those from the 11- to 16-year-olds. Apart from the challenges evidenced by their initial responses to the practice of silent sitting, the younger group commented about their improved implementation of values such as patience, positivity, love, caring, and gratitude to the teacher. Two of the younger students commented that they could control their anger after the practice. The 22 students (51%) whose ages ranged from 11 to 16 indicated self-regulatory behaviors. Four students commented on changes in their integration of values into their everyday lives, such as being more loving, truthful, polite, and caring.

13.5.3 Examining Individual Development

The discussion above focused on the number of responses that fell into each of the five hierarchical categories shown in Table 13.1. In the previous section, the responses from a selection of individuals have been selected to examine how they changed as they developed through the five levels of acceptance of silent sitting/visualization and the affective awareness that evolved through these changes. After their initial responses clearly revealed that the majority found it challenging, boring, or difficult to deal with, their reflections on the benefits changed over time.

There was also evidence of individual development not only in cognitive and behavioral learning as a result of regular silent sitting practice (consistent with Shephard and Fasko 1999) but also in ethical effects (Salzberg 2011) or values effects (Jumsai 2003; Parahakaran 2013).

13.6 Conclusion

This chapter has documented a group of Malaysian students' reflections on their experiences with silent sitting/visualization and characterized their acceptance of this technique according to Krathwohl's hierarchy of affective domains Two important themes that emerged at the higher levels suggested signs of self-regulation and self-awareness, consistent with earlier mindfulness studies (Flook et al. 2014; Hölzel et al. 2011; Kaunhoven and Dorjee 2017; Menezes et al. 2012; Vago and Silbersweig 2012).

More investigations should be carried out in depth to explore the different stages of development when students use the practice of silent sitting. The participants were only asked to respond to two questions, and there is scope to explore more deeply with a broader range of questions. The sample was small and cannot be generalized, although the results suggest that the silent sitting/visualization experiences may have contributed to cultivation of well-being and emotional balance (Menezes et al. 2012) and that, if the curriculum integrates pedagogical instruction with techniques such as silent sitting and visualization, students' affective capacities could be enhanced.

References

Bandura, A. (1986). *Social foundations of thought and action: A social cognitive theory*. Englewood Cliffs, NJ: Prentice Hall.

Bandura, A. (1991). Social cognition theory of self-regulation. *Organizational Behaviour and Human Decision Processes, 50,* 248–287.

Flook, L., Goldberg, S. B., Pinger, L., & Davidson, R. J. (2014). Promoting prosocial behavior and self-regulatory skills in preschool children through a mindfulness-based kindness curriculum. *Developmental Psychology, 51*(1), 44–51.

Goleman, D., & Davidson, R. J. (2017). *Altered traits: Science reveals how meditation changes your mind, body, and brain*. New York: Avery.

Hölzel, B. K., Lazar, S. W., Gard, T., Schuman-Oliver, Z., Vago, D. R., & Ott, U. (2011). How does mindfulness meditation work? Proposing mechanisms of action from a conceptual and neural perspective. *Perspectives on Psychological Science, 6*(6), 537–559. https://doi.org/10.1177/1745691611419671.

Jumsai, A. (2003). *A development of the human values integrated instructional model based on intuitive learning concept*. Bangkok: Chulalongkorn University.

Kabat-Zinn, J. (1990). *Full catastrophe living*. New York: Delta Publishing.

Kaunhoven, R. J., & Dorjee, D. (2017). How does mindfulness modulate self-regulation in pre-adolescent children? An integrative neurocognitive review. *Neuroscience & Biobehavioral Reviews, 74,* 163–184. https://doi.org/10.1016/j.neubiorev.2017.01.007.

Krathwohl, D. R., Bloom, B. S., & Masia, B. B. (1973). *Taxonomy of educational objectives: The classification of educational goals: Handbook II: Affective domain.* New York: David McKay Company.

Massachusetts General Hospital. (2011). *Mindfulness meditation training changes brain structure in eight weeks.* Science Daily. www.sciencedaily.com/releases/2011/01/110121144007.htm. Accessed 5 May 2020.

Menezes, C., Pereira, M., & Bizarro, L. (2012). Sitting and silent meditation as a strategy to study emotion regulation. *Psychology and Neuroscience, 5,* 27–36. https://doi.org/10.3922/j.psns.2012.1.05.

Miller, M. (2005). Teaching and learning in affective domain. In M. Orey (Ed.), *Emerging perspectives on learning, teaching, and technology.* Bloomington, Indiana: Association for Educational Communications and Technology.

Neff, K. D. (2003). Development and validation of a scale to measure self-compassion. *Self and Identity, 2,* 223–250.

Neff, K. D., & Dahm, K. A. (2015). Self-compassion: What it is, what it does, and how it relates to mindfulness. In B. Ostafin, M. Robinson, & B. Meier (Eds.), *Handbook of mindfulness and self-regulation* (pp. 121–137). New York: Springer.

Parahakaran, S. (2013). *Human values-based water, sanitation and hygiene education: A study of teachers' beliefs and perceptions in some SEA countries* [Doctoral dissertation, University of Sydney].

Salzberg, S. (2011). Mindfulness and loving-kindness. *Contemporary Buddhism, 12,* 177–182.

Shapiro, S., Jazaieri, H., & Goldin, P. (2012). Mindfulness-based stress reduction effects on moral reasoning and decision making. *The Journal of Positive Psychology, 7*(6), 504–515. https://doi.org/10.1080/17439760.2012.723732.

Shephard, R., & Fasko, D. (1999). Intrapersonal intelligence: Affective factors in thinking. *Education, 119*(4), 633–642.

Storbeck, J., & Clore, G. L. (2007). On the interdependence of cognition and emotion. *Cognition & Emotion, 21*(6), 1212–1237. https://doi.org/10.1080/02699930701438020.

Tang, Y., Hölzel, B. K., & Posner, M. I. (2015). The neuroscience of mindfulness meditation. *Nature Reviews Neuroscience, 16*(4), 213–225. https://doi.org/10.1038/nrn3916.

Teddlie, C., & Tashakkori, A. (2009). *Foundations of mixed methods research.* Los Angeles, CA: Sage Publications.

Vago, D. R., & Silbersweig, D. A. (2012). Self-awareness, self-regulation, and self- transcendence (S-ART): A framework for understanding the neurobiological mechanisms of mindfulness. *Frontiers in Human Neuroscience, 6,* 296. https://doi.org/10.3389/fnhum.2012.00296.

Weare, K. (2010). Mental health and social and emotional learning: Evidence, principles, tensions, balances. *Advances in School Mental Health Promotion, 3,* 5–17.

Wrightsman, L. S., & Sanford, F. H. (1975). *Psychology: A scientific study of human behaviour* (4th ed.). California: Brooks/Cole Publishing Company.